THE STRATEGIC DEFENCE INITIATIVE

For my wonderful parents

Dane and Anda Duric

The Strategic Defence Initiative

US Policy and the Soviet Union

MIRA DURIC
Keele University

ASHGATE

Published by
Ashgate Publishing Limited
Gower House
Croft Road
Aldershot
Hampshire GU11 3HR
England

Ashgate Publishing Company
Suite 420
101 Cherry Street
Burlington, VT 05401-4405
USA

Ashgate website: http://www.ashgate.com

British Library Cataloguing in Publication Data
Duric, Mira
    The Strategic Defence Initiative : US policy and the Soviet
    Union
    1.Strategic Defense Initiative 2.National security - United
    States 3.Cold War 4.Detente 5.United States - Foreign
    relations - 1981-1989 6.United States - Foreign relations -
    1989- 7.United States - Foreign relations - Soviet Union
    8.Soviet Union - Foreign relations - United States 9.United
    States - Military policy
    I.Title
    327.7'3'047'09045

Library of Congress Cataloging-in-Publication Data
Duric, Mira, 1975-
    The Strategic Defence Initiative : US policy and the Soviet Union / Mira Duric.
        p. cm.
    Includes bibliographical references and index.
    ISBN 0-7546-3733-6
    1. Strategic Defense Initiative. 2. United States--Foreign relations--Soviet Union. 3.
    Soviet Union--Foreign relations--United States. I. Title.

    UG743.D87 2003
    358.1'74--dc21
                                                                            2003056048

ISBN 0 7546 3733 6

Printed and bound in Great Britain by MPG Books Ltd, Bodmin, Cornwall

Contents

Acknowledgements

I am extremely grateful to a number of people who assisted and supported me during the writing of this book. First, I wish to thank John Dumbrell. His work has always has been an inspiration to me and his comments on the early draft of my manuscript have been invaluable. I would like to thank all my colleagues at the David Bruce Centre for American Studies, Keele University, England. They are too numerous to mention but include Robert A. Garson, Chris Bailey and David Adams.

Special thanks are extended to all the former US politicians, scientists and academics whom I interviewed for the writing of this book. They are Caspar W. Weinberger, Raymond L. Garthoff, Richard V. Allen, William Graham, Keith B. Payne, Richard N. Perle, Edwin M. Meese III, Peter Schweizer, Martin Anderson and William (Bill) T. Lee. I will always appreciate them taking time to meet/talk to me. They were gracious and generous with their time, and helped me with my work tremendously. I will always be grateful to them.

I would like to record a special thank you to Peter Schweizer. I will always be indebted to Peter Schweizer, – whose work is an inspiration to me – and who has helped and supported my research. I wish to express my appreciation to everyone – all the reference staff and librarians – at the Library of Congress, Washington D.C., USA, – including Tom Mann – who were efficient, diligent and assisted me in my research. They made the task of finding information far easier than would have otherwise been.

I deeply appreciate material which I was sent/given by a number of people. Amongst them, I would like to express my thanks to Bill Lee for sending me the information that he did. I would like to thank William Graham for the General Advisory Committee on Arms Control and Disarmament report entitled 'A Quarter Century of Soviet Compliance Practices Under Arms Control Commitments: 1958-1983' (also known as the GAC report). I wish to express my appreciation to Donald Rumsfeld's office for sending me a copy of 'The Report of the Commission to Assess the Ballistic Missile Threat to the United States' (The Rumsfeld Report). I wish to thank everyone at the Ronald Reagan Presidential Library, at Simi Valley, California, and everyone at the National Archives and Records Administration for sending me the information that they sent.

I am extremely grateful to Donald T. Regan for granting me permission to have access to his papers held at the Library of Congress. I am grateful to the Library of Congress for granting me permission to examine the Samuel C. Phillips Papers, held at the Manuscript Division, Library of Congress.

I wish to thank everyone at Ashgate Publishing Limited for their encouragement and efficiency, especially Kirstin Howgate, Irene Poulton, Amanda Richardson, Anne Keirby, Nicola Sheldrake, Kerrie-Anne Hughes, Donna Hamer, Pauline Beavers, Rachel Keane, Carolyn Court and Thomas Gray.

I wish to thank Derek H. Aldcroft who encouraged me over the last year and a half not to give up on academia. His work and character have been an inspiration to me. My thanks are extended to my cousin, Andelka Srdic-Mitrovic, who played a key role in sending me material – books, journal articles, newspaper articles – over from Arizona, USA, which I was unable to locate/buy in England. I would like to thank very much my friend Martin Clegg for his computer assistance. Many thanks go to Jeetander Ghag; my best friend whom I have known since primary school for being there for me always. Finally, but by no means the least, I would like to specially thank my wonderful parents, Dane and Anda Duric, for financing my work and for all their support throughout my life. I am truly blessed to have them as my parents. This book is dedicated to them.

Introduction

Located in an endnote at the back of his book *The United States and the End of the Cold War: Implications, Reconsiderations, Provocations*, one of the leading scholars in US foreign policy John Lewis Gaddis, makes a striking (and wholly accurate) claim. It appears to have gone unnoticed in the debates regarding the Strategic Defence Initiative (SDI) in US–Soviet relations and the end of the Cold War. It has not been repeated in any subsequent books or journal articles. Gaddis states that it is worthwhile considering the contention that 'there are moments in history when a single dramatic development can galvanize a country into taking action – *Sputnik* had this effect on the United States in 1957 – and the reaction to SDI inside the Soviet Union may have been an example of that'.[1]

Writing after the end of the Cold War, many commentators have dismissed the importance of the Strategic Defence Initiative. They argue that because it was not ready for imminent deployment after US President Ronald Reagan had proposed it (on March 23 1983), and was 'not technically feasible', therefore it was 'not important'. SDI critics believe that there is 'no substantial evidence to show that the SDI ended the Cold War'. This book is a response to these critics.

During the beginning of the end of the Cold War (in the early 1980s) the film 'The Day After' (which President Reagan saw on October 10 1983) dealt with the horror of a nuclear war.[2] Advertisements came through letterboxes advising the British public what to do in the event of a Soviet first-strike nuclear attack. Nearly two decades later, the September 11 2001 attack on the World Trade Center and Pentagon (orchestrated by Osama Bin Laden) occurred. A realization during the 1983, and after the 2001, case that the threat of attack – albeit nuclear or non-nuclear – was apparent. In the early 1980s the threat of a nuclear war hung over the world because of the intensification of the Cold War between the US and the Soviet Union.

SDI critics fail to acknowledge the fear felt by the masses of a nuclear attack (during the early 1980s) in their accounts. It was a time when the mere suggestion of a space-based defence (the SDI) was perceived with very great alarm by the Soviet Union. If only because of the environment of the Cold War, the SDI – a product of this environment – would inevitably impact greatly on the Soviet Union. That is why when the US President took to the airwaves to announce a space-based defence shield which could render nuclear missiles impotent, the General Secretary of the Soviet Union Mikhail S. Gorbachev took the so-called SDI 'threat' extraordinarily seriously. The SDI, when viewed against the psyche of the Cold War of the early 1980s, could only appear important. The SDI in reality was not a threat. It was proposed to deal with the threat of a nuclear war.

True that in the later years of the Reagan administration Congressional constraints on the SDI programme, and the 'altered' perception of it by the Soviet Union rendered the likelihood of SDI deployment unlikely. The Reagan administration's last two years in office were dominated by the Iran–Contra affair. However, there is evidence that as late as 1988 Gorbachev was still concerned about the SDI. The initial fear of it had subsided since the first few years of the Reagan administration, owing to the Reagan–Gorbachev summit meetings. At them, the two leaders saw that they 'could do business with each other'. Gorbachev also came to recognize that Reagan was serious to diminish the threat of nuclear war, which he inherently disliked. So why is it that in today's post-Cold War, post-September 11 world, SDI's successor – National Missile Defence (NMD) – continues to remain a controversial issue between US President George W. Bush and Russian President Vladimir Putin?

SDI and NMD both have far reaching consequences for security policy. Working on such defences would mean the death of the 1972 ABM Treaty which has kept the peace for the last thirty years. So it is in the light of the US decision to abandon this ABM Treaty (from which the US withdrew in June 2002) that additional relevance is placed on NMD's predecessor, the SDI, and, consequently, its role in US–Soviet relations and the Cold War's end.

Volumes have been written on the various factors accounting for the end of the Cold War. Books and articles highlighting whether it was the US defence build-up, the Soviet internal problems, the new 'enlightened' policies of Mikhail Gorbachev, or other forces, which led to the end of the Cold War. Each work tells its own unique persuasive story. Yet, we are still none the wiser in attributing the end to one factor alone.

The end of the Cold War was the outcome of a series of complex inter-related factors. It was one of the most complex and profoundly important historical events this century. Its denouement can be accounted for with great difficulty as it is rendered improbable by the lack of access to Soviet archives as well as the general information regarding US positions. It is the contention here that one explanation alone is not sufficient to explain the end of the Cold War. A variety of forces must explain it. This book does not aim to analyse these debates.

By focusing exclusively on the SDI, this book aims to document the role of the SDI in US–Soviet relations during the Reagan–Gorbachev era, and afterward. This work is a US foreign policy history. It does not examine Soviet documents, which are still classified. Yet, even if they were not classified some of the most important decisions of state are not committed to paper.[3] SDI was such an example.

This book examines why the SDI was introduced, how the Soviet Union reacted to it, and what role SDI played at the Reagan–Gorbachev summits. The Reagan administration's decision to launch the SDI, and the Soviet response to it, is critical to the debate whether SDI contributed to the Cold War's end. It is by examining the motivations for the introduction of the SDI that can one begin to consider was it part of the 'squeeze' strategy. This squeeze strategy was designed to get the Soviets to overspend, and consequently bankrupt them, ending the Cold War in the process.

The Soviet response to the SDI was crucial. Did the SDI cause the Soviets to end the Cold War through overspending, or seeking conciliation with the US? What role did the SDI play at the US–Soviet summits? American debates regarding the 1972 ABM Treaty are discussed. Gorbachev's motivation for delinking arms control (INF/START) from his government's opposition to SDI is analysed. What relevance did these two factors have for SDI? By documenting the importance of the SDI in the 1980s, and afterwards, inevitably the contribution to the historical discourse is widened.

To determine whether the SDI facilitated the Cold War's end a range of resources would be required. Statements from both US and former Soviet Union officials, statistics on Soviet defence expenditure (as well as from the US to determine whether the SDI 'cost' the American economy), private Reagan–Gorbachev correspondence, and minutes from the Soviet Politburo. Presenting all these is not the aim of this volume. This book aims to show the role of the SDI in US–Soviet relations, and to conclude whether it is possible to assert that the SDI influenced Gorbachev in the lead up to the Cold War's end. This is achieved by presenting both oral evidence from former Reagan administration officials, examining official government publications, and presenting a coherent account of both the Soviet reactions to the SDI, as well as the role of SDI at the US–Soviet summit meetings. Oral history is an indispensable source. Richard Ned Lebow, writing in December 1999, contended that the '[p]rocess tracing of the decisions that led to the end of the Cold War must rely on oral as well as written evidence'.[4]

Notes

[1]   Gaddis, John Lewis, *The United States and the End of the Cold War: Implications, Reconsiderations, Provocations*, New York, Oxford University Press, 1992, p. 225 83n.

[2]   Fischer, Beth A., *The Reagan Reversal: Foreign Policy and the End of the Cold War*, Columbia, University of Missouri Press, 1997, pp. 115-120.

[3]   Pipes, Richard, 'Review Essay: Misinterpreting the Cold War: The Hard-Liners Had it Right', *Foreign Affairs*, Vol. 74, No. 1, January/February 1985, p. 159.

[4]   Lebow, Richard Ned, 'The Rise and Fall of the Cold War in Comparative Perspective', *Review of International Studies*, Vol. 25, Special Issue, December 1999, p. 38.

Chapter 1

The Strategic Defence Initiative

Introduction

Addressing the nation on 23 March 1983, President Ronald Reagan launched the Strategic Defence Initiative (SDI), a defensive system which would make nuclear weapons 'impotent and obsolete'.[1] The system would form a space-based defensive shield – a kind of an invisible astrodome – using the high technology of futuristic space and ground-based laser weapons, and particle beams. Providing a layered defence, the objective of SDI would be to protect the US from nuclear attack by intercepting incoming missiles at various points along the missile trajectory high above the earth.[2] SDI was dubbed 'Star Wars' by critics.

The Evolution of Ideas

History of SDI

Defence against ballistic missiles started in the late 1940s, and early 1950s. By the mid-1950s, work on the actual systems was substantially underway.[3] The origin of ballistic missile development could be traced back to Adolf Hitler's Germany and the September 1944 launch of the V-2 ballistic missile against London, England. Research by the German physicists eventually led to work on anti-ballistic missiles (ABM) in the US in the 1960s. The origins of this development was the exodus of scientists from Germany in the 1930s. Amongst these was Hungarian Edward Teller, who played a significant role in the origin of the SDI.[4] The idea of laser defence emerged out of the 'Manhattan Project' on which some of these scientists were working, though Dr Edward Teller continued to insist that the 'technical initiative for the X-ray laser came from the Soviet Union'.[5]

The Soviet ABM Development: The Leningrad System and the Moscow ABM System

Anti-ballistic missile (ABM) work (which featured the launching of ground-to-air missiles) benefited from German scientists who perfected the Wasserfall surface-to-air missiles in Germany during the Second World War. The Germans reported that a Soviet ABM program was underway.[6] US U-2 confirmation of this, in April 1960, revealed Soviet progress in developing the Sary Shagan (Khazakhstan) test complex for anti-ballistic missiles. Near the Kapustin Yar ballistic missile test range impact area, on the periphery of Lake Balkhash, Siberia, very large phased-array radars were detected which set a precedent in ballistic missile early warning. By the early 1960s, nuclear test chambers at Sary Shagan were constructed. Both the Leningrad system and the Moscow (or 'Galosh') system were developed there.[7]

The Leningrad system was deployed in the early 1960s and removed in 1963. Although debate continues on whether it was an advanced air defence system, whether it had an ABM mission, or had the capability to do both, it was an integral development which led to later ABM systems. The developers of the system continued to work on advanced defensive systems.[8] Moscow's Galosh system – the city's own mini SDI – was deployed in the early 1960s and continues to remain in operation. Sixty-four above-ground launchers and nuclear-armed interceptors, and several radars were situated at four complexes around a ring forty to fifty miles from the centre of Moscow. Two immense radars south-west of Moscow and larger radars on the periphery of the Soviet Union completed the world's only operational ballistic missile defence (BMD) system.[9] This remains in operation today. On December 18 2002, *The Daily Telegraph* stated (regarding the Moscow ABM system) that a 'nuclear defence system remains in use by Russia to defend Moscow'.[10]

The nuclear power work programme carried out by the Russians was viewed by observers as work having strong relevance to research into particle beams, which were one of the main SDI technologies. Similarly, research into the hydrogen bomb (which scientist Edward Teller wanted to build) was invaluable for some aspects of the SDI. Research into fusion weapons was vital to understanding the behaviour of high energy particles.[11]

Edward Teller and the US ABM System: From 'Sentinel' to 'Safeguard'

The technology of the SDI was the dream of Edward Teller, who wanted nuclear weapons to stop ballistic missiles in flight. However, his proposal was different to that of the SDI. Teller favoured a defence system powered by a nuclear X-ray laser which would set off explosions in space. The nuclear system would be launched from missiles on submarines. Reagan never liked the idea of using nuclear explosions. He wanted a non-nuclear defence. Teller later revealed that Reagan had a better idea than him. Reagan wanted 'a defensive screen that could intercept those missiles when they came out of the silos'.[12] Teller helped to establish the Lawrence Livermore National Laboratory in Livermore, California, in 1951–52. It was a special research laboratory. On Teller's affirmation that the USSR could build a shield against nuclear missiles, the government consequently spent millions of dollars on Safeguard, the US ABM system.[13]

During John F. Kennedy's presidency, Teller's campaign for research into nuclear anti-missile systems led to Operation Starfish; on July 9 1962, the US detonated a nuclear bomb in space from a missile launched from Johnston Atoll in the Pacific. The explosion, according to David Baker, marked the beginning of the secret work on the SDI.[14] In the Lyndon B. Johnson administration (in the late 1960s), the US was proceeding with its own ABM system, known as the 'Sentinel', as protection against a possible Chinese intercontinental ballistic missile (ICBM) attack. President Richard Nixon transformed Sentinel to the 'Safeguard' system. The ABM system was deployed in 1973 to protect missile silos at Grand Forks, North Dakota. It was deactivated months later.[15]

US deployment of the Safeguard ABM system alarmed the Soviets (who had their own Galosh ABM system) about American technology. Negotiations proceeded to insist on a limitation on ABM systems, which resulted in the 1972 ABM Treaty. Official historian of the Strategic Defense Initiative Organization (SDIO), Donald R. Baucom, states that the 'use of Safeguard as a bargaining chip was the principal US strategy in the 30 months of SALT talks that culminated in May 1972 with the signing of the ABM Treaty'.[16] President Nixon insisted there would be no treaty unless the Soviets agreed to limitations on offensive forces, a condition which the Soviets disliked. However, their eagerness for the 1972 Treaty forced them to accept the Interim Agreement on Offensive Missiles.[17] Strong public and Congressional opposition to ABMs of any kind compelled the Nixon administration to reach an accord.[18] The precedent for the Sentinel and Safeguard system was the US Army's 1960s anti-ballistic missile called NIKE-ZEUS.[19]

The Political Will: Ronald Reagan

The Pentagon needed to protect its missiles and this provided Edward Teller with the military interest in ballistic weapons research and development. All that was needed was a political commitment, and for this, Teller gathered a group of people from the defence and intelligence community. To secure political commitment to BMD, the Air Force Intelligence assembled evidence for Teller to convince the President that Soviet technological breakthrough was militarily an imminent threat. President Jimmy Carter was unconvinced of this.[20]

Teller's most successful political alignment began when Teller invited then Governor of California, Ronald Reagan, to Livermore in 1967. Although at the time Reagan did not express either support or opposition to missile defence, Lou Cannon argues that it is conceivable that the briefing on defensive technologies, at the Livermore Laboratory, planted in Reagan's mind the seeds of an alternative concept to the doctrine of mutual assured destruction (MAD).[21]

Breakthroughs in laser engineering by the 1960s occurred at Livermore. Such successful research results provided Teller and General George J. Keegan Jr., (Head of US Air Force Intelligence) with the means to attract funds from the White House, thereby bypassing the usual route of funding of Congressional committees. A Keegan/Teller–CIA group was formed. In the late 1970s, laser and beam weapons emerged, under names 'Chair Heritage', 'White Horse' and 'Sipapu'.[22]

SDI Lobbying: The Hertz Foundation, the Heritage Foundation, the White House 'Kitchen Cabinet'

Teller was involved with the Hertz Foundation which played a key role in organising the campaign to fund beam research.[23] In 1981, the members of the foundation included friends of President Reagan; businessmen J. Coors, J. Dart and J. Hume. The foundation was divided on the issue of the SDI. In early 1982, one of the groups led by General Daniel Graham favoured immediately starting to build a 'space shield' over the US on the basis of available technology. Another group, headed by Former Deputy Secretary of Defense Karl Bendetsen, believed in continuing preliminary research, and not rushing ahead with immediate deployment. Teller, a member of the latter group, met with President Reagan in September 1982.[24] According to Reagan's National Security Adviser (1981–1982) Richard V. Allen, Daniel Graham and Karl Bendetsen were the early heroes of SDI.[25]

Several Heritage Foundation contacts got Teller access to President Reagan. The President's dream of SDI became US policy once Teller had convinced Reagan the feasibility of an Astrodome defence against nuclear weapons.[26] President Reagan's 'kitchen cabinet' had met with Teller, Dr Lowell Wood (his Lawrence Livermore colleague) and other influential scientists and aerospace experts at the Heritage Foundation since 1981 to consider the future of BMD.[27] Key Pentagon officials joined the scientists and industrialists at the Heritage Foundation (in Washington D.C.) who were lobbying the White House for a new strategy of defence; a public open anti-missile programme. The Heritage Foundation group received top security clearance and met Ronald Reagan in January 1982. Teller consulted Reagan several times including a private session in September 1982.[28]

After Reagan's election as President, 'a small, informal group' was 'formed within the White House' known as the 'Kitchen Cabinet'. It was formed by Counselor to President Reagan (and later Attorney General), Edwin M. Meese III, Richard V. Allen, Presidential aide (Reagan's chief domestic consultant) Martin Anderson, and George Keyworth (Reagan's science adviser) who were committed to providing a strategic missile defence for the US. Edward Teller, Karl Bendetsen and General Daniel Graham joined the group at their first White House meeting, on September 14 1981, to consider the future prospect for BMD. Bendetsen and Graham were military experts. Graham was head of the High Frontier organization which promoted space-based missile defence. He was a famous advocator of BMD.[29] The second meeting was held on October 12 1981 and consisted of a smaller group. Martin Anderson regarded the meeting of the group with Reagan, on January 8 1982, as a 'critical turning point' for the SDI.[30]

General Graham, who described himself as 'the midwife, but not the father' of the SDI, presented the case for space-based defences to the American public. He delievered personally his High Frontier (a missile defence programme) idea to General John Vessey, who later became Chairman of the Joint Chiefs of Staff (JCS), and briefed Admiral James D. Watkins.[31] The High Frontier study was published under the sponsorship of the Heritage Foundation.[32] In January 1981, when Ronald Reagan became President, he immediately requested a meeting with Teller.

Background to the SDI Speech

Technological Improvements: Lawrence Livermore's Dauphin Device Detonation and the Soviet Union's ABM Improvement

Jeff Hecht states that the nuclear X-ray laser (the concept of which evolved at the Lawrence Livermore Laboratory in the 1970s and was promoted by Edward Teller) helped launch Reagan's SDI speech.[33] Livermore's successful detonation of the Dauphin device, on November 14 1980, (and other technological improvements on both the US and Soviet side) contributed towards making SDI a reality. They demonstrated the feasibility of ballistic missile defence. Dauphin worked on the principle of the H-Bomb developed by Teller in the 1940s and combined Teller's dream weapons: nuclear bombs in an anti-missile system.[34]

The Soviets made great advances in their defence system. The Soviet Union's substantial improvement programme in 1980 for its Moscow BMD system,[35] to overcome vulnerabilities and increase its capability to respond to limited nuclear attack, alarmed the US. The expanded Moscow system involved two, instead of one layer of defence, and radars were deployed on the borders of the Soviet Union. The new developed ABM system – known as the ABM-X-3 system – had an advanced phased array engagement radar and a high acceleration interceptor missile. This discriminates against penetration raids.[36] Technological improvements in the Soviet Union contributed to the US motivation to introduce the SDI. Science Adviser to President Reagan, William Graham, stated that: 'I believe the Soviet Union assigned more importance to national missile defense than any administration other than Ronald Reagan'. According to Graham the Soviets were much more concerned for the need of national missile defence than the US.[37]

Strategic Concerns

The SDI was motivated by political aswell as strategic factors. It was viewed as a piece of electoral politics. Walter LaFeber argues that Reagan proposed the SDI because he was preparing to run for a second term in office, and wanted to counter criticisms of his first administration.[38] Michael Deaver, the President's confidant, saw SDI as 'a campaign issue because it held out hope to American voters that the nuclear threat would be neutralized, blunting Democratic attacks on Reagan as a warmonger'.[39]

The SDI was proposed as a means of strengthening strategic stability. The SDI was proposed because Reagan was dissatisfied with the US policy of deterence which was mutual assured destruction (MAD). This was based on the premise that if the US and Soviet Union were mutually vulnerable to each other could they be perfectly safe. Neither would launch an attack against the other. According to Secretary of Defense (1981–1987) Caspar W. Weinberger, Reagan did not agree with MAD when he was governor of California back in 1972 when it was proposed and never has since. Reagan was 'always anxious' to know if the US 'could and should develop defences'.[40] In his SDI speech, Reagan pointed out the dangers of the MAD doctrine of 'mutual assured destruction' which he called 'a sad commentary on the human condition'.[41]

The competition in strategic offensive forces had adversely affected the US, as the Soviets had increased their forces. The US was competing with the Soviet Union in offensive arms production whilst simultaneously was attempting to negotiate limits on the same arms. This increased the numbers of nuclear weapons and failed to produce a way out from the mutual vulnerability 'trap'. The SDI was the solution to both problems; it reversed the shift in offensive forces and led away from mutual vulnerability.[42] The SDI could appease the public who were dissatisfied with the arms competition and nuclear threat.

'The Greatest Sting Operation in History'

Robert C. ('Bud') McFarlane (who worked in the State Department in 1981–1982, was deputy National Security Adviser in 1982–1983, and became National Security Adviser from 1983–1985) was a key figure in the SDI proposal. He believed that the SDI could turn out to be 'the greatest sting operation in history' for the US could politically trade away or limit the SDI for a reduction in already produced and deployed Soviet nuclear weapons (ICBMs). Although this 'arms control' potential was McFarlane's central motive, he did not hint at using it to advance this strategic arms control. Nevertheless, according to McFarlane, the SDI was 'a way of recovering the negotiating leverage in arms control that the US had lost as a result of congressional opposition to the MX missile'.[43] McFarlane recalled that his desire to use SDI to leverage Soviet behaviour was 'lost' on President Reagan.[44] This corroborates the interpretation that Ronald Reagan was genuine in his ideal that the SDI should be used to make nuclear weapons obsolete. To Reagan, the SDI was not a bargaining chip.

The SDI as a Response to the Anti-Nuclear and 'Nuclear Freeze' Movement

The SDI was also a response to the increasing anti-nuclear movement which captured the public mood, and the 'nuclear freeze' movement. Ronald Reagan's SDI speech can be understood in terms of his desire to respond to the public and nuclear freeze movement in relation to the 'Three Mile Island' incident involving civilian nuclear power. Occurring in Philadelphia in 1978, the incident – a near meltdown of a nuclear power plant – caused a lot of worry about nuclear power. Reagan wanted to respond to such public anxieties. In proposing the SDI, Reagan was responding to Congressional opposition to nuclear development. The SDI addressed the concern of the anti-nuclear movement which was the threat of nuclear war. Reagan was able to respond to these anti-nuclear and 'freeze groups' in a new way; by proposing the possibility of directly countering the nuclear threat and not just requiring new forces to maintain deterrence.[45]

It is argued that Robert McFarlane pushed the SDI because McFarlane was worried that the increasing nuclear freeze movement in the US jeopardized the administration's strategic offensive arms build-up. McFarlane saw an opportunity to counter this nuclear freeze movement in the programme and drew Reagan's attention to it.[46] The nuclear freeze movement in late 1982 and early 1983 had 'greatly worried' the Chiefs of staff of all service branches. Their recommendation was to shift the emphasis into the 'defensive' side of the US military–political strategy.[47]

The SDI and the MX Missile: 'Operation MX Plus'

The Ronald Reagan–Joint Chiefs of Staff meeting on February 11 1983 was primarily intended to discuss ways to speed up the deployment of the new MX intercontinental ballistic missile. Attention focused on strategic defence only when the idea was mentioned.[48] MX was 'Missile Experimental' – a large, 'heavy' successor to the US 'Minuteman' ICBM, with MIRV capability, conceived during the 1970s. It was a counter to the Soviet SS-17s, SS-18s, and SS-19s which were perceived to be targeting the Minuteman silos.[49] After 1981, Reagan favoured the MX system, also known as the 'Peacekeeper' for it would 'keep the Soviets moving at the negotiation tables'.[50]

  Reagan (in late March) spoke in defence of his administration's military programmes, especially the MX missile. Consequently, the SDI was perceived as a cover – known as 'Operation MX Plus' – for pushing military programmes (such as the MX missile) with greater ease through Congress, for the March 23 1983 speech justified these military programmes. Ovinnikov affirmed that the SDI programme can, therefore, be seen as a 'distracting propaganda ploy'. It was only after that, that the strategic feasibility of SDI was pursued.[51] (President Reagan's SDI speech was intended to rally US support for his submitted defence budget in Congress).

  On December 8 1982, the House of Representatives defeated the Reagan administration's 'Dense Pack' proposal. By a vote of 245–176, the House dropped all funding for the production of the MX missile from the budget. Lou Cannon asserts that this set in motion the events that created the SDI, for had the MX funding been obtained SDI would not have come into being.[52] The SDI offered a way of responding to Soviet strategic capabilities.

The Joint Chiefs of Staff and the SDI

An advocate on the Joint Chiefs of Staff was necessary for developing any strategic defence system. Robert McFarlane found an advocate in Chief of Naval Operations, Admiral James D. Watkins.[53] McFarlane suggested to Watkins that the Chiefs discuss a ballistic missile defence proposal with the President on February 11 1983. Charles Gabriel, Air Force General, and John Vessey, Army General and then Chairman of the Chiefs, were too alarmed by the defeat of the Dense Pack and were receptive to a new strategic approach.[54] According to Donald R. Baucom, the decision for Reagan's SDI announcement was a response to a 'strategic crisis' – namely the 'increasing vulnerability of US ICBMs to a Soviet first strike'. It was taken on the 'advice of the nation's top military advisers, the Joint Chiefs of Staff and the National Security Council'.[55]

The Joint Chiefs of Staff did not believe in a total ballistic missile defence. Nor did they propose funding it. Watkins, however, remarked that 'its possibly within reach that we could develop systems that would defeat a missile attack'.[56] Weeks earlier (on January 20 1983) Watkins had lunch with several high-level advisers that including Edward Teller who explained to his 'Excalibur' plan. This would be 'launched into space from a submarine to defend against a Soviet ICBM attack'.[57] Although Teller's advocacy of defence by nuclear means was not shared by either Reagan or Watkins, Watkins was impressed with Teller. Several of Teller's points were noted in the 'White Paper' prepared for briefing the President.[58]

Reagan had proposed the SDI publicly – on March 23 – before the JCS had confirmed to him, (in their subsequent meeting with him at the White House on April 4) the feasibility of SDI based on the immediate technology available.[59] Evidence clearly points to Reagan's enthusiasm for the SDI as of paramount importance in its launch. At the earlier Reagan–JCS February 11 1983 meeting, Watkins asked 'Would it not be better if we could develop a system that would protect, rather than avenge, our people?'.[60] President Reagan was later to elaborate on this in his March 23 1983 speech.[61] According to Caspar Weinberger in his memoirs *Fighting For Peace: Seven Critical Years in the Pentagon*, the decision to extend the work on strategic defence was 'finally and completely decided in the President's mind after a meeting in the Cabinet room that he and I had with the Joint Chiefs of Staff on February 11 1983'.[62]

Assistant Secretary of Defense (for International Security Policy) Richard N. Perle later said that:

> Admiral Watkins, Chief of Naval operations took the lead in ballistic missile defenses and briefed Reagan on this. Reagan grabbed the idea. Reagan was influenced by Edward Teller and Lowell Wood.[63]

Secretary of State (1982–89), George P. Shultz, speaking at the February 1993 'Retrospective on The End of The Cold War' Princeton University Conference, New Jersey, revealed that although what the Joint Chiefs of Staff told Reagan triggered Reagan's March 1983 SDI speech, the Joint Chiefs of Staff 'didn't realise that anybody took them seriously'.[64] National Security Adviser to President Reagan in 1987–88 (and Secretary of Defense in 1988–89) Frank C. Carlucci III, similarly stated that the Chiefs 'had a lot of reservations about SDI when it was first announced' as they 'didn't expect to happen what happened'.[65] After some studies the JCS 'became satisfied' that SDI would add to the US deterrent capability.[66]

Ronald Reagan

His background in Hollywood It is argued that the SDI was the product of Ronald Reagan's imagination, influenced by the Hollywood film 'Murder in the Air' which the President had once starred in when he was an actor. In the 1940 movie, Reagan played hero secret service agent Brass Bancroft who prevented a spy stealing the 'Inertia Projector' which could knock down distant enemy airplanes.[67] National Security Adviser in 1987–1989 Lieutenant-General Colin Powell believed that the anti-war science-fiction film 'The Day the Earth Stood Still' (in which the alien hero has the utopian dream of a renunciation of atomic weapons) was the inspiration for Reagan's idea of sharing SDI technology with Moscow.[68] Reagan was greatly influenced by his Hollywood past.[69] Robert McFarlane believes that Reagan's background in Hollywood was possibly the reason why Reagan saw himself as a 'heroic figure' who wanted to avert Armageddon, in which he firmly believed in. The President believed in the power of a person to avert (or mitigate) even pre-ordained catastrophes.[70]

The NORAD visit Ronald Reagan was sympathetic to strategic defence before his March 23 1983 speech. On July 31 1979 (during his presidential campaign), Reagan visited NORAD – the North American Aerospace Defense Command. Located inside Cheyenne Mountain, Colorado, NORAD was the North American attack warning centre.[71] According to Martin Anderson, Reagan was aware of ballistic missile defence when he was Governor of California, 'yet the NORAD visit was the first time that the need for ballistic missile defence was driven home to him'.[72]

Interviewed in 1998, Martin Anderson spoke of Reagan's NORAD visit; when Reagan asked what would happen if a missile was fired at the US. According to Anderson, the General [James Hill] said 'the US could tell if the Soviets launched a missile and what city it would hit eight to ten minutes ahead of time'. Anderson explained that 'they could tell the people they'd die eight to ten minutes ahead of time but we couldn't stop it'.[73] Reagan told Anderson that the United States had spent billions on national security, yet were powerless to protect the country and its people.[74] Anderson later revealed that:

> Reagan had two important choices if the Soviets launched an attack. The first was to let it happen; which was unacceptable. The second was launch a retaliatory strike; which was unacceptable. The third choice was to have a missile defence; which was acceptable.[75]

In 1979, after the NORAD visit, Anderson wrote 'Policy Memorandum No. 3'. In it, he proposed the development of a 'Protective Missile System'.[76]

The SDI as his 'idea' According to Caspar Weinberger, the SDI programme was 'Reagan's idea'.[77] George Shultz also contended that 'I think that the SDI programme was very much driven by Ronald Reagan. It was personal'.[78] President Reagan's claims that the SDI was his idea to begin with[79] is plausible. As a science fiction enthusiast he had always been interested in anti-missile defence. The scientists and advisers who advised Reagan that technological advancement meant that ballistic missile defences were feasible, prompted Reagan to announce the SDI. Reagan, writing in his memoirs, *An American Life*, stated that the SDI 'wasn't conceived by scientists, although they came on board and contributed greatly to its success'.[80]

By the time Reagan announced his SDI proposal there were some important Senators on Capitol Hill ready to provide enthusiastic support. In 1979 four technical experts from the aerospace industry known as the industrial 'Gang of Four' managed to present the case for BMD to the Senate. Many of the Senators were enthusiastic about the prospect, especially Senator Malcolm Wallop, who became an advocator of BMD in Congress.[81]

Ballistic missile defences were not exclusively Reagan's idea. BMD technology had a long history to it. There were many individuals and groups who pushed for ballistic missile defence. However, Reagan embraced the idea of the SDI. He believed in it and announced it. The SDI really was in a sense Reagan's idea. Above all, he was responsible for the SDI becoming a national issue and US policy. His enthusiasm for the SDI was of paramount importance.

Ronald Reagan campaigns Martin Anderson recalled that the issue of 'missile defence was never raised by Reagan during the 1980 presidential campaign' for reasons of political strategy. Reagan's 'main political advisers especially Michael Deaver, argued against it'.[82] According to Richard V. Allen:

> President Reagan was interested in ballistic missile defence when campaigning. He wanted SDI and moved ahead with it effectively. Reagan's position was upheld by Edwin Meese III, the Attorney-General.[83]

According to Edwin Meese III, 'Ronald Reagan was interested in SDI for a long time'. Meese III revealed that:

> Reagan thought about it in the 1970s; when he visited Cheyenne Mountain in 1979. Then by 1981, beginning of 1982, he had been convinced in the idea, that the technology of SDI was feasible, by Edward Teller.[84]

Meese III further added that in 1982 Ronald Reagan asked the Joint Chiefs of Staff to give an assessment of the total strategic defence system. Meese III affirmed that 'Simultaneously also a small task force in the National Security Council staff were set up looking at this'. The Joint Chiefs of Staff at the end of 1982, beginning of 1983, felt that the ABM programme had military standing and was 'advisable and necessary from a moral standpoint. This led to the March speech that announced the SDI'.[85]

Retired Army General Daniel O. Graham served as campaign adviser to Reagan in 1976 and 1980. Graham described that Reagan was displeased with MAD during his campaign for the Republican nomination in 1976.[86] Graham stated that Reagan had compared MAD to a situation where two men trained loaded pistols on each other's heads. If either sneezed they would kill each other.[87] George Shultz, speaking at the 'Retrospective on the End of the Cold War' conference, in New Jersey, February 1993, explained that in his opinion, SDI's impact on the Soviet Union was a secondary question for Reagan. Reagan's primary motivation was to advance the defence of the United States. Nevertheless, the SDI 'did turn into a terrific bargaining chip'.[88]

Soviet Non-Compliance with Arms Agreements and Violation of the ABM Treaty

Official government publications issued a few years after the SDI was announced provide a strategic analysis as to why the SDI was introduced. A June 1986 *Report to the Congress on the Strategic Defense Initiative* stated that the SDI was an:

> important effort to find a fundamental improvement in the long-term security of the US and its Allies, and to provide a better response to the growing Soviet offensive and defensive threat.[89]

According to the report, since 1969 when the SALT I process was beginning, the Soviet Union 'built five new classes of intercontinental ballistic missiles (ICBMs) and upgraded these seven times'.[90] The increasing growth in both the quality and quantity of such ballistic missiles could 'significantly' degrade the US 'land-based retaliatory capability'.[91] Consequently, the resulting asymmetry between Soviet and US force structures led to a destabilising situation which the Reagan administration 'strongly' believed 'must be redressed'.[92] Interestingly, 'the U.S. fielded only one ICBM since 1969 – the Peacekeeper – and only in limited numbers'.[93] According to a 1989 report issued to Congress, the Soviet Union did not just have the world's only operational anti-ballistic missile system but had a wealth of the operational anti-satellite (ASAT) capability.[94]

According to the report, aside from the improvements in Soviet strategic offensive and defensive forces, there was the Soviet research programme in 'many of the same basic technological areas that the SDI Program addresses'. There was a 'continuing pattern of Soviet non-compliance with existing arms control agreements'. This included a 'significant violation of a central provision of the Anti Ballistic Missile Treaty'.[95] Soviet violations of agreements were documented in the General Advisory Committee on Arms Control and Disarmament report, of October 1984, entitled *A Quarter Century of Soviet Compliance Practices Under Arms Control Commitments: 1958–1983*. It stated that Soviet:

> activities, as well as other concealment activities, may be intended to raise the level of U.S. confusion in order to hide more serious covert activities, such as development and deployment of a ballistic missile defense system.[96]

According to Defense Intelligence Analyst William (Bill) T. Lee, the Soviets 'violated the ABM Treaty'.[97] According to William Graham, the Soviets had violated arms control by their mass biological weapons programme; by increasing biological weapons. By the early 1980s, the US knew that the Soviets violated the biological weapons convention of the 1970s. This was 'typical Soviet behaviour under agreements'.[98]

According to Caspar Weinberger, the Soviets had 'been working to get the strategic defence for many, many years'. They violated the ABM treaty many times by 'installing radars and other equipment that could only be used to assist a defense capability'.[99] The Krasnoyarsk radar in Central Siberia could be used in an ABM defence of the central USSR. Due to its 'location, orientation and capability' it was a 'significant violation of a central element of the ABM Treaty'.[100] In 1986, Soviet Foreign Minister Eduard Shevardnadze accepted that the Krasnoyarsk phased-array radar station had violated the ABM Treaty.[101] The *1989 Report to the Congress on the Strategic Defense Initiative* stated that the SDI was a 'powerful deterrent' to any 'Soviet decision to expand rapidly its ABM capability beyond that permitted by the ABM Treaty'.[102]

To Eliminate the Threat Posed by Ballistic Missiles and to Strengthen Strategic Stability

Strategic defence was designed to enhance deterrence by denying the Soviets the confidence in their ability to 'plan or execute a successful attack'.[103] The SDI would eliminate the threat posed by ballistic missiles and thereby 'support a better basis for deterring aggression; strengthen strategic stability; increase security of the United States and its Allies'.[104] The SDI research was promoted as being conducted in a manner fully consistent with all US treaty obligations including the 1972 ABM Treaty.[105]

The *President's Strategic Defense Initiative* report of January 1985 stated that in the near term, the SDI responded to the 'extensive' Soviet ABM 'effort' which included 'actual deployments'. The SDI provided a 'powerful deterrent' to 'any Soviet decision to expand' its BMD capability 'beyond that permitted by the ABM Treaty'. In the long-term it was hoped that the SDI could induce the US and the Soviets to agree to 'very deep reductions, and eventually, even the elimination of ballistic missiles and the nuclear weapons they carry'.[106]

This is important as it shows the SDI was more than just a defence for the US. It was pursued because it was believed that it could ultimately contribute to successful arms control, improving US–Soviet relations. However, although it was hoped that the SDI would later eliminate ballistic missiles, its principal objective was to defend against them, just like the President said. He was prompted to announce the SDI due to the Soviet activities in this research area. This was evident by *The President's Strategic Defense Initiative* report of January 1985. It stated that the SDI was being pursued because technological breakthroughs 'suggested' that the difficulties in BMD could be 'overcome'. According to the report BMD could enhance deterrence and stability. The report stated that 'the Soviets have long been hard at work in this area'.[107]

In Reagan's SDI speech the President documented the Soviet Union's modernization of strategic weapons.[108] Reagan stated that if the Soviet Union joined the US in achieving 'major arms reductions, we will have succeeded in stabilising the nuclear balance'.[109] The President affirmed that in proposing the SDI the US sought 'neither military superiority nor political advantage'. The US wanted to 'search for ways to reduce the danger of nuclear war'.[110]

The SDI could contribute to arms control. It could be a way of taking arms control talks to a new level following the stalemate in US–Soviet negotiations. Reagan acknowledged such a proposition. This was evidenced by his SDI speech. In it, he referred to the SDI as paving 'the way for arms control measures to eliminate the weapons themselves'.[111] The US's 'only purpose' here was to 'search for ways to reduce the danger of nuclear war'.[112]

The 'Red Shield': The Soviet SDI

The Soviet research on its own anti-missile system was called 'Red Shield'. President Ronald Reagan contended that 'Red Shield' 'actually dwarfs our S.D.I'.[113] In March 1988, President Reagan declared that:

> The Soviet defense effort, which some call 'Red Shield', is now over 15 years old and they have spent over $200 billion on it – that's 15 times the amount that we have spent on SDI.[114]

It is argued that Reagan's statement is 'seriously misleading'. The premise of this argument is that the $200 billion estimate is not only the amount that the Soviets spent on strategic defence alone. The $200 billion sum is the amount that the Soviets spent against ballistic missiles plus Soviet expenditure 'for air defense against bombers and cruise missiles and for antisatellite applications' too.[115]

Ronald L. Tammen, James T. Bruce and Bruce W. MacDonald, writing in their article 'Star Wars After Five Years: The Decisive Points', contend that:

> There is no doubt that the Soviets have been quite active in ballistic missile defense research, and there has been limited development and deployment of terminal ABM systems – those systems that are targeted on the last segments of the ballistic missile flight trajectory.[116]

This, in essence, means that the Soviets' ABM system is a ground-based defence only. However, Tammen, Bruce and MacDonald, point out that:

> there is a major difference between the Soviet orientation and a full SDI program. The latter of necessity must be a multi-tiered approach composed of a variety of sensor and weapons platforms based on the ground and in orbit. The Soviet 'SDI' effort lacks this broad focus.[117]

The precis of this statement is that the Soviets do not have a space-based ABM system. They only have a ground based system.

Writing in *Arms Control Today*, in 1998, Tammen, Bruce and MacDonald affirmed that analyses from the Strategic Defense Initiative Organization (SDIO) stated that the US would be ahead of the Soviets in developing a space-based defence. The Soviets were ten years behind in crucial SDI 'sensor technologies, and nearly as far behind in computers'. The Soviet efforts to modernize its Moscow ABM system included 'The Pill Box' radar. This was part of 'Red Shield'. Interestingly, the technology of the new Soviet system was similar to the technology of the US Safeguard system, which was briefly deployed in the mid-1970s.[118]

Notwithstanding the difference between the Soviet ground-based ABM system and a space-based ABM system, the Soviets had its own operational SDI;

the Moscow ABM system. The US did not have an ABM defence. One can argue that the Soviets were working towards a 'full' (space-based) SDI programme anyway. Since the *Arms Control Today* article was written, presumably, the Soviets must have improved their Moscow ABM system. This system remains operational. The Soviets are very secretive regarding their work, especially concerning the issue of strategic defences. It can be resolutely asserted that information on the Soviet 'Red Shield' is not well documented. What is documented, is that General Secretary of the Communist Party of the Soviet Union, Mikhail Gorbachev, admitted the Soviet strategic defence effort.

Views of the SDI by Reagan Administration Officials and Scientists

The Background to the SDI

The introduction of the SDI   According to Martin Anderson, in 1983 'several things were happening at the same time which we realise in retrospect'. The first was the SDI speech which was Reagan's decision and was a classic example of a decision coming from the top down as 'the Secretary of State and Defence didn't know'. The second was the US was negotiating privately with the Soviets. Anderson added that 'Bill Clark was sending messages to Andropov about negotiations to get rid of all nuclear weapons'.[119] The third factor was that Reagan called into question the moral basis of the Soviet Union. He publicly called the Soviet Union 'bad people'. Anderson declared that 'I would argue that all three were very important. They conveyed to the Soviets that Reagan was very serious to diminish the number of nuclear weapons'. He added that, 'all these things gave credence to move ahead with SDI'.[120]

Reagan's understanding of the SDI concept   Interestingly, Richard V. Allen revealed that contrary to the views of:

> many who believe that Reagan thought he would presses a switch for SDI and it would happen; that was not Reagan's thinking at all. He understood the concept of SDI.[121]

Reagan believed that 'there might be something' in the idea of ballistic missile defence; that 'it might be possible to defend people against incoming missiles'. Allen further added 'but whether or not it would work was less important than the fact that the Soviets believed that it could work'.[122] That Reagan understood the feasibility of ballistic missile defence was evident by what Reagan wrote in his diary. On March 23 1983 – the night he unveiled his SDI proposal to the nation – Reagan wrote 'I made no optimistic forecasts – said it might take 20 years or more but we had to do it'.[123] Reagan, according to Allen wanted to disarm, 'He didn't want to arm, but he believed that if there was an arms race we didn't want to lose it'.[124]

A benefit to deterrence Like Richard V. Allen, William Graham later revealed that 'Ronald Reagan did not believe in an astrodome' version of SDI, for the astrodome has limits. The SDI was, nevertheless, a benefit to deterrence.[125] William Graham cited an example; if the Russians with their 15,000 to 20,000 strategic warheads were to shoot more missiles than the US could intercept. The consequent academic view would be that the 'SDI is/was not/could never be viable'. However, 'by that criterion no military system performs that well'. A contrasting polemical view to the example is that 'even if the SDI keeps one nuclear weapon from hitting the civilian US, that would be of benefit. There is clearly room between these two extremes'.[126]

According to Graham 'we are capable of building ballistic missile defenses capable of intercepting ballistic nuclear warheads, but we could not intercept everyone'. The 'Astrodome' view, is the view of a system that would intercept most ballistic missiles. However, the SDI would make a strike unpredictable because the enemy's 'risk return calculation would be higher'. In other words, to the enemy, the risk would outweigh the benefit of launching an attack.[127] Reagan understood this.

William Graham contended that the argument that the enemy would deploy counter-measures, thereby negating the SDI and making US defences not work, is not convincing. He stated that 'most countries have a higher regard for US technology than the US does because we're surrounded by our technology every day and take it for granted'.[128] Regarding the technology of the SDI, Journalist and author Peter Schweizer believed in the US developing the SDI. According to him, in the Soviet mind there was 'no question that we could, as the Soviets had an exaggerated view on everything. Even the Soviet Politburo said that SDI would work'.[129]

The Feasibility of the SDI

The US could field a BMD system Martin Anderson contended that the US was technologically far ahead of the Soviet Union but 'did still not make a missile intercept so far'. It was clear that if the US used its power and technology it could 'in a short period of time put together a missile defense system'.[130] Anderson added that the Soviets did in the 1970s with their ABM system. The only thing holding SDI up was 'purely a political problem'. He asserted that the US was very close to a defence which would stop missiles. They could build against one missile coming in 'but with two or three missiles it was more difficult'.[131]

Richard Perle later revealed that he believed that it was possible to 'develop and deploy a system which would destroy a significant fraction of ballistic missiles'.[132] He never believed in a full defence and this would not be necessary to justify deployment. If the SDI could intercept as little as half of the missiles, the Soviets could never be as confident to strike at the US.[133]

Advocacy groups Interviewed in 1998, Washington based defence expert, Keith B. Payne stated that 'there were a number of very prominent studies who were very supportive' of the SDI. Payne cited the Fletcher study and the Hoffman study. He recalled that:

> One of the statements from Dr Fletcher a year after the Fletcher study, or during its course, was to the extent that he was absolutely certain that the US could field a missile defense system that would work to a very high level of effectiveness.[134]

Payne added that there were advocacy groups such as the Union of Concerned Scientists 'who essentially let their own campaign against the SDI'. However 'their particular approach to it was that it would not work to their level of satisfaction'. The Union of Concerned Scientists was not other than an advocacy group; 'it's not as if you had an independent scientific commission called the Union of Concerned Scientists that then puts out an independent non-partisan report'.[135] It was an advocacy group in support of arms control. They thought that the SDI would have challenged arms control as arms control was practised. Although there were a 'good number of organizations that had scientists as part of them come out in opposition to missile defense' such an opposition was generated because 'ballistic missile defense was seen as a challenge to arms control'. A particular tool these groups used against the SDI was to suggest it could never work.[136] William (Bill) Lee stated that proponents of arms control – who were critics of SDI – were 'screaming murder' at the SDI proposal.[137]

The technology of SDI Caspar Weinberger, in 1998, recalled that a lot of scientific people believed that the SDI:

> could not be done; that there were too many rockets for the Soviets, – thousands of them – and that we would not be able to discriminate or distinguish between real and decoys; that they came in too fast to re-entry and that we could not do it.[138]

However, 'Mr Reagan had great faith in America's capabilities and believed if we could put a man on the Moon, we could probably do this too'. According to Caspar Weinberger, the US had established the feasibility of SDI, yet a large number of things remained to be done. The US had to develop a very sensitive 'battle management plan'.[139] There had to be:

> radar that could pick up the course, speed and direction of the missiles right after they were launched and track them through the various stages and course directions that were made.[140]

Caspar Weinberger affirmed that the US had to discriminate between real and decoy missiles 'because one of the plans of the Soviets was to launch a very large number of decoys and other things that would look like missiles on our radar screens'.[141] Weinberger asserted that people in the US were 'outraged', and said that the SDI was 'an awful thing to do' and would violate the ABM Treaty. He contended that Ronald Reagan had a policy of defending rather than avenging people. Weinberger stated that 'The ABM Treaty was based on avenging people'. This ABM Treaty had 'established the whole mutual assured destruction theory as part of our law'. Under the treaty, working on the SDI would 'be bad', but the US nevertheless persisted with it.[142] According to Weinberger, the US made 'very great progress' on the SDI. Weinberger stated that the Soviets 'during the last few years of the Cold War, and afterwards according to some of the documents', regarded the SDI 'with very great alarm'.[143]

According to Caspar Weinberger one of the demands that the Soviets insisted on in the various discussions they were having with the US, on 'reducing the number of weapons of all kinds' was that the US should give up working on strategic defence. Weinberger added that the Soviets 'had a couple of other demands; that we should give up work on stealth technology and that we should also decouple ourselves, or be decoupled from Europe'. These were three military objectives which the Soviets never obtained because 'the US never gave in'.[144]

The ABM treaty is 'undeclarable' Caspar Weinberger stated that 'Administrations followed Reagan policy up until 1993 when Clinton said we were basing our security on the ABM Treaty'. The ABM Treaty is 'based on the premise that the Soviets behave how we do which isn't the case'. Regarding President Bill Clinton's decision to adhere to the ABM Treaty, Caspar Weinberger, in 1998, revealed 'Well I think he has made a serious mistake. We still have no defense. We're doing worse trying to expand the ABM Treaty'.[145] The new provisions were allowing the Soviets to build-up their defences. Weinberger attested that 'Congress was unhappy about trying to extend the treaty'. He added that 'In common law, legally the ABM Treaty is undeclarable because the Soviet Union died. It was based on two superpowers; now one is dead'.[146] Speaking in 1998, Martin Anderson prophesized that in the following few years there would be a 'greater effort to build a limited defense system consistent with the ABM Treaty'. A missile defence system was a guarantee and insurance that no one would threaten the US. According to Anderson, this should make Japan more secure, and would make Israel more secure in the Middle East.[147]

The SDI

Soviet work on ballistic missile defence According to William Graham, by virtue of internetting all radars, and peripheral radars, – the RS-300, SA-10, SA-12s – upon which significant numbers have nuclear interceptors on them, and in conjunction with the Moscow system deployed, 'the Soviets have a reasonably proficient national defense system. You can argue they had it since the 1970s'.[148] Similarly, Keith Payne stated that the:

> Soviets had been working on ballistic missile defense for many years and they probably devoted more resources to it than did the US. They obviously had an operational system in Moscow and still do, as a matter of fact.[149]

Richard V. Allen affirmed that 'the Soviets were actively working on ballistic missile defenses since the 1960s and had their own SDI'.[150]

The SDI as part of 'competitive strategies' and the 'revolution of military affairs'
The SDI was part of the US policy of 'competitive strategies'. According to Keith
Payne, 'the SDI was – really – a reflection of the US decision not to compete in
areas of Soviet strength any more'. He further added that:

> The US had something called 'competitive strategies'. It was actually a planned idea
> to compete in those areas that we knew that the Soviets could not compete very well
> in. We actually had an office of competitive strategies.[151]

Instead of focusing on areas where the Soviets had an advantage in – which was
fairly simple technologies and then mass producing the simple technologies – the
US moved to work in areas which were much more technologically sophisticated,
'that the Soviet economy essentially could not compete in'.[152]

According to Keith Payne 'A number of Soviet military leaders, probably
beginning with Ogarkov' recognized that, that was what the US was beginning to
do. This US new course of action was called the 'revolution of military affairs'.[153]
This is also substantiated by Peter Schweizer. Payne contended that the 'SDI was
the perfect example of the fact that the US was going to move into areas that did
not lend themselves to Soviet competition'. They did not lend themselves to Soviet
competition because in Soviet industry everything, except the fairly narrow
military fields that the Soviets had been pursuing, was so 'abysmally primitive'.[154]

The Soviets 'could not take anything out of commercial industry and use it'
as the 'commercial industry was not lenient to Soviet military research,
development and deployment'. The Soviet economy could produce virtually
nothing for the international consumer market.[155] On the other hand, in the US and
Western countries, the consumer industry lead in terms of advanced technology:

> and so the US was able to exploit consumer industry and technology, and transfer
> that to the military, whereas the Soviets just could not do that, because their
> consumer industry was so primitive.[156]

Payne added that in the US (and the West) there was a 'thriving robust industry
that was not focused on military procurement per se'. However, the 'transfer to
military procurement was obvious and gave a huge advantage to the West. People
such as Ogarkov – and others in the Soviet Union – figured that out'. As part of
competitive strategies, the SDI 'very neatly demonstrated to the Soviet leadership
that it was no longer competitive, and the Soviet leadership understood that'.[157]

Peter Schweizer stated that the US had a 'revolution in military affairs' as
well as direct spending on strategic defence. The Soviets were worried that the tank
would become obsolete because of the investment in technologies which
Weinberger was making.[158] The Soviets were spending money not just on strategic
defence but also on conventional weapons. The SDI was important, but, according
to Peter Schweizer, should not be separated from conventional weapons spending.
Schweizer declared that the 'SDI by itself was not a large proportion of the budget
but it was substantial proportion if you look at the Soviet budget'. Schweizer added
that 'it stretched Soviet capabilities in the area of high technology'.[159] According to

Martin Anderson, from the viewpoint of the Soviets 'they strongly believed in missile defense'. The Soviets 'were convinced that if the US put money into it, the US would have not only a massive capability but a missile defense capability'.[160]

'Hit to kill' technology   Keith Payne recalled the Soviets' reaction, when the Soviets saw what the US was looking at in terms of goals for missile defence, their space-based sensors and interceptors; 'hit to kill' technology. Those were the very advanced technologies which the Soviets could not do, and knew they could not do. Keith Payne revealed that a number of Soviet scientists and military specialists told him that:

> we cannot do hit to kill, we just can't do it. We believe you can do it, maybe, but we know we can't do it – which is why our missile defence will be nuclear armed because we cannot do hit to kill.[161]

The Soviets, stated Payne, 'knew their own limitations in the area of missile defense although they were putting a lot of effort into it'. According to Payne 'In terms of how effective a missile defense system might be; an intercept armed with a nuclear weapon for missile defense purposes can be a very effective intercept'. The fact that the West, and in particular the US wanted to move towards 'hit to kill' technology was driven by a lot of reasons, 'but it wasn't because nuclear armed interceptors don't make good interceptors'.[162]

Richard Perle identified that 'Things had gone on in ballistic missile defense before the President's speech'. Perle declared that 'two thirds of the technology projects which were part of the SDI were projects which were going on before'.[163] According to Edwin Meese III, the 'High Frontier' was the name under which work in ballistic missile defence had previously gone on. The SDI was the new name for the project from March 23 1983, but the technology and people involved in the High Frontier was the same technology and people involved in the SDI.[164] Meese III pointed out that the SDI was a significant factor in the total improvement in US capabilities. The US was 'filling a hollow military force since the 1970s' by going ahead with civil and air defence improvements, building up forces in strategic competition both air-borne and sea-borne and increasing its conventional forces.[165]

Why the Soviets feared the SDI   According to William (Bill) Lee 'there is good evidence on the Soviet side why the SDI is important'. It was documentable that the Soviets had their own SDI programme and did not want any competition. The second important factor was that the US SDI, even if 30 per cent to 40 per cent effective (which were relatively low levels), would defeat the targeting strategy of the Soviet Union. William (Bill) Lee explained that 'if SDI was 23 per cent effective never mind 99 per cent, 50 to 60 per cent of the Soviet attack would fail'.[166] The third factor was that the Soviets had violated the ABM Treaty, totally. This, according to Lee, was another reason why they did not want the US to get involved in the ABM Treaty. Lee contended that 'The Soviets are still biding by

ABM Article 1 which forbids national and ABM deployment'. He added that the Soviets could not stand the cost of competition with the US.[167]

When the SDI would be operational Regarding the way in which SDI was sold to Congress and to the public, Richard V. Allen believed that the SDI was 'miserably defended'. He explained that SDI was called 'Star Wars' through the fault of the staff of the President who:

> announced it then did not have a vigorous program to sell it. They let it be criticised and demongated by the Union of Concerned Scientists who portrayed SDI as a hopeless 'Buck Rogers–Star Wars' thing.[168]

According to Allen 'Reagan did not mind that, but he was disturbed by the lack of a strong sales campaign for SDI'.[169] Richard Perle affirmed that although the SDI programme was a 'vigorous program' it was ill-defined.[170] Similarly, William (Bill) Lee expressed that the SDI was 'badly managed in my view'. As the programme was 'never administered in an appropriate manner', Lee could not tell when he believed that the system would have been operational. However, he stated that 'if you apply the usual criteria, SDI would probably be operational within ten years or so. SDI would have been fielded now'.[171] Caspar Weinberger also believed that the SDI would have been deployed in the period 1997–9.[172]

Keith Payne commented that it was 'impossible' to answer the question when he believed that the SDI would have been operational. This was because 'there was never a specific US system that was scheduled for deployment'. Payne asserted that there was 'always research and development' in SDI technologies. Before the Clinton administration, the 'closest' that the US came to deploying these technologies was 'with the GPALS program'. However, 'When the Clinton administration came in, it basically cut back on that program'.[173]

The GPALS programme was discontinued. Regarding the feasibility of ballistic missile defence, Keith Payne remarked:

> Do I think it can work? Against the kind of threats that the US is going to confront in the foreseeable future – sure. By that what I mean is the emerging missile threats from places like North Korea.[174]

Edwin Meese III believed in the feasibility of the SDI.[175] Regarding the US expenditure on the SDI, Caspar Weinberger revealed that the 'SDI was four to five per cent of the US military budget. We should never have given it up'.[176] Keith Payne remarked that the US spent 'somewhere between $45 to 50 billion on SDI since its inauguration'.[177] Peter Schweizer similarly stated that the 'US spent $40 billion research on SDI'.[178] Richard V. Allen put this figure at $50–60 billion.[179] Richard Perle, speaking in 1998, stated that 'there is still work going on' the SDI.[180]

The US Offer to Share SDI Technology

In his memoirs, *An American Life*, Ronald Reagan stated that 'Privately, I had made a decision: I was going to offer to share SDI technology with the Soviets. This, I thought, should convince them it would never be a threat to them'.[181] The US offer to share SDI technology was made to the Soviets on November 19 1985, the first day of the Geneva summit.[182] In his memoirs, Reagan revealed that he said that it would be years before the US knew whether the SDI would be practical or not. If it were, the US would discuss with other countries how the SDI would be used. The US would 'open its laboratories to the Soviets, and offer the fruits of its research to all countries, so the entire world could enjoy security against a nuclear holocaust'.[183] Reagan continued:

> Gorbachev, without saying it in so many words, suggested that when I'd made my offer to share SDI research and open our laboratories to the Soviets so they could see that the SDI was not designed for offensive purposes, I was lying.[184]

In attempting to discern whether the offer to share SDI research was due to Ronald Reagan's own initiative or as part of the American strategy, the argument that Reagan acted instinctively when he made his offer to the Soviets is more plausible. It was his personal 'pet project'. The offer made by Reagan was an instinctive casual thing, which was later embellished. Critics argue that because Caspar Weinberger and George Shultz did not know about the offer of sharing SDI technology, this substantiates the argument that the offer Reagan made was not a serious offer. This not plausible as Reagan's failure to discuss it with Weinberger or Shultz does not negate the validity of his proposal. More so, it substantiates the assertion that it was a genuine offer made and proposed by Reagan. An example of the President instigating policy.

The reason why Mikhail Gorbachev did not accept Reagan's proposal (or even the 'zero option' offer) is because Gorbachev was skeptical of the proposal, given the history of American offers to the Soviet Union. A similar US offer to the Soviets to share technology was made during the Dwight D. Eisenhower Presidency, with the 'Open Skies' proposal. This proposed that Soviet spy planes could look at US installations and vice versa. The proposal had never really been taken seriously, although it was claimed that the offer was genuine.

Caspar Weinberger revealed that Ronald Reagan wanted to share the technology of the strategic defence against intercontinental and intermediate range strategic missiles because 'we didn't want for any military advantage. He wanted to make useless these terrible weapons'.[185] Reagan felt by sharing that defence there would be:

> somewhat the same situation as when gas masks were invented. That made it basically militarily irrelevant to have a gas attack because everyone would have defenses against it. That was this same theory that he used.[186]

Having obtained Soviet concessions and even his ideal of a nuclear-free world – the elimination within ten years of all ballistic missiles (nuclear weapons) – made at the 1986 Reykjavik summit, Reagan refused to compromise and abandon his SDI programme. Reagan stated that he wished to offer to share SDI technology with the Soviets in order to convince them that it was not a threat to them. Such an argument is persuasive when viewed within the context of Reagan seeking better relations with the Soviet Union (This was especially evident in his second term). Reagan's offer of sharing SDI technology was revived at the Reykjavik summit.[187]

The Reagan–Gorbachev Correspondence: The Importance of the Issue of Defensive Systems in Space

The Ronald Reagan–Mikhail Gorbachev private correspondence from the *Donald T. Regan Papers* is significant as it shows the importance of the issue of space-based defensive weapons. It shows that the SDI was a crucial issue in US–Soviet relations, as other issues (regional issues) were delegated as subordinate to the issue of 'weapons' in space. Gorbachev's letter of December 24 1985 to President Reagan went against what he himself said about not being bothered about the SDI. The letter clearly shows that Gorbachev was greatly concerned about the SDI.

Gorbachev's December 24 1985 Letter

Mikhail Gorbachev stated that he did not doubt that Ronald Reagan himself had no intention of using the SDI to obtain military superiority. However, Gorbachev stated that a country's leadership had to evaluate the actions of another country regarding the development of new 'types' of weapons in accordance with 'potential capabilities' rather than intentions. Gorbachev wrote that:

> only a country which is preparing for a first (disarming) strike needs a 'space shield'; a country which does not base its actions on such a concept should have no need for such a weapons system.[188]

He added that the 'space-strike weapons' which were being created in the US could destroy objects both in and from space which were 'thousands of miles away'.[189]

Gorbachev wrote that space weapons could only deprive the other side of the 'possibility of countering a nuclear strike'. He added that if such weapons were developed, the process of perfecting them would immediately begin.[190] This would involve 'an ever-increasing arms race' which would have unpredictable consequences for mankind.[191] Gorbachev stated that the USSR would not reduce its nuclear weapons 'to the detriment of its security' whilst the US implemented its SDI programme. He stated that the Soviet Union would be forced to:

develop and improve our strategic nuclear forces and increase their capability of neutralizing the U.S. 'space shield' ... we would also have to develop our own space weapons inter alia for the purpose of a territorial ABM defense.[192]

Gorbachev was convinced that the only 'sensible way out is not to engage in this at all'. Gorbachev wanted the US and Soviet Union to discuss the 'prevention of an arms race in space and its cessation on earth'.[193]

Gorbachev called on Reagan to 'prevent the development of offensive space weapons' which could 'destroy targets in space and from space'. Gorbachev declared that 'this issue has now become very acute' and stated that 'we must not permit anything to go beyond the walls of the laboratory'. Gorbachev also wanted to discuss with Reagan the issue of eliminating the 'danger of a first (disarming) nuclear strike'.[194] He reiterated that the Soviet Union did not have any intention to prepare for a first nuclear strike.[195]

Reagan's Draft Reply Letter, February 12 1986

In his draft reply, February 12 1986, to the handwritten letter from Mikhail Gorbachev, Ronald Reagan wrote that ballistic missile defences could help in reducing nuclear weapons. Reagan contended that he recognized that adding defensive systems to weapons with a first-strike capability could be destabilising but this was why the US proposed that they and the Soviet Union concentrate on reducing such first-strike weapons.[196]

Reagan perceived that 'directed-energy and kinetic devices' used in ballistic missile defence would be 'ill-suited for mass destruction on earth'. He made the point that 'if one were planning to strike earth targets from space, it does not seem rational to resort to such expensive and exotic techniques'.[197] Reagan stated that the Soviet Union was the only country to have 'space strike weapons'. He stated that the Soviet ABM system deployed around Moscow could 'strike targets beyond the atmosphere and has been tested in that mode'. Furthermore, the Soviet 'co-orbital anti-satellite weapon is designed to destroy satellites'. Reagan attested that:

> the Soviet Union began research in defenses utilizing directed energy before the United States did and seems well along in research (and – incidentally -- some testing outside laboratories) of lasers and other forms of directed energy.[198]

Reagan wrote that the US saw the Soviets devote 'enormous resources into defensive systems'. Also, the Soviet Union had built up 'its counterforce weapons in numbers far greater' than the US.[199]

According to Reagan the US was deeply concerned with this situation, but not because the Soviets were 'developing -- and unlike us deploying -- defensive weaponry'. The US was concerned because the Soviet Union deployed a larger number of first-strike weapons than had the US. He stated that there may well have been other reasons for this aside from seeking a 'first-strike advantage'. However, the US similarly had to 'look at capabilities rather than intentions'. The fact was that the US were concerned that the Soviets had 'an advantage in this area'.[200]

Synopsis

Ballistic missile defence (BMD) was not a new idea. It had a history spanning several decades. Much progress had been made on BMD since work on such defences started in the late 1940s. The Moscow or 'Galosh' system highlighted the need for a comparable US system. This was one of the best reasons for the development of the US SDI. As an idea which emerged from Germany and the Soviet Union, ballistic missile defence appeared a feasible concept. This was further evidenced by the development and existence of Moscow's ABM system which is still in operation today.

The SDI had the potential to be both a defensive shield, and as part of the 'squeeze strategy' (to destroy the Soviet Union by bankrupting them). Some saw the SDI as a bargaining chip and as part of the squeeze strategy. Ronald Reagan did not see it this way. President Reagan was motivated by a desire to protect America. His understanding of the purposes of SDI was different from his associates. Ronald Reagan saw the SDI as a genuine defense shield. He had an idealistic notion and great faith in the technology of BMD. To him, SDI was a genuine attempt to secure US invulnerability to missile attack, and to supersede nuclear weapons altogether. He did not see it as a way of destroying the Soviet Union, as Richard Perle did. Reagan did not perceive the SDI in the sceptical way that George Shultz did. Ronald Reagan did not intend to destroy the Soviet Union via the SDI.

It is difficult to conclude anything other than, regardless of whichever factors led to President Reagan's announcement of the SDI, his belief and support of the proposal was the most significant factor. Reagan had announced the SDI before the Joint Chiefs of Staff had confirmed to him the feasibility of it. Although he is often portrayed as being naive in his outlook regarding the SDI, Reagan understood the concept (and some of the limitations) of the SDI. He acknowledged that it could not be immediately deployed. Examining his March 23 address to the nation, that introduced the SDI, this could be deduced. Reagan referred to the SDI as a 'long-term research and development program'.[201] Critics, however failed to acknowledge this and portrayed Reagan as believing in a 'star wars' fantasy. However, the crucial fact was that the Soviets believed that the SDI would work. The Soviets objected to the US work on strategic defence, yet they themselves were building up their own defence capability and had an operational BMD system in Moscow.

Mikhail Gorbachev's anxiety about the SDI was evidenced by his December 24 1985 letter to Ronald Reagan. For a country so advanced in defensive weapons systems, the Soviets were concerned about the SDI. Yet the SDI was not a finished product, ready for imminent deployment, but a project based on technological developments to be deployed at a future date. This demonstrates the degree of fear that the Soviets felt. Their own technology in ballistic missile defences and their own ABM system demonstrated that such technologies were possible.

Notes

1   'Address to the Nation on Defense and National Security, March 23 1983', *Public Papers of the Presidents of the United States: Ronald Reagan, 1983, (Book I: January 1 to July 1983)*, Washington, US Government Printing Office, 1984, pp. 442-443.

2   Payne, Keith B., *Strategic Defense: 'Star Wars' in Perspective*, London, Hamilton Press, 1986, p. 20.; Chalfont, Alun, *SDI: The Case for the Defence*, Occasional Paper No. 12, Institute for European Defence and Strategic Studies, London, Alliance Publishers Ltd., 1985, pp. 23-24, 19-30.; Jones, R. V., Prof., *New Light on Star Wars: A Contribution to the SDI Debate*, Policy Study No. 71, Centre for Policy Studies, London, Donald and Co. Ltd., 1985, pp. 7-23.

3   Stevens, Sayre, 'The Soviet Factor in SDI', *Orbis: A Journal of World Affairs*, Vol. 29, No. 4, Winter 1986, p. 693.; For the history of ballistic missile defence see the following: Baucom, Donald R., 'Hail to the Chiefs: The Untold History of Reagan's SDI Decision', *Policy Review*, No. 53, Summer 1990, pp. 66-73.; Baucom, Donald R., *The Origins of SDI, 1944–1983*, Kansas, University Press of Kansas, 1992.

4   Baker, David, 'The Making of Star Wars', *New Scientist*, July 9 1987, pp. 36-37.

5   Edward Teller quote stated in Brown, Neville, 'A Soviet SDI?', *The World Today*, Vol. 43, December 1987, p. 213.

6   Stevens, 'The Soviet Factor in SDI', p. 693.; That 'the Soviets had begun basic research on ballistic missile defense right after World War II', see Baucom, *The Origins of SDI*, p. 27.; For 'the origins of the Soviet ABM program', see Baucom, *The Origins of SDI*, pp. 27-30.

7   All information taken from the following: Stevens, 'The Soviet Factor in SDI', p. 693.; Baker, 'The Making of Star Wars', p. 39.

8   All information taken from Stevens, 'The Soviet Factor in SDI', p. 693.

9   All information from the following: Ibid., pp. 693-694.; Payne, *Strategic Defense*, pp. 52-53, 59.; For information on the world's only ballistic missile defence (BMD) system in Moscow, and the Soviet work on strategic defence, see McFarlane, Robert C., 'Remarks Delivered to the Overseas Writers Association', March 7 1985, pp. 42-48, especially p. 43, in Jones, *New Light on Star Wars*.; Brown, 'A Soviet SDI?', pp. 212-215, especially p. 212.; Lord Thomas of Swynnerton, 'Preface', p. 1, in Jones, *New Light on Star Wars*, p. 1.; Chalfont, *SDI: The Case for the Defence*, pp. 31-35, especially p. 33.; Chapter 4, 'The Soviet Union and Strategic Defense', in Payne, *Strategic Defense*, pp. 52-60, especially p. 52, 53, 59, 60.; Perle, Richard N., 'The Strategic Defense Initiative: Addressing Some Misconceptions', *Journal of International Affairs*, Vol. 39, No. 1, Summer 1985, p. 27.; Jastrow, Robert, 'The Technical Feasibility of Ballistic Missiles Defense', *Journal of International Affairs*, Vol. 39, No. 1, Summer 1985, pp. 49-50, 52.; Early in September 1984, Dr Edward Teller at his televised speech to the American Defense Institute, argued that it was essential that the US began work on strategic defence, especially since 'the Soviet Union is already working on such defenses', consequently reliance on deterrence was no longer feasible. Stated in Garwin, Richard L., 'Star Wars: Shield or Threat?', *Journal of International Affairs*, Vol. 39, No. 1, Summer 1985, p. 36.; For the Soviet history of strategic defenses at the beginning of the 1970s, see O'Neill, Bill, 'Fear and Laughter in the Kremlin', *New Scientist*, March 20 1993, p. 35.; That the 'Russian antimissile work has a very long history and is very aggressive and threatening', see Broad, William J., 'Experts Say Soviet Has Conducted Space Tests on Anti Missile Weapons', *NYT*, October 15 1986, p. A14.; For US Government reports that state that the Soviets have the world's only ABM system, see

the following: Department of Defense, Strategic Defense Initiative, *Report to the Congress on the Strategic Defense Initiative*, June 1986, pp. III–3 and B–3.; *The President's Strategic Defense Initiative*, January 1985, pp. 2, 7, 9.; Strategic Defense Initiative Organization, *1989 Report to the Congress on the Strategic Defense Initiative*, March 13 1989, pp. 1–5 and A–2.

[10] Rennie, David, in Washington, 'British Puts Base in Front Line', *The Daily Telegraph*, December 18 2002, p. 4.

[11] All information taken from Baker, 'The Making of Star Wars', pp. 38-39.

[12] All information taken from Cannon, Lou, *President Reagan: The Role of a Lifetime*, New York, Simon and Shuster, 1991, p. 321.; See also Hecht, Jeff, 'Blinded by the Light', *New Scientist*, March 20 1993, p. 31.; Herken, Gregg, 'The Earthly Origins of Star Wars', *Bulletin of The Atomic Scientists*, October 1987, p. 28.

[13] Baker, 'The Making of Star Wars', p. 38.

[14] Ibid., pp. 38, 36.

[15] Slater, Jerome and David Goldfischer, 'Can SDI Provide a Defense?', *Political Science Quarterly*, Vol. 101, No. 5, 1986, p. 847.; Schlesinger, James R., 'Rhetoric and Realities in the Star Wars Debate', *International Security*, Vol. 10, No. 1, Summer 1985, pp. 3-4.; 'SDI: Star Wars Comes to Earth', *The Economist*, January 30, 1988, p. 19.; Anderson, *Interview*.; For information on Safeguard, see 'Safeguard: What US Got for $5.4 Billion', *USNWR*, June 30 1975, pp. 42-43.; That the 'Johnson administration announced plans to build an ABM system called Sentinel, to protect against a future missile threat from 'Red China'', see MacDonald, Bruce W., 'Falling Star: SDI's Troubled Seventh Year', *Arms Control Today*, September 1990, p. 8.

[16] See Schlesinger, 'Rhetoric and Realities', p. 12.; Baucom, Donald, 'Hail to the Chiefs', p. 67.; According to William (Bill) Lee, the Soviet Union was 'frightened into SALT by the U.S. antiballistic missile (ABM) program' which Defense Secretary McNamara announced in September 1967. The Soviets perceived that the US NIKE-X ABM could give America an 'intolerable advantage over the USSR'. The NIKE-X ABM system was technically 'more than a decade ahead' of the Soviet programmes 'under development at the time'. It was 'more than two decades ahead' of the Moscow ABM system which the Soviets deployed in the late 1960s. Lee, William T., 'US–USSR Strategic Arms Control Agreements: Expectations and Reality', *Comparative Strategy*, Vol. 12, No. 4, October/December 1993, p. 418.

[17] Schlesinger, 'Rhetoric and Realities', p. 12.

[18] Slater and Goldfischer, 'Can SDI Provide a Defense?', p. 848.

[19] Baucom, *The Origins of SDI*, p. 1.

[20] Baker, 'The Making of Star Wars', pp. 38-39.

[21] Cannon, *President*, p. 319.

[22] All information from Baker, 'The Making of Star Wars', pp. 39-40.

[23] Ibid., p. 39.

[24] Ovinnokov, R., '"Star Wars" Programme – A New Phase in Washington's Militaristic Policy', *International Affairs*, Moscow, No. 8, August 1985, p. 18.

[25] Allen, *Interview*.

[26] Mayer, Jane and Doyle McManus, *Landslide: The Unmaking of the President 1984-1988*, London, Collins, 1988, p. 32.

[27] Payne, *Strategic Defense*, p. 39.

[28] Baker, 'The Making of Star Wars', p. 40.

[29] All information taken from Anderson, Martin, *Revolution: The Reagan Legacy*, Stanford, California, Hoover Institution Press, 1990, p. 94.

[30] Ibid., pp. 95-96.

[31]   Payne, *Strategic Defense*, pp. 39-40.

[32]   Baucom, 'Hail to the Chiefs', p. 70.

[33]   Hecht, 'Blinded by the Light', p. 31.

[34]   Baker, 'The Making of Star Wars', p. 40.

[35]   See Gates, Robert M., *From The Shadows: The Ultimate Insider's Story of Five Presidents and How They Won The Cold War*, New York, Simon and Schuster, 1996, p. 265.

[36]   Payne, *Strategic Defense*, p. 53.; Stevens, 'The Soviet Factor in SDI', p. 695.; That the Soviets were upgrading their ABM (Galosh) system around Moscow, see Thatcher, Margaret, *The Downing Street Years*, London, Harper Collins, 1993, p. 465.; For the interview British Prime Minister Margaret Thatcher gave Soviet television, whereby she said that the Soviet Union was ahead of the US in ABM defenses, see Thatcher, *The Downing Street Years*, p. 483.; For information on the Moscow ABM system, see Lee, William T., 'US–USSR Strategic Arms Control Agreements: Expectations and Reality', *Comparative Strategy*, p. 427.; That the Soviets have the world's only operational ABM system in Moscow and are upgrading the system is documented in Department of Defense, *Soviet Military Power 1985*, Washington D.C., US Government Printing Office, 1985, p. 47.; For the Soviet improvements in their deployed strategic defenses and investments in ABM related developments, see Department of Defense, *Soviet Military Power 1985*, p. 43. See 'Chapter III: Strategic Defense and Space Programs', pp. 43-59.; Soviet Military Power 1985 states that the Soviets could 'be ready to deploy a ground-based laser BMD by the early-to-mid 1990s'. The publication states that 'the Soviets have a vigorous program underway for particle beam development and could have a prototype space-based system ready for testing in the late 1990s'. Department of Defense, *Soviet Military Power 1985*, p. 44.; That the 'Soviets were modernising their Galosh system' and were 'adding SAMs', see FitzGerald, Frances, *Way Out There in the Blue: Reagan, Star Wars and the End of the Cold War*, New York, Simon and Schuster, 2000, p. 561 52n.; That the Soviet Union was hard at work on its own SDI, see Lee, William T., 'US–USSR Strategic Arms Control Agreements: Expectations and Reality', *Comparative Strategy*, p. 432.

[37]   Graham, *Interview*.

[38]   LaFeber, Walter, *America, Russia, and the Cold War 1945-1990*, 6th Ed., New York, McGraw-Hill, Inc., 1991, p. 304.

[39]   Dobrynin, Anatoly, *In Confidence: Moscow's Ambassador to America's Six Cold War Presidents 1962–86*, New York, Random House, 1995, p. 529.

[40]   Weinberger, *Interview*.

[41]   'Address to the Nation on Defense and National Security, March 23 1983', *Reagan Public Papers*, p. 442.

[42]   Payne, *Strategic Defense*, p. 38.

[43]   Talbott, Strobe, *The Master of the Game: Paul Nitze and the Nuclear Peace*, New York, Vintage Books, 1989, p. 204.

[44]   FitzGerald, *Way Out There in the Blue*, p. 198.

[45]   Payne, *Strategic Defense*, p. 38.

[46]   Ovinnokov, '"Star Wars"', p. 18.

[47]   Ibid.

[48]   Talbott, *Master of the Game*, p. 201.; Ovinnokov, '"Star Wars"', p. 18.

[49]   Young, John W., *Cold War And Detente 1941–1991 (The Longman Companion to)*, London, Longman, 1993, p. 295.

[50]   Ibid., p. 295.; Dumbrell, John, *American Foreign Policy: Carter to Clinton*, London, Macmillan Press Ltd., 1997, p. 72.

51 Ovinnokov, '"Star Wars"', pp. 17-19.
52 Cannon, *President*, p. 323.
53 Ibid., p. 327.
54 Ibid, pp. 327-328.
55 Baucom, 'Hail to the Chiefs', p. 66.
56 Cannon, *President*, p. 329.
57 Baucom, 'Hail to the Chiefs', p. 71.; Baucom, *The Origins of SDI*, p. 188.
58 Cannon, *President*, p. 328.
59 Ibid., p. 330.
60 Weinberger, Caspar, *Fighting For Peace: Seven Critical Years in the Pentagon*, New York, Warner Books, 1990, p. 304.
61 Ibid.
62 Ibid.
63 Perle, *Interview*.
64 These revelations were made at the February 1993 Princeton University conference. See Wohlforth, William, C., (ed.), *Witnesses to the End of the Cold War*, Baltimore, The John Hopkins University Press, 1996, p. 45.
65 Ibid.
66 Ibid.
67 Cannon, *President*, pp. 292, 319.
68 Ibid., p. 292.
69 For information on Dr Michael Rogin's thesis that Ronald Reagan was influenced by the movies he starred in, see FitzGerald, *Way Out There in the Blue*, pp. 22-23.; That Alfred Hitchcock's 1966 film *Torn Curtain* (about 'an attempt to develop an anti-missile missile') influenced 'Reagan's thinking about missile defenses', see FitzGerald, *Way Out There in the Blue*, p. 23. Quotes and words are by Frances FitzGerald.; That 'Reagan saw the presidency as one big movie', see Greenberg, David, 'Review Essay: The Empire Strikes Out: Why Star Wars Did Not End the Cold War: A Review of FitzGerald, Frances, 'Way Out There in the Blue: Reagan, Star Wars and the End of the Cold War', New York, Simon and Schuster, 2000', *Foreign Affairs*, Vol. 79, No. 2, March/April 2000, p. 138.
70 Cannon, *President*, p. 290.
71 Payne, *Strategic Defense*, pp. 36-37.
72 Anderson, *Interview*.
73 Ibid.
74 Anderson, *Revolution*, p. 83.
75 Anderson, *Interview*.
76 Anderson, *Revolution*, pp. 85-86.
77 Weinberger, *Interview*.
78 Wohlforth, *Witnesses to the End*, p. 35.
79 FitzGerald, *Way Out There in the Blue*, p. 19.
80 Reagan, Ronald, *An American Life*, London, Hutchinson, 1990, p. 547.; Dr George A. Keyworth contended that President Reagan was not the first person to raise the issue of strategic defence. Nevertheless, 'The question of raising it to public attention as a major strategic goal, the first step of which would be a research program, was the President's own initiative'. Dr Keyworth affirmed that 'The President did not invent the concept of ballistic missile defense'. However, Keyworth stated that 'the giving of the speech, its content and its timing, was the President's own initiative and objective'. See 'Strategic Defense and Anti-Satellite Weapons', *Hearing Before The Committee on Foreign*

        Relations, United States Senate, Ninety-Eighth Congress, Second Session, April 25
        1984, Washington, US Government Printing Office, 1984, pp. 83 and 84, respectively.

[81]   Payne, *Strategic Defense*, p. 41.

[82]   Anderson, *Revolution*, p. 80.

[83]   Allen, *Interview*.

[84]   Meese III, *Interview*.

[85]   Ibid.

[86]   Baucom, 'Hail to the Chiefs', p. 69.

[87]   Ibid.

[88]   Wohlforth, *Witnesses to the End*, p. 6.

[89]   Department of Defense, Strategic Defense Initiative, *Report to the Congress on the
        Strategic Defense Initiative*, June 1986, p. III–8.

[90]   Ibid., p. III–2.; For the Soviet modernization of its intercontinental ballistic missiles
        (ICBMs) see Department of Defense, *Soviet Military Power 1985*, p. 25.

[91]   Department of Defense, Strategic Defense Initiative, *Report to the Congress on the
        Strategic Defense Initiative*, June 1986, pp. III–2 and III–3.

[92]   Ibid., p. III–3.

[93]   Strategic Defense Initiative Organization, *1989 Report to the Congress on the Strategic
        Defense Initiative*, March 13 1989, p. 1–3.

[94]   Ibid., pp. 1–4, 1–5 and A–4.; That the Soviet Union had the world's only operational
        ABM system is also stated by Gates, *From The Shadows*, p. 265.; That the Soviet Union
        has an operational ASAT capability, see 'Statement of Hon. Richard N. Perle, Assistant
        Secretary of Defense for International Security Policy', in 'Strategic Defense and Anti-
        Satellite Weapons', *Hearing Before The Committee on Foreign Relations, United States
        Senate*, Ninety-Eighth Congress, Second Session, April 25 1984, Washington, US
        Government Printing Office, 1984, p. 28.; That the Soviet Union have the 'world's only
        operational ABM system, and are continuing to modernize it' and that the 'Soviets also
        have the world's only extensively tested and fully operational anti-satellite system. And
        their own research efforts into SDI technologies' is quoted in 'Remarks and Question
        and Answer Session by the Honourable George P. Shultz, Secretary of State, Before the
        North Atlantic Assembly, St. Francis Hotel, San Francisco, California, Monday October
        14 1985', in 'Strategic Defense Initiative', *Hearings Before the Subcommittee on
        Strategic and Theater Nuclear Forces of the Committeee on Armed Services, United
        States Senate*, Ninety-Ninth Congress, First Session, October 30, November 6, 21,
        December 3, 5, 1985, Washington, US Government Printing Office, 1986, pp. 156, 157
        respectively.; That the Soviet Union has the world's only deployed antisatellite weapons
        system and deployed ABM system is stated in Preface, Department of Defense, *Soviet
        Military Power 1985*.; That Moscow has 'the world's only operational antisatellite
        weapon', see Broad, 'Experts Say Soviet Has Conducted Space Tests on Anti Missile
        Weapons', *NYT*, p. A14.

[95]   Strategic Defense Initiative Organization, *1989 Report to the Congress on the Strategic
        Defense Initiative*, March 13 1989, p. 1–2.

[96]   General Advisory Committee on Arms Control and Disarmament, *A Quarter Century of
        Soviet Compliance Practices Under Arms Control Commitments: 1958-1983*,
        Washington D.C., October 1984, p. 14.

[97]   Lee, *Interview*.

[98]   Graham, *Interview*.

[99]   Weinberger, *Interview*.

[100] Strategic Defense Initiative Organization, *1989 Report to the Congress on the Strategic Defense Initiative*, March 13 1989, p. 1–5.; See also *The President's Strategic Defense Initiative*, January 1985, p. 2.

[101] Ekedahl, Carolyn McGiffert and Melvin A. Goodman, *The Wars of Eduard Shevardnadze*, London, Hurst, 1997, p. 88.

[102] Strategic Defense Initiative Organization, *1989 Report to the Congress on the Strategic Defense Initiative*, March 13 1989, p. 1–6.

[103] Ibid., p. 1–4.

[104] Department of Defense, Strategic Defense Initiative, *Report to the Congress on the Strategic Defense Initiative*, June 1986, p. IV–1.

[105] Ibid., p. C–1.; *The President's Strategic Defense Initiative*, January 1985, p. i.

[106] *The President's Strategic Defense Initiative*, January 1985, p. i.

[107] Ibid., p. 9.

[108] 'Address to the Nation on Defense and National Security, March 23 1983', *Reagan Public Papers*, pp. 438-439.

[109] Ibid., p. 442.

[110] Ibid., p. 443.

[111] Reagan, *An American Life*, p. 443.

[112] Ibid.

[113] Brinkley, Joel, 'Reagan Reaffirms 'Star Wars' Stand', *NYT*, November 24 1987, p. A14.; That the Soviets had their own Galosh ABM system around Moscow, see Baucom, *The Origins of SDI*, pp. 30, 34, 46, 56-57, 67-68.; For Soviet ABM work, see FitzGerald, *Way Out There in the Blue*, pp. 560-561 51n.; That the Soviets were working on their own 'Star Wars' defence system, see Patman, Robert G., 'Reagan, Gorbachev and the Emergence of "New Political Thinking"', *Review of International Studies*, Vol. 25, No. 4, October 1999, p. 596.

[114] Tammen, Ronald L., James T. Bruce, and Bruce W. MacDonald, 'Star Wars After Five Years: The Decisive Points', *Arms Control Today*, July/August 1988, p. 7.; Reagan affirmed that the Soviets had 'spent billions and billions of dollars developing and deploying their own antiballistic missile defenses'. Brinkley, 'Reagan Reaffirms 'Star Wars' Stand', *NYT*, p. A14.; That the Soviets spent '$240 billion more than the U.S. on defense', see FitzGerald, *Way Out There in the Blue*, pp. 109-110.; That the backwardness of the Soviet SDI programme is the reason why the Soviets wanted a ban on SDI testing outside of the laboratory as Gorbachev requested, see Broad, 'Experts Say Soviet Has Conducted Space Tests on Anti Missile Weapons', *NYT*, p. A14.

[115] All information taken from Tammen, Bruce, and MacDonald, 'Star Wars After Five Years: The Decisive Points', p. 7.

[116] Ibid.

[117] Ibid.

[118] Ibid.

[119] Anderson, *Interview*.

[120] Ibid.

[121] Allen, *Interview*.

[122] Ibid.

[123] Reagan, *An American Life*, p. 571.; Ronald Reagan, in his memoirs, stated that 'I never viewed the SDI as an impenetrable shield – no defense could ever be expected to be one hundred percent effective'. Ibid., p. 608.

[124] Allen, *Interview*.

[125] Graham, *Interview*.

[126] Ibid.

[127] Ibid.
[128] Ibid.
[129] Schweizer, *Interview.*
[130] Anderson, *Interview.*
[131] Ibid.
[132] Perle, *Interview.*
[133] Ibid.
[134] Payne, *Interview.*
[135] Ibid.
[136] Ibid.
[137] Lee, *Interview.*
[138] Weinberger, *Interview.*
[139] Ibid.
[140] Ibid.
[141] Ibid.
[142] Ibid.
[143] Ibid.
[144] Ibid.
[145] Ibid.
[146] Ibid.
[147] Anderson, *Interview.*
[148] Graham, *Interview.*
[149] Payne, *Interview.*
[150] Allen, *Interview.*
[151] Payne, *Interview.*
[152] Ibid.
[153] Ibid.
[154] Ibid.
[155] Ibid.
[156] Ibid.; That the Soviet Union lags in computer technology and that their technology is inferior to the US, see Broad, 'Experts Say Soviet Has Conducted Space Tests on Anti Missile Weapons', *NYT*, p. A14.
[157] Payne, *Interview.*
[158] Schweizer, *Interview.*
[159] Ibid.
[160] Anderson, *Interview.*
[161] Payne, *Interview.*
[162] Ibid.
[163] Perle, *Interview.*
[164] Meese III, *Interview.*
[165] Ibid.
[166] Lee, *Interview.*
[167] Ibid.
[168] Allen, *Interview.*
[169] Ibid.
[170] Perle, *Interview.*
[171] Lee, *Interview.*
[172] Weinberger, *Interview.*
[173] Payne, *Interview.*
[174] Ibid.

175 Meese III, *Interview*.
176 Weinberger, *Interview*.
177 Payne, *Interview*.
178 Schweizer, *Interview*.
179 Allen, *Interview*.
180 Perle, *Interview*.
181 Reagan, *An American Life*, p. 631.
182 Ibid., p. 637.; For the Reagan–Gorbachev summit meeting at Geneva, where Reagan said he would share SDI technology, see Dobrynin, *In Confidence*, p. 589.; That Ronald Reagan promised, at the Geneva summit, to share SDI technology with the Soviets, see Gorbachev, Mikhail, *Memoirs*, London, Bantam Books, 1997, p. 524.; Ronald Reagan stated to Mikhail Gorbachev, regarding the SDI defensive shield, 'We don't know if it is possible, but we are optimistic. You've been researching such a system also ... If either of us comes up with a solution, let's share it, make it available to everyone. Remove all fear of a nuclear strike'. Morris, Edmund, 'Saving The World', *The Sunday Times*, September 26 1999, p. 2.
183 Reagan, *An American Life*, p. 637.; That Ronald Reagan would share SDI technology with 'all nations once all nuclear missiles had been scrapped', see ibid., p. 665.
184 Ibid., p. 639.
185 Weinberger, *Interview*.
186 Ibid.
187 See Shultz, George P., *Turmoil and Triumph: My Years as Secretary of State*, New York, Charles Scribner's Sons, 1993, p. 761.; Ronald Reagan reiterated, at the Reykjavik summit, 1986, his promise that the US would share its SDI technology with the Soviet Union. 'Gorbachev refused to believe it, insisting that SDI would just take the arms race into space, whereupon the meeting adjourned'. Sicherman, Harvey, 'Review Essay: The Rest of Reagan. Review of Morris, Edmund, 'Dutch: A Memoir of Ronald Reagan', New York, Random House, 1999', *Orbis: A Journal of World Affairs*, Vol. 44, No. 3, Summer 2000, p. 493.; Gorbachev, however, 'held firm on no SDI testing outside the lab. "It's laboratory or nothing" said Gorbachev. Said Reagan after consulting with Shultz: "The meeting is over"'. Sicherman, 'Review Essay: The Rest of Reagan. Review of Morris, Edmund, 'Dutch: A Memoir of Ronald Reagan', New York, Random House, 1999', p. 493.
188 'Letter From Mikhail Gorbachev to Ronald W. Reagan', Moscow, December 24 1985, p. 2, *Regan, Donald T., Papers*, Box 214, Folder 9, 'Soviet Union, Reagan–Gorbachev Correspondence', Library of Congress.
189 Ibid.
190 Ibid.
191 Ibid., p. 3.
192 Ibid., pp. 2-3.
193 Ibid., p. 3.
194 Ibid.
195 Ibid., p. 4.
196 Reagan, Ronald, 'Draft Reply to Handwritten Letter From Gorbachev', February 12 1986, p. 1, *Regan, Donald T., Papers*, Box 214, Folder 9, 'Soviet Union, Reagan–Gorbachev Correspondence', Library of Congress.
197 Ibid.
198 Ibid, p. 2.
199 Ibid.
200 Ibid.

[201] 'Address to the Nation on Defense and National Security, March 23 1983', *Reagan Public Papers*, p. 443.

Chapter 2

The Soviet Reaction to the SDI

Introduction

The US bureaucracy, the American public, Congress and the allies were all surprised by President Ronald Reagan's SDI announcement. However, the most interesting reaction was from the Soviet Union.

The World Reacts

The Bureaucracy's Reaction to the SDI

The SDI speech was a surprise to the Washington defence and foreign policy bureaucracy, apart from National Security Adviser (1982–1983) William Clark, John Poindexter (who was NSA in 1985–1986) and Robert McFarlane.[1] That the SDI speech was a surprise to the bureaucracy is evidence that the introduction of the SDI was very much due to President Reagan. George Shultz and Frank C. Carlucci III's statements (in the previous chapter), that the Joint Chiefs of Staff did not expect the SDI to be announced (as they did not believe anyone 'took them seriously'), is corroborated by Chairman of the Joint Chiefs John Vessey's disclosure that 'the speech caught us all by surprise'. Vessey expected more emphasis on defence following the February 11 1983 meeting, not a new initiative. To Vessey it was apparent that Reagan as Commander-in-Chief wanted to announce it and that was enough.[2]

The Public Reaction to the SDI

The American public was surprised to learn that the US had no defence against Soviet or other missiles.[3] Approximately 75 per cent to 85 per cent of the population – in all national opinion polls – had indicated support for 'star wars' (SDI) weapons as protection against nuclear attack.[4] The public, however, disputed a SDI driven by nuclear means.[5] The public during the Cold War was consistently worried about the Soviet Union. This accounts for the public's support of the SDI. Although the public tends to support the government in foreign policy issues through a sense of patriotism, their interest in foreign affairs is primarily overshadowed by their interest in domestic issues.

The Congressional Reaction to the SDI

In Congress, the day after the SDI announcement several Democratic members of the House responded with sharp criticisms of the SDI. Congressman Ted Weiss (Democrat–N.Y.) contended that it was clear that Reagan 'seeks to elevate the current nuclear madness to a new dimension'.[6] Democrat Congressman Howard Wolpe stated that 'Last night the American people were treated to one of the most outrageous and misleading pieces of political propaganda that this Nation has seen in many years'.[7]

Congress tabled (defeated) amendments reducing SDI funding, though it was not happy about the rapid increases in the project that Reagan sought. From 1984 to 1988 (Fiscal 1985 to Fiscal 1989), Congress increased the funds for the SDI.[8] Proposals rejected by Congress included the Bumpers–Proxmire amendment (38–57), the Gore proposal (36–59) and the Glenn proposal (36–59).[9] According to Edwin Meese III, the Congressional reaction to SDI was mixed. Malcolm Wallop was interested in SDI; a lot of other people felt it was 'unwise'.[10]

The Allies' Reaction to the SDI

The allies were concerned about the SDI because they feared that the US would become less interested in NATO's security,[11] consequently threatening the alliance. (The SDI threatened to overturn MAD (mutual assured destruction), upon which NATO's security was based.) The allies felt that the SDI would exacerbate the arms race with the Soviet Union, thereby ending arms control and detente.[12] SDI threatened to render nuclear missiles obsolete thereby negating the nuclear threat which was the principal deterrent in NATO's 'flexible response'.[13]

The SDI proposed to render impotent the very missiles which were being deployed in Western Europe. (The SDI proposal increased the difficulties which the INF (Intermediate Nuclear Force) deployment programme faced. The European governments faced difficulty in justifying to the public why the missiles which the US President was proposing to render 'impotent and obsolete', were being placed on their soil.)[14] SDI also jeopardized the effectiveness of the Trident programme that the British government was undertaking.[15] The SDI threatened to degrade the credibility of this British defence. West German Chancellor Helmut Kohl urged his government to participate in the SDI, whilst France rejected participation in the SDI.[16]

By de-emphasising the importance of the SDI announcement, the allies played an important role in defusing Soviet criticism of the SDI.[17] The allies legitimized the case for the SDI by referring to the Soviet missile defence research, which Reagan failed to mention in his March 23 1983 speech. (Reagan had portrayed the SDI as a US initiative, rather than a response to extensive Soviet BMD programmes.) By correcting Reagan's ommission, the allies directly countered the Soviet argument against SDI that Washington was initiating a new phase in the arms race (rather than responding to Moscow BMD programmes).[18]

British Prime Minister Margaret Thatcher, at Camp David, on December 22 1984, warned Ronald Reagan that although she would support research on strategic defences, any implication made of her approval of advanced development and deployment would result in her repudiating the SDI.[19] The allies were responsible for the US agreeing to specific parameters for SDI. Formulated by President Reagan and Prime Minister Thatcher at Camp David on December 22 1984, the 'SDI Charter' was the 'credo' of the European allies. The charter was a guarantee to the allies that SDI would not lead to the deployment of ballistic missile defences.[20] The 'SDI Charter', signed at Camp David, was an extraordinary coup for Margaret Thatcher. She single handedly was responsible for Reagan agreeing to strict parameters for the SDI.

According to Caspar Weinberger, the US encouraged 'a great many' of the European nations to help support the SDI and 'got them interested in it'.[21] Caspar Weinberger had in 1985 invited Japan, as well as the NATO allies and other countries, to participate in SDI research. Japanese companies did not want to be left out of any potential technological advances. The Japanese public reaction was, however, 'not altogether positive'.[22] Weinberger had justified the rationale behind the SDI as wholly defensive 'to make the use of nuclear weapons much less likely'.[23] Caspar Weinberger later revealed that England, Italy, Japan and the other allies were interested in 'trying to work out the technology' of the SDI.[24] He stated that:

> The idea of contracts being awarded, and funding by the US, was attractive to them, but I think they were also interested in the idea of seeing whether a defense could be developed. In any event, we made very great progress on it.[25]

The Soviet Union's Reaction to the SDI

Former Reagan Officials' Analysis of the Soviet Reaction to the SDI

According to Martin Anderson, the initial reaction to the SDI speech was 'vehement and furious'. He added that:

> The worlds of many people were turned upside down. The Soviets were stunned and angry, and fearful. Soon Reagan's missile defense program became their number one political target.[26]

After a few years 'The Soviets remained angry and fearful, but within three years they began to seriously discuss nuclear arms reduction, just as Reagan predicted'.[27] Keith Payne stated that 'The Soviet immediate reaction to SDI was very negative. It became a number one focus of their propaganda efforts to discredit it, and to stop it'. Also 'It became the number one goal of the Soviet arms control efforts to stop it. That's what the Reykjavik summit was all about'.[28]

Richard Perle recalled that it was very clear in all dealings with the Soviets that they attributed the highest priority to stopping the SDI. Perle declared that 'the Soviet priority number one was to get rid of SDI'. The reason was that the Soviets believed that they would have a difficult time in maintaining land-based ballistic

missiles in the absence of strategic defenses if the US deployed against them.[29] The SDI 'shook the confidence in the Soviet ability to prevail in the long-term'.[30] The immediate reaction, according to Perle, was a 'flat rejection of SDI'. The Soviets started a major diplomatic campaign against the SDI, and accused the US of 'militarizing the heavens'.[31]

Regarding the Soviet work on their own SDI, Richard Perle stated 'When it comes to a focused effort on SDI, they are doing a very considerable amount'.[32] Perle affirmed that: 'Up until the spring of 1983', the Soviets were the only ones who were working on strategic defences. 'They were busy at work on SDI' whilst the US were 'not making any comparable effort'. Perle stated that the Soviets 'liked that situation' and wanted it to continue. According to him 'The only way they know to continue it is to stop the American program while they continue their own'. Perle believed that the Soviet 'slogans about demilitarizing space' were 'nothing more than slogans'.[33]

Edwin Meese III attested that the:

> Soviet reaction was very aggressive. There was opposition to the SDI on the grounds that it was destabilizing; was a pretence to give the US the strategic offensive edge; was technologically infeasible and cost too much.[34]

Recalling the Soviet response to the SDI, Richard V. Allen declared that:

> Actually, it scared the hell out of the Russians. They were not sure whether they should believe it or whether it was a massive hoax. They rolled out all their propaganda tools to counter it, they blustered and threatened, but to little avail.[35]

According to Caspar Weinberger, 'Unquestionably, the Soviet Union was most afraid of the SDI. The Soviets were afraid of the US dedication to maintain parity'. Recalling the Soviet reaction, Caspar Weinberger explained that:

> the Soviets were very angry because they feared the SDI would render impotent their missiles. Their actions were of a warlike gesture. They paid no attention to the US offer of sharing the technology.[36]

Richard V. Allen affirmed that the Soviet reaction to the SDI was to 'rip up the peace mix: the world peace congress in Prague. The Soviets threw everything they could against SDI. They acted provocative'.[37] William (Bill) Lee declared that the SDI was a 'bad blow' to the Soviets.[38] Recalling the Soviet reaction, Martin Anderson contended that there is 'increasing evidence' that the Soviet Union were concerned about the SDI.[39] According to William Graham, the SDI was important to Mikhail Gorbachev to 'table it' as the price of denuclearizing the Soviet Union and the United States. Graham commented that the Soviet Union did not demilitarize but Gorbachev was willing to demilitarize in exchange for the SDI.[40] Graham added:

> How the Soviets responded to the prospect of SDI; they signed Soviet ballistic missile defense and acted in an offensive program to face the prospect of US

ballistic missile defense even when one did not exist. It was important to the credibility of the US to conduct their own ballistic missile defense.[41]

According to William Graham, from a militarily perspective, 'if the SDI proceeded, the Soviets perceived that we could launch pre-emptive strikes from the US. This would mean defense from the majority of Soviet missiles'. [42]

The Soviet Perception of SDI's Motivation and the Issue of Weapons in Space

The Soviets perceived that the SDI would invoke the nuclear war they had sought to avoid and had consequently reflected in their change in ideology since the 1970s.[43] On March 26 1983, General Secretary Yuri Andropov condemned the US administration. He stated:

> Let there be no mistake about it in Washington. It is time they stop devising one option after another in their search for best ways of unleashing nuclear war in the hope of winning it. Engaging in this is not just irresponsible, it is insane.[44]

Andropov accused the US of seeking a first-strike capability. The USSR perceived this as SDI's primary motivation. Andropov declared that the Soviet Union would never let the US could achieve military superiority. This statement was representative of the Soviet military's reaction to the SDI.

Yuri Andropov's statement (released a few days after Reagan's SDI speech) said that President Reagan's plan would appear truly defensive only to 'someone not conversant with these matters'; SDI was actually 'a bid to disarm the Soviet Union in the face of the United States' nuclear threat'.[45] Andropov's advisers believed that the SDI was feasible as a partial defence against a second strike.[46] The Soviets 'considered SDI a destabilizing threat to land-based ICBMs, the main part of their nuclear arsenal'.[47]

The Soviets argued that the SDI contradicted its basic logic of averting a nuclear war, for it would escalate the arms race which the Soviet Union wished to avoid. Consequently, Andropov proposed a treaty which would ban the militarization of space. To Anatoly Dobrynin, Soviet ambassador to the US from 1962–1986, the SDI looked like the US was 'launching another round of the arms race in a new field, namely, in space'.[48] Yuri Andropov's successor, Konstantin Chernenko, on May 19 1984, proposed talks to prevent the militarization of space before it became irreversible. The Soviets, on June 29 1984, publicly demanded arms control discussions with the US in Vienna to be held in mid-September.[49]

On August 18 1983, the Soviet Union formally disqualified itself from being the first country to place anti-satellite systems (ASAT) in space. Washington had acknowledged that the proposal of banning ASAT weapons was an early attempt to 'nip SDI in the bud', since some forms of ASAT might have much in common with some forms of SDI. This was because intercepting a satellite in orbit was similar to destroying a missile warhead at certain points in its trajectory.[50] The Soviets had successfully tested ASAT systems since the 1960s and had the comparative advantage in space weaponry. Consequently, their response can be viewed as a concession made from a position of strength, not weakness, which represented the Soviet desire for conciliation. This need for cooperation was evident by Andropov's private letter, dated 4 July 1983, to President Reagan in which he said that the two leaders should focus 'on the elimination of the nuclear threat'.[51] By January 13 1985, Andrei A. Gromyko (Foreign Minister from 1957–1985, and President from July 2 1985) asserted that there would be no agreement on nuclear disarmament unless the US limited its SDI.

The Soviets had responded to SDI in *Tass* by comparing Ronald Reagan to Adolf Hitler.[52] Soviet news agency *Tass*, on March 24 1983, asserted that the SDI would violate the 1972 ABM Treaty, which, along with SALT, the Soviet Union used as a legal justification in its campaign against the SDI. The SDI was seen as the product of reactionary imperialist circles in the US and the military–industrial complex that had a stake in the project which the SDI would bring.[53] The SDI speech was designed to secure Congressional support for further military programmes (which 'Operation MX Plus' justified).

Yevgeny Velikhov – a Vice-President of the Russian Academy of Sciences in Moscow, and Gorbachev's personal scientific adviser in 1984 – reconciled the SDI announcement to the fact that the Reagan re-election campaign was getting underway and some new policies were needed to take to the public. Velikhov stated that 'one possibility for his administration was to go for real, drastic disarmament'. This was precluded by the fact that the President's closest advisers, notably Caspar Weinberger and Richard Perle, were 'completely against any agreement with the Soviet Union, and not ready for any radical steps'. Consequently, Reagan adopted the alternative idea of strong defence as 'there were only two choices'.[54]

Yevgeny Velikhov claims that only days before Reagan's speech he asked scientists in Washington whether Reagan was about to propose 'something like a big anti-ballistic missile system in space'. They dismissed such a proposal as 'nonsense'.[55] Similarly, he was reassured a year earlier by Edward Teller and other scientists, that there were no plans for the development of space weapons. Yet in 1982, Velikhov claims that he sensed 'something big was happening in the United States – that was my feeling'.[56]

Yevgeny Velikhov was chairing the Committee on International Security and Arms Control (CISAC) – a joint commission from both the US and Soviet science academies. 1983, Velikhov asserted, 'was a very important year for us [because it saw] the completion of an agreement not to put weapons in space'. Both superpowers called for moratoria on the development of anti-satellite weapons.[57]

The Soviet Union's Contradictory Stance: The SDI was 'Technically Infeasible' and 'Easily Neutralised'

The Soviet Union's contradictory stance of seeking conciliation with the US whilst, simultaneously, espousing hostility to the SDI could only be reconciled with a genuine fear of SDI technology. In 1984, The Committee of Soviet Scientists for Peace Against the Nuclear Threat reported that the SDI as 'a salvation from nuclear missiles for mankind', was 'perhaps the greatest ever deception of our time' for it was too expensive, technically unattainable and could easily be defeated by counter-measures.[58]

Such a conclusion was denied by Nikolai Basov of the Soviet Academy of Sciences, in January 1985. Basov announced that the Soviet Union would have no difficulty in matching the SDI. The claim has subsequently been endorsed by Marshall Sergei Sokolov, the Soviet Defence Minister (1984–1987).[59] Similarly, the conclusion from the Committee of Soviet Scientists for Peace Against the Nuclear Threat was also repudiated by the considerable Soviet research in ballistic missile defence technology since the 1970s. Basov's statement, and those who assert that the SDI would provoke the Soviets to develop a similar system overlook the fact that the Soviet Union had already progressed beyond research in laser weapons to deployment, for Moscow has the only ground tested system in existence today.[60]

Within a month of President Reagan's SDI speech, a letter signed by 244 Soviet scientists appeared in *The New York Times* attacking the initiative. A closer inspection of the signatories revealed that it was signed by a substantial number of prominent Russian scientists who had spent their entire professional lives designing Soviet strategic missile systems as well as military and nuclear systems.[61] Among those who had signed the letter were Basov and Prokhorov. The most interesting signature was that of the leading figure in strategic defence research in the Soviet Union, Yevgeny Velikhov. Nikolai Basov was one of the driving forces behind the Soviet strategic defence programme.[62] According to George Shultz:

> Indeed, some of the Soviet scientists most active in declarations against our SDI Program are themselves the men leading the Soviet military research in the same technologies.[63]

The Soviet scientific declaration of SDI's unfeasibility would, in itself, have been a reason for the Soviets to drop their own strategic BMD programme and encourage the US in this 'futile enterprise',[64] devoting resources on a wasted programme that would otherwise have been employed elsewhere. Yet, Moscow had for years worked on its own SDI. Debate has centered upon the effectiveness of Moscow's Galosh system. It is argued that it did not emphasize the initiative and creativity that the western high technological economy did, but was, instead, plagued by technical problems.[65] Sayre Stevens argues that in several technological areas (such as computer hardware and software) the Soviets were behind the US, whose technology, industrial infrastructure and economic resources would only further improvements in the American SDI.[66]

Although Alun Chalfont states that the Soviet Union feared that it would be overtaken by a western space-based defence system with this western technology, industrial infrastructure and economic resource, he documents the impressive Soviet progress with particle beams. Chalfont elaborated that 'the Soviet Union's expertise in microwave weapon technology is at least as great as that of the United States'.[67]

The Soviet Union was simultaneously arguing that the SDI was both 'dangerous, destabilising and provocative' and was 'useless, expensive and easily neutralised'. They were saying that the SDI was 'technologically infeasible' and 'well within the reach of Soviet military scientists'.[68] Alun Chalfont reconciles this contradiction in Soviet attitudes to the fact that the Soviets genuinely feared the SDI, for they were working on their own system and feared that it may be overtaken by the US challenge to it.[69] Others argue that the Soviets have difficulty in making the transition from pure science to technology. That is, they are as capable of research as the Americans, but are unable to translate their research results into technically viable systems.[70]

Deputy Foreign Minister of the Soviet Union in 1986–1987 and Foreign Minister in 1991, Alexander Aleksandrovich Bessmertnykh, reconciled the contradiction in Soviet attitudes towards the SDI as due to the fact that different people in the government felt differently about the SDI.[71] Those in the foreign ministry including Bessmertnykh, Eduard Shevardnadze and Gorbachev himself, believed that because of the SDI there was a 'good opportunity to work with the military and with the defense sectors of the economy to go further with arms control'.[72] In contrast, the military (defence) part of the government wanted to 'increase the production of their offensive weapons' to counter the SDI.[73]

The Soviet Union on the Offensive

Yevgeny Velikhov asserts that military hawks in Moscow, on hearing President Reagan's SDI speech, 'immediately called for the development of a comparable defence system for the Soviet Union'. The Soviet Defence Minister, Dimitri Ustinov, appointed Velikhov to chair a commission to evaluate the SDI threat and propose a response. 'The commission's conclusions were not published and remained classified',[74] precluding an accurate analysis of the Soviet Union's true reaction to the SDI. Such accuracy is similarly precluded by the lack of access to Soviet archives.

Declarations of prominent military officials (as well as prominent Soviet scientists) appeared to recognize the potential feasibility of SDI. In 1985, intelligence officer and Soviet military attache Col. A. Sazhin revealed that military officials believed that the SDI system might prove 90 per cent effective.[75] Similarly, KGB defector Oleg Gordievsky revealed that the consensus in the Soviet Union was that the SDI might really work and could pose a fundamental challenge to the Soviet strategic arsenal.[76]

Consequently, Soviet military officials, such as former Defence Minister S.L. Sokolov, threatened to match American military developments with those of their own, including upgrading their own SDI.[77] Privately, Vladimir Shcherbitsky informed the President that the US SDI would be countered by the Soviet Union's offensive and defensive measures. Nikolai Shishlin and Soviet arms control spokesman Nikolai Chervov continued this. Referring to an increase in offensive missile production, to overwhelm the SDI, Shishlin stated that the Soviet Union would 'do its best to get a sharper and heavier sword'.[78]

Even at the Geneva summit, Gorbachev looking Reagan 'squarely in eye' stated that he could and would do everything necessary to counter SDI with more offensive weapons.[79] Yet, the Soviet Union was still prepared to decrease these offensive forces in exchange for the SDI. (Its highest officials reiterated there would be no reduction of offensive forces unless there was a simultaneous agreement to curb the planned US defensive forces.)

The possibility of negotiation was further demonstrated by the February 1985 KGB report which unquestionably revealed that Soviet intelligence was curious to obtain information on the potential of including SDI and ASAT in negotiations.[80] The report stated possible active measures on the Soviet side to promote opposition to America's SDI plans and support the attitude of the USSR at the Geneva talks. The report also acknowledged the possibility of the SDI being a giant sting operation to induce concessions from the Soviet Union in the field of nuclear weapons.[81]

The Arms Control Implications of the SDI

The SDI had ramifications for arms control.[82] The new General Secretary, Mikhail Gorbachev, perceived the SDI as an American plan to further burden the Soviet economy. He stated that:

> The US wants to exhaust the Soviet Union economically through a race in the most up-to-date and expensive space weapons. It wants to create various kinds of difficulties for the Soviet leadership, to wreck its plans, including the social sphere, in this sphere of improving the standard of living of our people, thus arousing dissatisfaction among the people with their leadership. [83]

The SDI would force the Soviet Union to divert their resources to arms. In a letter which Gorbachev wrote to Reagan on December 24 1985, Gorbachev stated that space strike weapons possessed the capability of being used for 'defensive and offensive arms' and 'represent in the final analysis an extremely dangerous build-up of offensive potential' which could further escalate the arms race.[84] *Izvestiya* stated that SDI was intended to:

> impose on us an even more ruinous arms race. They calculate that the Soviet Union will not last the race ... They hope that our country's economy will be exhausted.[85]

Gorbachev wanted to accelerate the country's economic and social development for he realized the extent of the Soviet economic crisis and understood that to maintain geographical–political strength the economy had to be strengthened.[86] Falling behind the US in this sphere of military technology threatened the Soviet Union's superpower status.[87]

Although Gorbachev believed that science and technology, particularly in the military field, could lead to a new phase in the arms race,[88] he began investing in such technologies. SDI supporters here would assert that his motives for doing so was to embrace the SDI challenge. They point to Gorbachev's convention of a ific–technical conference in June 1985 as an attempt to invest in the key SDI industries, for the conference's aim was to accelerate the development of the machine tool industry, and modernize computer technology and the electro-technical industry. Also, the subsequent Eleventh Five Year Plan allocated research and development funds to be concentrated on high-technological projects.[89] Even Gorbachev's Perestroika plan, according to General Dmitri Yazov, was the 'intensification of production based on the newest achievements in science and technology'.[90] It was more than a modernization of the Soviet civilian economy.

Eduard Shevardnadze in his memoirs, *The Future Belongs to Freedom*, asserted that the SDI could 'alone destroy everything that had been achieved in limiting strategic offensive arms and antimissile systems'.[91] Anatoly Dobrynin stated that the introduction of the SDI meant that:

> All the parity and stability created over many years through arms procurement and negotiations were disrupted. It meant that we too would need to spend huge amounts of money. It would begin a new phase in the arms race.[92]

The view that the SDI would be detrimental to the Soviets is also supported by Margaret Thatcher. Thatcher in her memoirs, *The Downing Street Years*, states that SDI's technological and financial implications for the USSR 'were devastating'.[93]

Gorbachev and the SDI: The Antisymmetrical Response and Gorbachev's Admittance of Strategic Defence Research

According to Anatoly Dobrynin, Mikhail Gorbachev:

> made SDI the number one target of his diplomatic and public attacks and proceeded with a cheaper Soviet version, though his main target always remained the same: to kill or neutralize Star Wars through diplomatic negotiations.[94]

Dobrynin recalled that Gorbachev convinced himself and the Soviet leadership that the SDI 'had to be thwarted at all costs'.[95] Dobrynin believed that Gorbachev overdid his criticisms of the SDI. However, this 'would merely reinforce Reagan's belief in its importance'.[96]

Peter Schweizer states that the SDI and the US military build-up contributed to, if not, forced Gorbachev to continue the increase in defence expenditure, which he later admitted that he increased eight per cent per annum from 1986 to 1990. This was twice the rate of national income growth. Defence expenditure would rise 45 per cent from 1990 to 1995.[97] Interestingly, Yevgeny Velikhov claims that Gorbachev, since becoming leader in March 1985, promulgated a strategy of 'antisymmetrical, or asymmetrical' defence. The essence of the view was that:

> the Soviet Union was not going to compete with the US in a symmetrical way, matching military development for military development, which has been the traditional approach.[98]

Instead, the Soviet Union 'would do only enough to negate the current level of development of the threat'.[99]

Regarding the Soviet expenditure on their own SDI, Keith Payne contended that 'The Soviet statistics that are publicly available stated many times that the Soviets spent as much or more on their strategic defense as they did on their strategic offense'. He added that 'We know that the level of resources they put into strategic offense was enormous'.[100] According to William (Bill) Lee, the 'estimates of Soviet defense spending on SDI are few and far between'.[101] Lee stated that 'Despite his public statements, Gorbachev did not reduce FSU [former Soviet Union] military expenditures significantly, if at all'.[102]

In contrast to these views, historian, Sovietologist and ex-diplomat Raymond L. Garthoff stated – regarding the Soviet statistical expenditure on SDI – that 'There was really nothing measurable to speak about'. Garthoff commented that the US 'understanding of Soviet military spending' was 'imprecise'.[103] Consequently, it 'would be hard to see and particularly to know' whether SDI had any affect on Soviet defence expenditure. Garthoff stated that the Soviets 'did not engage in additional expenses as a number of Soviet people involved in the program at the time had said'.[104]

Gorbachev perceived Reagan's advocacy of the SDI as being 'bizarre'.[105] It was a 'continuation of the arms race into a different, more dangerous sphere'.[106] The SDI could only 'foment mistrust and suspicion' but, if the Americans chose to continue with the programme and fail to reduce nuclear weapons the Soviet Union would 'have no choice but to accept the challenge'.[107] Regarding counter-measures to the US SDI, Gorbachev announced to Reagan: 'I think you should know that we have already developed a response. It will be effective and far less expensive than your project, and be ready for use in less time'.[108] In his book *Memoirs*, Gorbachev stated that he could not reveal details regarding this to the reader but guaranteed that the Soviets 'were not bluffing'. He affirmed that 'Our studies had proved that the potential answer to SDI could meet the requirements I had mentioned'.[109] On November 30 1987, Gorbachev acknowledged that the USSR was involved in strategic defence research.[110] He announced that:

> The Soviet Union is doing all that the United States is doing, and I guess we are engaged in research, basic research, which relates to these aspects which are covered by the SDI of the United States.[111]

William D. Jackson stated that Gorbachev indicated that the 'SDI should not be a subject of inordinate concern', for the Reagan administration was 'deliberately disseminating exaggerated and false claims of progress in the development of such weapons'.[112] Gorbachev asserted that:

> You will note that the United States is quite exclamatory on everything concerning SDI – the successes and accomplishments of the program. If everything was as they say, and they were accomplishing some superiority, then there would be more secrecy.[113]

ccording to Anatoly Dobrynin, by the end of February 1986, Gorbachev said that: 'Maybe it is time to stop being afraid of SDI?'. Gorbachev perceived that the US was 'counting' on Soviet 'readiness to build the same kind of costly system, hoping meanwhile that they will win this race using their technological superiority'. Dobrynin revealed that Soviet scientists told Gorbachev that if the Soviets wanted to 'destroy or neutralize the American SDI system, we only would have to spend 10 percent of what the Americans plan to spend'.[114] Gorbachev added that the cost of the Soviet SDI system would 'be more than 500 billion rubles, a huge sum'.[115]

Alexander Bessmertnykh believed that the SDI programme evolved. According to him, 'SDI I' was 'too fantastic, so the fear of it evaporated pretty soon'.[116] It was not feasible to build a dome protecting the US.[117] Bessmertnykh said that 'It only took us several months to calculate that was a fantasy'.[118] However, when the US realized this they started work on a SDI II option, then there was SDI III. With the development of these, SDI looked 'more and more feasible'.[119] Bessmertnykh added that once the military part of the Soviet government realized this, they wanted to find a counter-measure against the SDI.[120] This accounted for Gorbachev mentioning several times 'We are working on a counter measure and we do already have something'.[121] According to Bessmertnykh, Gorbachev never revealed what that was, but the main counter-measure was the modernization of the ICBM programme.[122]

Yevgeny Velikhov states of the Soviet response to the SDI 'Because the threat never developed, we didn't need to make any real countermeasures' and 'We needed only to spend some time and money on understanding the scientific part of the job, not on the production'.[123] Velikhov reveals that the huge spending on higher energy lasers that dominated the SDI was 'nonsense'. He dismissed the feasibility of the free electron or X-ray lasers as strategic weapons. Although 'Moscow did not respond with a similar programme to develop lasers for space' the lasers developed were 'mostly for tactical purposes'.[124] Velikhov contended that Moscow watched Washington spend $32 billion on SDI since 1983, while investing little itself in a response. As an idea to hasten the economic collapse of the Soviet Union, the SDI 'was a good idea, but really we were quite capable of bankrupting ourselves. It wasn't necessary'.[125]

The 'Retrospective on the End of the Cold War' Princeton University Conference

Former Soviet officials' disclosures at the conference   On February 26 1993, former high officials from the former Soviet Union came to the Princeton University Conference, New Jersey, and admitted that the Soviet Union's attempt to match the SDI was the primary cause of the collapse of the Soviet Union and that SDI helped end the Cold War.[126] Speaking at the 'Retrospective on the End of the Cold War' conference, the officials said that Soviet leader Mikhail Gorbachev was convinced that 'any attempt to match' the SDI 'would do irreparable harm to the Soviet economy'.[127]

Alexander Bessmertnykh told the gathering 'We were told, even before the SDI, the US had suddenly changed course away from a defensive posture and began an enormous build up'. Then came the SDI which Soviet officials perceived as a 'something very dangerous'.[128] Bessmertnykh stated that the 'SDI made us realise we were in a very dangerous spot'. Further, 'The atmosphere in Moscow was very tense for the first few years of the Reagan administration, especially because of the SDI system: it frightened us very much'.[129] Bessmertnykh added that when the Soviets talked about the SDI, the thought of getting involved in the 'SDI arms race' of trying to emulate what the US was about to do with its 'space-based weapons' programme, 'looked like a horror to Gorbachev'.[130] Gorbachev tried to avoid this by attempting to negotiate a reduction in armaments, whilst trying to persuade the US side to abandon SDI.[131]

A couple of months after the conference, Roald Z. Sagdayev, who headed the Soviet Space Research Institute in the 1980s, was reported in *The New York Times* as stating that Moscow spent billions of dollars it could ill afford responding to SDI. Sagdayev attested that 'This program became priority No.1 after Mr Reagan's announcement of the Star Wars in 1983'. Sagdayev believes that the spending weakened the Soviet Union and may have contributed to its demise.[132]

The Soviets were misquoted at the conference According to Raymond Garthoff, (who was interviewed in 1998) the Soviets were misquoted at the 1993 Princeton University conference. According to Garthoff (in all three cases he was aware of), the accounts published of Soviet leaders who were cited as saying that the 'SDI was the main thing' in the dissolution of the Soviet Union and the end of Cold War, were a 'misrepresentation' of what the Soviets said.[133] Robert C. McFarlane quoted Soviet Chief of General Staff Sergei F. Akhromeyev as having said that the SDI was a 'key thing'. However, Garthoff revealed that, that is not what Akromeyev said and 'he did not say it to McFarlane anyway'. Sergei Akhromeyev said what he said to 'General Davy Jones'.[134] Garthoff talked to both Marshal Akhromeyev and General Jones. Akhromeyev's statement was 'exaggerated, but not intentionally'. It was a 'misstatement'.[135]

Raymond Garthoff wrote to Roald Sagdayev and he replied to Garthoff that he was completely misquoted and misrepresented in *The New York Times* article (where he allegedly stated that the SDI caused a 'very great, heavy burden' on the Soviet Union). Sagdayev said that 'he did not say that at all'. Sagdayev thought that there was virtually no Soviet increase in expenditure in response to the SDI, and he was involved in the studies as the Head of the Institute for Space Research, at the time in the Soviet Union.[136]

The third case is Alexander Bessmertnykh. Raymond Garthoff was present at the Princeton University conference when Bessmertnykh made a statement that Garthoff 'knew right away would be sought of misconstrued'.[137] Garthoff talked to Bessmertnykh about it later and Bessmertnykh agreed that he did not mean that the SDI was the decisive factor for the Soviet collapse and the end of the Cold War. What he said was that the 'SDI was a big shock' to the Soviets and 'represented a major challenge'.[138] Garthoff stated that Bessmertnykh 'did not mean it in the way that some people seized upon his remark'. Regarding the statements that the SDI caused the collapse of the Soviet Union, Garthoff stated 'so in fact the alleged sources of confirmation for that view on the Soviet side evaporate when one looks at them and knows more about them'.[139]

Keith Payne stated that disclosures by a number of senior officials from the Soviet Union influenced his view of the role of the SDI in the Cold War's end. Many of the officials had said that 'the SDI actually led to the ending of the Cold War'. Keith Payne attested that he was unsure whether this was a 'summary generalisation' or whether they meant it specifically that it was the SDI which led to the Cold War's end.[140] Payne added that he had a chance to ask some of the Soviet participants in the Cold War 'who had positions of leadership during the ending of the Cold War' about SDI. Essentially what they said was that the 'SDI was a reflection of the fact that they could not compete any more'. This was 'true in a number of areas' although the 'SDI was the most manifest of those areas'. [141]

The SDI Proposal: Defending the Soviet Side

The Soviet perception of the background to the SDI proposal   According to Raymond Garthoff, the Soviets were troubled by the SDI for a number of reasons. The SDI speech 'occurred at a time of rising tensions for a number of other reasons' like the 'evil empire' speech. The early 1980s and a couple of years preceding that the US began to 'exercise much more aggressive aerial and naval incursions around the Soviet Union'. The US was taking a more active role in the Third World, with what later was called the 'Reagan Doctrine'.[142] A couple of months after Ronald Reagan's SDI speech there was an important NATO exercise, Able Archer, in November 1983 that 'caused very real concern' to the Soviets. Consequently, it was in a context of growing hostility which led some people in the leadership, including Andropov, to perceive the SDI as a technical challenge and a possible heavy additional cost. They also perceived it 'as a political–military challenge'.[143]

The Soviet perception of the SDI   The SDI, according to Raymond Garthoff, 'represented a departure by the US from the position of being in favour of strategic arms control'. The SDI was predicated upon abandoning the ABM Treaty, which had been the largest success in the field of strategic arms control. Reagan did not just unratify SALT II, but with his SDI he appeared ready to abandon attempts to work at arms control.[144] According to Garthoff, Gorbachev's response to the SDI, the US positions in the START and INF talks was to make 'greater concessions on the Soviet side in order to reach agreements'. According to Garthoff, this was because of a change of understanding of the whole relationship of politics in the world, 'not because of some military–economic pressure from the SDI or arms race as a whole'.[145] Initially, 'many in the Soviet leadership' saw the SDI as 'another sign that the US was determined to proceed with a very hard-line of pressure on the Soviet Union and possibly even leading to war'. However, 'by the time Gorbachev came to power, he and most of the others in his leadership did not see it that way'.[146]

The Soviet Union's Political Concerns Regarding the SDI

Dmitry Mikheyev stated that the real Soviet concerns about the SDI were political.[147] The Communist Party was chiefly concerned that the SDI would give the Americans a 'first strike capability', or that it would lead to a militarization of space, or the effect it would have on the military balance per se.[148] The Soviets knew that the Americans would never launch a nuclear attack.[149] Instead, the Soviets were concerned about the:

> political ramifications of the technological lag behind the West ... the consequences of SDI for Moscow's ability to project power throughout the world; and ultimately, SDI's effect on the struggle between the two superpowers for world domination.[150]

According to Mikheyev, SDI posed the following problem for Moscow:

> to survive, it must compete; to compete, it must reform; yet to reform is to admit the bankruptcy of the communist regime, and to make clear the unwisdom of totalitarian control.[151]

The SDI, consequently, presented the Soviets with the choice of falling behind technologically or restructuring their political system.[152] Either way, the SDI could be the leading edge of the US policy towards Moscow.[153]

The New York Times journalist Leslie H. Gelb's recollection substantiates the argument that the SDI would affect the Soviet leadership politically. It corroborates the view that the Soviets lagged behind the West in technology. Recalling his meeting with Marshal Ogarkov, the Chief of Staff of the Soviet Armed Forces, Marshal Ogarkov said to Gelb:

> all modern military capability is based on the computer. You have little kids in America, three years old who know how to deal with computers. It takes years here to train Soviet recruits in the military to use them because they've never used them before. We're afraid of computers. If we start deploying computers it is going to mean loss of political control for the Soviet leadership.[154]

KGB General Nikolai Leonov stated that the SDI:

> played a powerful psychological role. And of course it underlined still more our technological backwardness. It underlined the need for an immediate review of our place in world technological progress.[155]

Robert G. Patman, writing in 1999, contended – regarding Leonov's statement – that:

> The last point assumes greater meaning in light of the fact that the Soviet Union had been working secretly on its own 'Star Wars' defence system since 1976 without success.[156]

The Economic Burden on the Soviet Union and the Soviet Theoretical Studies

Any shift in resources to the military sector was significant given the Soviet acknowledgement of their economic problems. Soviet defence expenditure, like US rearmament (including the SDI) perpetuated the Cold War in an end run competition where the greater economy would prevail. Defence as a share of Soviet GNP, however, was a burden that fell more painfully on the Soviet Union than on the US.[157]

Raymond Garthoff stated that although the prospect of SDI 'would imply an additional burden' on the Soviet Union, the reality was that there was 'no burden at all'. The Soviets 'had various countermeasures in mind and so, even the prospect' of the SDI 'was not as daunting as it seemed'. Garthoff believed that the 'SDI did not increase the economic burden on the Soviet Union because in never reached a point where the Soviets had a specific program to which they could react'.[158]

The Soviet response to the SDI proposal was important as for the first time 'people other than the professional military establishment, had a major role in formulating a response to SDI which the political leadership then accepted'. A number of scientists including Yevgeny Velikhov, Roald Sagdeyev, Andrey Kokoshin, (Deputy Director of the Institute for the Study of the USA and Canada of the USSR Academy of Sciences), and others worked out responses to SDI.[159] Raymond Garthoff said that:

> They would not emulate the US. They would not simply redouble their efforts in building up offensive arms, but they would respond depending upon the specific nature of SDI, which was a concept rather than a real concrete program.[160]

He added that 'There were a number of different possible ideas being examined under the SDI'. It was only when the US had clear which path it was going to take would the Soviets initiate the appropriate counter-measures. These, however, would be 'undertaken with much less cost and burden' on the Soviet Union itself.[161] The Soviets worked out theoretical studies; – responses of the kind of measures they would take to respond to 'one or another concrete program evolving out of SDI'. However, Garthoff asserted that 'it never reached the stage of even identifying such programs, so the only added expense they had were these paper studies not any costly hardware response'.[162]

Change in Soviet Perceptions of the SDI

To the Soviets the perceived threat of SDI had changed. Raymond Garthoff claimed that the Soviets 'were going to frustrate' the US plan of using the SDI to spend the Russians into bankruptcy. This was the thinking of the Soviet military as well.[163] According to Garthoff, in Geneva (1985) and Reykjavik (1986) Gorbachev saw that Reagan was determined to proceed with SDI. Gorbachev also came to realize that:

this was because of Reagan's own particular view of defense, and was tied to serious interest on Reagan's part in moving to drastically reduce or eventually eliminate nuclear weapons.[164]

Garthoff further added that 'While the technical challenge of SDI was still potentially there, the idea this represented an American policy of heavy hostility did not remain'.[165] According to Frances FitzGerald, Roald Sagdeyev, proclaimed that the Soviets had not helped themselves by 'screaming so much about SDI'. The Soviets encouraged the Americans to think that:

> anything the Russians hate so much can't be all bad. And we had overestimated how much damage SDI could do to strategic stability in the short and even the medium term.[166]

A Correlation Between the SDI and the End of the Cold War?

Yes, SDI Did End the Cold War: Former Reagan Officials' Views on the End of the Cold War

According to Caspar Weinberger, the SDI was 'one of the real factors, perhaps one of the major factors' in the ending of the Cold War. In reference to the 'zero option', Weinberger stated that 'In October 1987 we got precisely the treaty that we had asked for in October 1981'. Initially, the Soviets had said they would 'never even discuss' the 'zero option' treaty to get rid of all intermediate nuclear weapons. A lot of US experts said it was an 'absurd proposal' and that it was made because the US knew that the Soviets would never agree to it.[167]

Caspar Weinberger explained that there were a lot of conditions which the Soviets wanted to impose in the discussions. An example was when the Soviets said 'all right we'd do that but we'd have an exception to our missiles aimed at Asia' and, to this proposal, everyone would refuse. With the 'zero option' treaty which the US got, 'all the doomsayers who said this would destroy all the negotiations and discussions were proven wrong'.[168] Weinberger maintained that:

> one of the factors that went into the Soviets agreement – I think – was first of all the realisation we would never change, that we would never give up strategic defense, that we would never give up stealth, and that we would stay committed to NATO and Europe.[169]

He added that:

> One of the factors was they realised that we were working on strategic defense and they were sure and very much afraid that we would get it. We would get and develop a system and they were petrified about that.[170]

Weinberger stated that the SDI was 'I think, clearly, one of the factors that went into the winning of the Cold War'. Weinberger believed that the Cold War ended in 1988–1990. It ended in Eastern Europe; Hungary, Bulgaria and Czechoslovakia where Reagan was very popular. It ended with the free movement of people internally in the united Germany. Reagan himself asked for the Berlin Wall to be torn down before it was, and it was torn down. Interestingly, Weinberger revealed that he did not predict the break-up of the Soviet Union.[171]

According to Caspar Weinberger, 'bargaining from strength' won the Cold War. He certified that, 'Above all one man, Ronald Reagan, ended the Cold War, but he had help from others. Unquestionably, SDI was invaluable'.[172] Richard V. Allen attested that, 'SDI caused the end of the Cold War. It was the straw that broke the camel's back'. The Soviets began to believe that the SDI might work but 'they did not want to take the chance and threw in the towel. SDI broke the Cold War'.[173] According to Edwin Meese III from:

> what we understand by examining both the individual and documentary evidence from the Soviet Union was that the SDI played a major and significant role in bringing about the end of the Cold War.[174]

One of the reasons, for the importance of the SDI, was that the Soviet Union was working for 10-15 years on ABM defences in violation of the ABM Treaty. The Soviet realized after a few years that; 1) US technology was more advanced and 2) that the US demonstrated the will to go forward.[175]

Edwin Meese III believed that a 'combination of factors led to the end of the Cold War'. The first factor was the military build-up. The second was the Strategic Defence Initiative as a new venture. The third was the way in which world opinion changed. Meese III affirmed that:

> Ronald Reagan engaged the Soviets on a moral plane. The Soviets were depriving people of liberty. Before, the US had to be seen to deal with the Soviet Union as a moral equivalency. Now that had changed.[176]

The fourth factor was the containment of the Soviet Union. The fifth was 'rollback'; the US support for freedom fighters around the world.[177] According to Martin Anderson, the 'SDI was not a total factor in the explanation of the end of the Cold War'. However, 'given everything else, SDI made US actions appear very credible and significant'. The SDI was a possible factor in why the Cold War ended; it 'hastened things up a bit'.[178]

William (Bill) Lee highlighted the importance of the SDI. Lee believed that the 'SDI was one of the most important things we did. It helped end the Cold War'. The Soviet reaction demonstrated at Reykjavik was 'centrepiece evidence of the importance of SDI'.[179] Lee stated that 'Gorbachev could not get Reagan to agree with his view of abandoning SDI. Gorbachev had no choice but to cave in on arms control'. Lee added that the 'SDI helped negotiations'. Given the fact that Gorbachev could not get Reagan to abandon the SDI, and the problems that Gorbachev inherited in the Soviet Union (which made his problems worse), Gorbachev had no choice but to do what he did.[180] Lee asserted that:

those who gave Gorbachev credit to the policies fail to recognise that it was Ronald Reagan's policies which Gorbachev was agreeing to. All Gorbachev was trying to do was to salvage his domestic problems, which were a disaster. SDI helped in getting Gorbachev's concessions.[181]

Edwin Meese III stated that 'it was good that SDI was not given up by President Reagan at Reykjavik. SDI was not a bargaining chip'.[182]

According to William Graham, 'Gorbachev was concerned enough about the SDI to make an offer of doubtful believability' which Reagan refused. He added that 'we can only speculate what was in Gorbachev's mind'.[183] Graham further added that 'The Soviet Union before decided they had an advantage in ballistic missile defense, when the US was constrained'. However, Reagan with the SDI 'laid the foundations for breaking' that arrangement. The Soviets realized that if the US laid its strength it would be:

> impossible for the Soviet Union to keep up in terms of resources and advanced technology – in comparison with the US – for the US was more technologically advanced.[184]

Graham added that the 'SDI exacerbated the financial strain in Russia. It highlighted the technological difference'.[185] Richard Perle, stated that a combination of factors led to the end of the Cold War. He added that the 'SDI caused Gorbachev to consider whether Soviet ambitions to achieve military superiority were feasible'.[186]

According to Peter Schweizer, documents from the Soviet GRU (Soviet military intelligence) showed that the SDI was something to be 'very frightened about'. The SDI was the largest component of the new US revolution in military affairs. The SDI was part of a 'larger puzzle'. It was one factor amongst several things which the Pentagon was doing. There were three things Reagan did. He increased deterrence and economic warfare by increasing the general military budget overall. The second thing was there was the focus on high technology weapons. Finally, there was the change in the strategic doctrine. [187]

Raymond Garthoff: No, SDI Did Not End the Cold War

Raymond Garthoff contested the view that Gorbachev turned to Perestroika because he was 'forced to do so' by the disadvantageous situation for the Soviet Union in the arms race'. According to him, this view was 'incorrect'. Garthoff explained that the Reagan build-up meant the US moved from being the world's largest creditor nation to the world's largest debtor. However, the burden of the arms race on the Soviet Union was greater than on the US. America had 'underestimated the weakness of the overall Soviet economy'.[188]

According to Raymond Garthoff, the Soviet Union could have survived for many years. He asserted that today, the Soviet Union could still have been a global superpower competing with the US had they chosen to do so. Garthoff acknowledged that the arms race in the new technological areas – a competition in space weapons, and a competition between strategic offensive and defensive arms – had the 'potential of greatly increasing the burden on the Soviet Union'. However, according to him, this depended on how the Soviet Union would react.[189] Garthoff affirmed that 'Gorbachev did not lose the arms race; he just opted out of it'. Gorbachev decided that the Soviets would not continue to compete or 'outdo' the US in the arms race. To quote Garthoff, Gorbachev decided it was 'necessary to entirely refashion the relationship between the Soviet Union and the rest of the world and he did that'.[190]

Raymond Garthoff attested that the SDI was an obstacle, not a 'source' to the programme that Gorbachev and others were thinking about and were ready to pursue. Garthoff maintained that although the SDI was announced and began before Gorbachev came to power, there were people already thinking – at that time – in the leadership and the general political establishment, about the 'new thinking' which Gorbachev later advocated.[191] According to Garthoff, it is by exaggerating the importance of the SDI – and 'misunderstanding its impact on Soviet political and military planning and thinking' – that leads to the 'erroneous view' that 'SDI played a decisive role in helping end the Cold War'.[192]

The Soviets: SDI Did Contribute to the Soviet Reassessment

The Soviets contentions at the 1993 Princeton University Conference (that SDI ended the Cold War) were taken out of context. What was accurately documented was the effect that the SDI had on the Soviet positions of strategic and arms control policy. Alexander Bessmertnykh said at the conference that the beginning of the SDI programme was 'one of the major moments when the strategists in the Soviet Union started maybe even to reconsider their positions'.[193] The SDI 'had a long-lasting impact on US'.[194]

Anatoly Dobrynin similarly stated that 'one of the moments at which strategists in the Soviet Union started to reconsider their positions was when Reagan announced his SDI program in 1983'. According to him, the Soviets realized that they and the US were 'approaching a very dangerous situation in the strategic balance'.[195] Dobrynin believed that although the Soviets had possibly 'overestimated the military significance' of SDI, nevertheless, 'its unveiling made us think about the situation once again and thus bought us closer to arms control'.[196]

Synopsis

The advent of a second Cold War, initiated by the most ideologically anti-Communist President in US history, could only have increased Soviet fears of the possibility of the SDI deployment. The SDI was perceived by the Soviet Union as rejuvenating the possibility of nuclear war which their ideology had repudiated. As a result of the SDI, whether the Soviets fell behind technologically, or restructured their system, the SDI gave US policy the leading edge. The Soviet response to the SDI was, clearly, concentrated to prevent SDI's ultimate implementation. For a programme that the Soviets deemed unfeasible, their response to it was contrary to their contentions. The Soviets argued that the SDI was 'technically unattainable', yet they also declared that the Soviet Union would be able to counter the US SDI programme.

The Soviets had been engaged in ballistic missile defence research for decades and had their own BMD system. Viewed within this prism, one can only conclude that they feared that they would be overtaken by the US SDI. Had SDI technology been unfeasible, the Soviets would not have engaged in their own ballistic missile defence programme, and would have encouraged the US to waste resources on theirs. On November 30 1987, Mikhail Gorbachev admitted Soviet strategic defence research. Gorbachev also stated that he believed that the US was exaggerating the success of its system. However, the Soviets were still prepared to decrease its offensive forces in exchange for such a system.

Raymond Garthoff attested that the Soviet statements at the Princeton University conference were misconstrued. Notwithstanding, this does not diminish the fact that the SDI was discussed at length in the conference which shows the importance which the SDI played in US–Soviet relations. Any admittances do not detract from the fact that both the Americans and Soviets were engaged in ballistic missile defence research. This shows the importance of the SDI. The SDI would inevitably have provoked a Soviet response, albeit a rhetorical or material response; investing in a counter-measure to the SDI/improving its own BMD system. The SDI was an important factor in US–Soviet relations, as would later be evidenced by the US–Soviet summits.

The Soviet perception of the SDI changed, as Gorbachev came to realize that Ronald Reagan was serious about eliminating nuclear weapons. Stating that is not to deny that Gorbachev continued making reductions in Soviet forces conditional upon SDI withdrawal. Soviet ballistic missile defence research similarly continued. Were the Soviets still scared of the SDI being a first-strike weapon or were they just seeking to maintain a monopoly on strategic defences? The latter argument is more persuasive. They Soviets had to be seen to be a world superpower. The survival of their political system depended on it.

The significance of the SDI was that it was perceived that it would be deployed and would work. Perceived threats in international diplomacy are as important as actual threats. The unavailability of Soviet statistical defence expenditure allocated to their SDI response prevents a detailed analysis of their response. Whilst any response would have been substantial, a purely aggressive stance was to be rejected by the new leader of the Soviet Union, Mikhail Gorbachev. By negotiating significant arms reductions, Gorbachev hoped to defeat the SDI by non-aggressive diplomatic means, in the newly agreed negotiations with the US.

Notes

1   Payne, Keith B., *Strategic Defense: 'Star Wars' in Perspective*, London, Hamilton Press, 1986, p. 41.; Cannon, Lou, *President Reagan: The Role of a Lifetime*, New York, Simon and Schuster, 1991, p. 331.
2   Cannon, *President*, p. 331.
3   Weinberger, Caspar, *Fighting For Peace: Seven Critical Years in the Pentagon*, New York, Warner Books, 1990, pp. 307-308.
4   Payne, *Strategic Defense*, p. 23.
5   Ibid., p. 244.
6   Pressler, Larry, *Star Wars: The Strategic Defense Initiative Debates in Congress*, New York, Praeger, 1986, p. 66.
7   Ibid.
8   According to *Congressional Quarterly Almanac*, the final sum figures which Congress appropriated for SDI are as follows: in 1984 (Fiscal Year 1985), $1.4 billion; 1985 (FY 1986), $2.75b; 1986 (FY 1987), $3.5b; 1987 (FY1988), $3.9b; 1988 (FY 1989), $4.08b; 1989 (FY 1990), $3.8b; 1990 (FY 1991), $2.89b; 1991 (FY 1992), $4.15b; 1992 (FY 1993), $3.8b; In 1993, the SDI became the Ballistic Missile Defense Program. In 1993 (FY 1994), $2.59b. See *CQA 1984*, Vol. XL, p. 17. See also pp. 399, 403.; *CQA 1985*, Vol. XLI, pp. 360, 130.; *CQA 1986*, Vol. XLII, p. 16.; *CQA 1990*, Vol. XLVI, p. 691.; *CQA 1987*, Vol. XLIII, p. 421.; *CQA 1988*, Vol. XLIV, p. 651.; *CQA 1989*, Vol. XLV, pp. 760-761.; *CQA 1990*, Vol. XLVI, p. 812.; *CQA 1991*, Vol. XLVII, pp. 621, 630, 638.; *CQA 1992*, Vol. XLVIII, p. 592. See also pp. 594, 600.; *CQA 1993*, Vol. XLIX, p. 449.
9   Pressler, *Star Wars*, pp. 134, 150.
10   Meese III, *Interview*.
11   Payne, *Strategic Defense*, p. 194.
12   Hamm, Manfred R., and W. Bruce Weinrod, 'The Transatlantic Politics of Strategic Defense', *Orbis: A Journal of World Affairs*, Vol. 29, No. 4, Winter 1986, p. 713.
13   Payne, *Strategic Defense*, p. 195.
14   Hamm and Weinrod, 'Transatlantic', pp. 710-711.
15   Pressler, *Star Wars*, pp. 148-149.
16   Payne, *Strategic Defense*, pp. 195, 200.
17   Hamm and Weinrod, 'Transatlantic', p. 718.; Yost, David S., 'European Anxieties About Ballistic Missile Defence', *Washington Quarterly*, Fall 1984, pp. 112-129, 115.
18   Hamm and Weinrod, 'Transatlantic', p. 718.
19   Talbott, Strobe, *The Master of the Game: Paul Nitze and the Nuclear Peace*, New York, Vintage Books, 1989, pp. 206-207.; See also Thatcher, Margaret, *The Downing Street Years*, London, Harper Collins, 1993, pp. 466-468.
20   Hamm and Weinrod, 'Transatlantic', pp. 722-723.; For the Margaret Thatcher–Ronald Reagan discussions of SDI, at Camp David on December 22 1984, see Thatcher, *The Downing Street Years*, pp. 466-467.; For British Prime Minister Margaret Thatcher's speech to Congress in February 1985, where she urged strong support for SDI, see Thatcher, *The Downing Street Years*, pp. 468-469.; Thatcher differed from Reagan's view that 'SDI was a major step towards a nuclear weapon-free world'. She believed that this was 'neither attainable nor even desirable'. However, she believed that Reagan was right to introduce the SDI. Thatcher, *The Downing Street Years*, p. 463.
21   Weinberger, *Interview*.
22   All information from Weinberger, *Fighting For Peace*, p. 238.

23   Ibid.; For information on SDI and the allies, see Department of Defense, Strategic Defense Initiative, *Report to the Congress on the Strategic Defense Initiative*, June 1986, pp. B–1, B–2, B–3, B–4, B–5.

24   Weinberger, *Interview*.

25   Ibid.

26   Anderson, Martin, *Revolution: The Reagan Legacy*, Stanford, California, Hoover Institution Press, 1990. p. 76.

27   Ibid., p. 77.

28   Payne, *Interview*.

29   Perle, *Interview*.

30   Ibid.

31   Ibid.

32   'Strategic Defense Initiative', *Hearings Before the Subcommittee on Strategic and Theater Nuclear Forces of the Committee on Armed Services, United States Senate*, Ninety-Ninth Congress, First Session, October 30, November 6, 21, December 3, 5, 1985, Washington, US Government Printing Office, 1986, p. 87.

33   Ibid., p. 81.; Richard Perle added that 'The Soviets will continue to militarise space to the degree they are technologically able to do so. They prefer to do that without any competition from the United States'. Ibid.; Lieutenant-General James A. Abrahamson, Director of the Strategic Defense Initiative Organization, stated regarding Soviet work in ballistic missile defence, 'The evidence of massive Soviet investments and programs is overwhelming'. He added, 'However a US program capable of responding to Soviet deployment could lead to a safer world, with deterrence increasingly based on effective defenses for all sides'. See 'Strategic Defense and Anti-Satellite Weapons', *Hearing Before the Committee on Foreign Relations, United States Senate*, Ninety-Eighth Congress, Second Session, April 25 1984, Washington, US Government Printing Office, 1984, pp. 13, 14, respectively.; That the Soviet programme in strategic defence is 'in a number of respects much more comprehensive' than the US, see 'Strategic Defense Initiative [SDI] Program', *Hearing Before the Committee on Armed Services, House of Representatives*, Ninety-Ninth Congress, First Session, June 6 1985, Washington, US Government Printing Office, 1985, p. 4.

34   Meese III, *Interview*.

35   Allen, Richard V., 'The Man Who Changed the Game Plan', *The National Interest*, Vol. 44, Summer 1996, p. 64.

36   Weinberger, *Interview*.

37   Allen, *Interview*.

38   Lee, *Interview*.

39   Anderson, *Interview*.

40   Graham, *Interview*.

41   Ibid.

42   Ibid.

43   For the Soviet 'abandonment' of a 'nuclear war fighting strategy' see the following: MccGwire, Michael, *Perestroika and Soviet National Security*, Washington, The Brookings Institution, 1991, pp. 27, 48; Shenfield, Stephen, *The Nuclear Predicament: Explorations in Soviet Ideology*, London, Routledge and Kegan Paul, 1987, p. 13.; For the Soviet reaction to the SDI, see Patman, Robert G., 'Reagan, Gorbachev and the Emergence of "New Political Thinking"', *Review of International Studies*, Vol. 25, No. 4, October 1999, pp. 596-597.

44   'Replies by Yuri V. Andropov to Questions from a Correspondent of Pravda', *Pravda*, March 27 1983.

45 Talbott, *Master of the Game*, p. 209.; The Soviet perception that the US constantly sought nuclear victory was evident in the Dropshot US contingency plan in 1949, and more recently PD59, NSDD-32, the Pershing II missile deployment and even the Able Archer NATO exercise. See Garthoff, Raymond L., *The Great Transition: American–Soviet Relations and the End of the Cold War*, Washingon D.C., The Brookings Institution, 1994, pp. 171-3.; MccGwire, *Perestroika and Soviet National Security*, p. 135.

46 Bowker, Mike, *Russian Foreign Policy and the End of the Cold War*, Dartmouth, Aldershot, 1997, p. 81.

47 Ekedahl, Carolyn McGiffert and Melvin A. Goodman, *The Wars of Eduard Shevardnadze*, London, Hurst, 1997, p. 108.

48 Dobrynin, Anatoly, *In Confidence: Moscow's Ambassador to America's Six Cold War Presidents 1962–86*, New York, Random House, 1995, p. 527.

49 Talbott, *Master of the Game*, p. 209.

50 Ibid.

51 Cannon, *President*, p. 742.; Anderson, *Revolution*, p. xxxviii.

52 Cannon, *President*, p. 742.

53 Menshikov, S., 'What is Behind the "Star Wars" Debate', *International Affairs*, Moscow, No. 6. June 1985, pp. 74-75.

54 All information taken from O'Neill, Bill, 'Fear and Laughter in the Kremlin', *New Scientist*, March 20 1993, p. 36.

55 Ibid.

56 Ibid., p. 35.

57 Ibid.

58 Chalfont, Alun, *SDI: The Case for the Defence*, Occasional Paper No. 12, Institute for European Defence and Strategic Studies, London, Alliance Publishers Ltd., 1985, pp. 46, 10, 31.; According to William T. Lee, 'Although it often is alleged that countermeasures to SDI are many and cheap, this was not so'. Lee, William T., 'US–USSR Strategic Arms Control Agreements: Expectations and Reality', *Comparative Strategy*, Vol. 12, No. 4, October/December 1993, p. 422.

59 Chalfont, *SDI: The Case for the Defense*, p. 10.

60 Ibid., p. 32.

61 Chalfont, *SDI: The Case for the Defense*, p. 34.; Perle, *Interview*.

62 Chalfont, *SDI: The Case for the Defense*, pp. 32, 34.

63 'Remarks and Question and Answer Session by the Honorable George P. Shultz, Secretary of State, Before The North Atlantic Assembly, St. Francis Hotel, San Francisco, California, Monday, October 14 1985', in 'Strategic Defense Initiative', *Hearings Before the Subcommittee on Strategic and Theater Nuclear Forces of the Committee on Armed Services, United States Senate*, Ninety-Ninth Congress, First Session, October 30, November 6, 21, December 3, 5, 1985, Washington, US Government Printing Office, 1986, p. 157.

64 Jastrow, Robert, 'The Technical Feasibility of Ballistic Missile Defense', *Journal of International Affairs*, Vol. 39, No. 1, Summer 1985, p. 52.; Brzezinski, Zbigniew, *Game Plan*, New York, Atlantic Monthly Press, 1986, p. 153.; Chalfont, *SDI: The Case for the Defense*, p. 31.

65 Schweizer, Peter, *Victory: The Reagan Administration's Secret Strategy That Hastened the Collapse of the Soviet Union*, New York, Atlantic Monthly Press, 1994, p. 137.

66 Stevens, Sayre, 'The Soviet Factor in SDI', *Orbis: A Journal of World Affairs*, Vol. 29, No. 4, Winter 1986, p. 698.

67 Chalfont, *SDI: The Case for the Defense*, p. 32.

[68] Ibid., pp. 31-32.; Regarding the feasibility of the SDI, according to Lars-Erik Nelson 'Star Wars has never been built; after an expenditure of more than $60 billion, none of its variations has ever passed a realistic operational test'. Nelson, Lars-Erik, 'Fantasia: A Book Review of FitzGerald, Frances, 'Way Out There in the Blue: Reagan, Star Wars and the End of the Cold War', New York, Simon and Schuster, 2000', *The New York Review of Books*, Vol. XLVII, No. 8, May 11 2000, p. 4. See also p. 6.

[69] Chalfont, *SDI: The Case for the Defense*, p. 32.

[70] Pick, Otto, 'How Serious is Gorbachev About Arms Control?', *The World Today*, Vol. 43, April 1987, p. 68.

[71] Wohlforth, William, C., (ed.), *Witnesses to the End of the Cold War*, Baltimore, The John Hopkins University Press, 1996, p. 35.

[72] Ibid., pp. 34-35.

[73] Ibid., p. 34.

[74] O'Neill, 'Fear and Laughter', p. 36.

[75] Schweizer, *Victory*, p. 215.

[76] Ibid., pp. 249-250.

[77] Ibid., p. 238.

[78] Shishlin, Nikolai, 'Soviet Aims in Geneva', *NYT*, March 15 1985, p. 27.

[79] Schweizer, *Victory*, p. 245.

[80] Garthoff, *Great Transition*, pp. 515-516.

[81] Schweizer, *Victory*, p. 215.; Garthoff, *Great Transition*, p. 516.

[82] For the arms control implications of SDI, see 'Implications of the President's Strategic Defense Initiative and Antisatellite Weapons Policy', *Hearings Before the Subcommittee on Arms Control, International Security and Science of the Committee on Foreign Affairs, House of Representatives*, Ninety-Ninth Congress, First Session, April 24 and May 1 1985, Washington, US Government Printing Office, 1985, pp. 6-8.; For a 'Review of Arms Control Implications of the Report of the President's Commission on Strategic Forces' – commonly known as the Scowcroft Report – see *Hearings Before the Committee on Foreign Affairs, House of Representatives*, Ninety-Eigth Congress, First Session, May 17, 19 and 24 1983, Washington, US Government Printing Office, 1983.

[83] Schweizer, *Victory*, p. 240.

[84] 'Letter From Mikhail Gorbachev to Ronald W. Reagan', Moscow, December 24 1985, p. 1, *Regan, Donald T., Papers*, Box 214, Folder 9, 'Soviet Union, Reagan–Gorbachev Correspondence', Library of Congress.

[85] Schweizer, *Victory*, p. 136.; Alexander Bessmertnykh, reminiscing at the Princeton University Conference, revealed that the 'Soviet Union was already feeling the pressure of the arms race. Gorbachev wanted to go on with the reforms, and the continued arms race was a tremendous hindrance to the future of those reforms'. Stated in ibid., p. 246.; According to Eduard Shevardnadze, by engaging in the arms race the US and Soviet Union 'are beginning to lose the competition in other areas'. He added that 'Both of us have lost the arms race'. Shevardnadze, Eduard A., *The Future Belongs to Freedom*, New York, The Free Press, 1991, pp. 82, 83, respectively.

[86] On May 23 1986, Gorbachev stated that, 'Without an acceleration of the country's economic and social development, it will be impossible to maintain our positions on the international scene'. Quoted in Oberdorfer, Don, *The Turn: How the Cold War Came To An End, The United States and the Soviet Union, 1983–1990*, London, Jonathan Cape, 1991, p. 162.; Schweizer, *Victory*, p. 246.

[87] Schweizer, *Victory*, p. 240.

[88] Ibid., p. 238.

[89] Ibid., p. 239.

[90]   Ibid., p. 247.
[91]   Shevardnadze, *The Future Belongs to Freedom*, p. 80.
[92]   'Cold War: Star Wars 1981-1988', *Television Programme*, BBC2, Sunday April 25 1999, 8pm-8.50 pm.
[93]   Thatcher, *The Downing Street Years*, p. 451.
[94]   Dobrynin, *In Confidence*, p. 565.
[95]   Ibid., p. 561.
[96]   Ibid., p. 538.
[97]   Schweizer, *Victory*, p. 240.
[98]   O'Neill, 'Fear and Laughter', p. 36. Author's quote, information by Velikhov.
[99]   Author's quote, information by Velikhov. Ibid.
[100] Payne, *Interview*.
[101] Lee, *Interview*.
[102] Lee, William T., 'US–USSR Strategic Arms Control Agreements: Expectations and Reality', *Comparative Strategy*, p. 425.; For the Soviet strategic defence expenditures see ibid., pp. 424-425.
[103] Garthoff, *Interview*.
[104] Ibid.
[105] Gorbachev, Mikhail, *Memoirs*, London, Bantam Books, 1997, p. 524.
[106] Ibid., p. 525.
[107] Ibid.
[108] Ibid.; Gorbachev said, at the Geneva summit, regarding the US SDI, and possible Soviet countermeasures to it, 'The SDI is a terrible arms race – a race in space. We would have to take steps to smash your shield, like a porcelain plate'. Morris, Edmund, 'Saving The World', *The Sunday Times*, September 26 1999, p. 2.; Gorbachev told Reagan, at the Washington summit, regarding the SDI 'I think you're wasting money. I don't think it will work. But if that's what you want to do, go ahead'. Nelson, 'Fantasia: A Book Review of FitzGerald, Frances, 'Way Out There in the Blue: Reagan, Star Wars and the End of the Cold War', New York, Simon and Schuster, 2000', p. 4.
[109] Gorbachev, *Memoirs*, p. 525.
[110] Strategic Defense Initiative Organization, *1989 Report to Congress on the Strategic Defense Initiative*, March 13 1989, p. A–3.
[111] Ibid.; For the Soviet strategic defence programmes and the Soviet response to SDI, see ibid., pp. A–1 to A–12.; Caspar Weinberger states that many SDI opponents in the US 'disputed the U.S. Government's assessment that the Soviets had an SDI program of their own' until General Secretary Mikhail Gorbachev admitted this in his interview with Tom Brokaw on NBC on November 30 1987. Weinberger, *Fighting For Peace*, p. 298 4n. (See also pp. 298-299 4n).; The Soviet Union proceeded with their work on strategic defence in the 'greatest secrecy'. According to Weinberger 'it was, and is, a massive effort'. Weinberger, *Fighting For Peace*, p. 299.; In analysing Gorbachev's admission of the Soviet strategic defence research programme, it is important to recognize that there is a long tradition of Soviet Potemkinism regarding the issue of nuclear weapons. The Soviets on many occasions put up a smokescreen. The Soviets could have put up a smokescreen regarding their capabilities in this instance to make Soviet science and technology appear stronger than it actually was. During the Cold War the Soviets had exaggerated their state of technology and capability. For example, the Soviet Sputnik was good. Technologically it was very advanced. However, by the late Cold War technologically the Soviets were not very advanced in comparison with the US. This Soviet decline began in the 1960s. The Soviets had disguised this decline with propaganda. Perhaps by stating that the Soviets were working on their own strategic

defence programme, Gorbachev wanted to get the US to overstretch its capability. However, this cannot be proved. Soviet policy was extraordinarily difficult to understand. There is a danger in taking the alternative polemical view to an extreme. Looking back now one cannot say 'how could we have been so impressed with the Soviet Union?' This can only be said with the benefit of hindsight. Soviet technology can never be underestimated, especially in the area of space defences. During the Cold War, the Soviet Union was perceived to be strong, as it was a world superpower. It is only by looking at the overall Soviet response can a clear picture emerge regarding the Soviet response to the SDI. What can be asserted is that the Soviets had a strategic defence system around Moscow (its Galosh system) whilst the United States had no ABM defence. What can also be asserted is that both countries were working on ballistic missile (strategic) defences.

[112] Jackson, William D., 'Soviet Reassessment of Ronald Reagan, 1985–1988', *Political Science Quarterly*, Vol. 113, No. 4, Winter 1998–99, p. 626. Words are by Jackson.

[113] Jackson, 'Soviet Reassessment of Ronald Reagan', p. 626.

[114] Dobrynin, *In Confidence*, p. 620.

[115] Ibid.

[116] Wohlforth, (ed.), *Witnesses to the End of the Cold War*, p. 34.

[117] Ibid.

[118] Ibid.

[119] Ibid.

[120] Ibid.

[121] Ibid., pp. 34-35.

[122] Ibid., p. 35.

[123] Velikhov quoted in O'Neill, 'Fear and Laughter', p. 36.

[124] O'Neill, 'Fear and Laughter', p. 36.

[125] Ibid., p. 37.

[126] Reuter, 'SDI, Chernobyl Helped End Cold War, Conference Told', *The Washington Post*, February 27 1993, p. A17.; Pipes Richard, 'Review Essay: Misinterpreting the Cold War: The Hard-Liners Had it Right', *Foreign Affairs*, Vol. 74, No. 1, January/February 1985, p. 159.

[127] Reuter, 'SDI, Chernobyl Helped End', *The Washington Post*, p. A17.

[128] Ibid.

[129] Alexander Bessmertnykh, remarks at Princeton University Conference, 'A Retrospective on the End of the Cold War', February 23 1993, stated in Schweizer, *Victory*, p. 135.

[130] Bessmertnykh quoted in Wohlforth, (ed.), *Witnesses to the End of the Cold War*, p. 48.

[131] Ibid.

[132] Schweizer, *Victory*, p. 197.; That the head of Soviet strategic research in 1989, in his interview with *The New York Times*, revealed that 'tens of billions of dollars' was spent responding to SDI, is stated by Peter Schweizer. Schweizer, *Interview*.

[133] Garthoff, *Interview*.

[134] Ibid.

[135] Ibid.

[136] Ibid.

[137] Ibid.

[138] Ibid.

[139] Ibid.

[140] Payne, *Interview*.

[141] Ibid.

[142] Garthoff, *Interview*.

143   Ibid.

144   Ibid.

145   Ibid.

146   Ibid.

147   Mikheyev, Dmitry, *The Soviet Perspective on the Strategic Defense Initiative*, Washington, Pergamon–Brassey's, 1987, p. 2.

148   Ibid.

149   Ibid., p. 2.

150   Ibid., pp. 2-3.

151   Ibid., p. x.

152   Ibid., p. 3.

153   Ibid.

154   'Cold War: Star Wars 1981–1988', *Television Programme*, BBC2, Sunday April 25 1999, 8pm-8.50 pm.; That the Soviets feared US technology, see the following: Reagan, Ronald, *An American Life*, London, Hutchinson, 1990, p. 608.; Lee, William T., and Richard F. Staar, *Soviet Military Policy Since World War II*, Stanford, California, Hoover Institution Press, 1986, p. 189.; According to William T. Lee, the 'Fear of SDI forced the FSU [former Soviet Union] back into the START negotiations and to agree to deep cuts in its ready ICBM and SLBM warhead arsenal'. Lee, William T., 'US–USSR Strategic Arms Control Agreements: Expectations and Reality', *Comparative Strategy*, p. 433.

155   Patman, 'Reagan, Gorbachev and the Emergence of "New Political Thinking"', p. 596.

156   Ibid., p. 596 123n.

157   See Kaufmann, William W., *Glasnost, Perestroika, and US Defense Spending*, Washington, D.C., The Brookings Institution, 1990.; According to Eduard Shevardnadze, Soviet military expenditures 'as a percentage of gross national product were two and a half times greater than those of the United States'. Shevardnadze, *The Future Belongs to Freedom*, p. 54.

158   Garthoff, *Interview*.

159   Ibid.

160   Ibid.

161   Ibid.

162   Ibid.

163   Ibid.

164   Ibid.

165   Ibid.; For the Soviet reaction to SDI, with the evolution of the Soviet approach from a hardline to a softer position, see Puschel, Karen, 'Can Moscow Live With SDI?', *Survival*, Vol. XXXI, No. 1, January/February 1989, pp. 34-51. Puschel places the Soviet change towards SDI to a softer approach due to political expediency, as well as the change in Soviet perception of how SDI would affect Soviet security. See p. 42.

166   FitzGerald, Frances, *Way Out There in the Blue: Reagan, Star Wars and the End of the Cold War*, New York, Simon and Schuster, 2000. p. 411.

167   Weinberger, *Interview*.

168   Ibid.

169   Ibid.

170   Ibid.

171   Ibid.

172   Ibid.

173   Allen, *Interview*.

174   Meese III, *Interview*.

[175] Ibid.
[176] Ibid.
[177] Ibid.
[178] Anderson, *Interview*.
[179] Lee, *Interview*.
[180] Ibid.
[181] Ibid.
[182] Meese III, *Interview*.
[183] Graham, *Interview*.
[184] Ibid.
[185] Ibid.
[186] Perle, *Interview*.
[187] Schweizer, *Interview*.
[188] Garthoff, *Interview*.
[189] Ibid.
[190] Ibid.
[191] Ibid.
[192] Ibid.
[193] Wohlforth, (ed.), *Witnesses to the End of the Cold War*, p. 6.
[194] Ibid., pp. 6, 33.
[195] Dobrynin, *In Confidence*, p. 609.
[196] Ibid.

Chapter 3

The Reykjavik Summit:
October 11–12 1986

Introduction

That the Reykjavik summit, October 11–12 1986, took place was remarkable considering the plethora of ominous setbacks which plagued US–Soviet relations. Yet, despite the earlier stagnation – which included the failure of the Geneva summit[1] the previous year, the April 1986 Chernobyl nuclear accident, and the US Libyan air raid – the movement on arms control increased raising hopes for a meeting between President Ronald Reagan and Mikhail Gorbachev.[2] Most significantly, pressures in both capitals for such a meeting would not be deterred by even the arrest of American Nicolas Daniloff, upon whose fate the convening of the Reykjavik summit came to depend.

Daniloff–Zakharov affair Arrested in retribution for the earlier US arrest of physicist Gennadi Zakharov in New York City, August 23 1986, *US News and World Report* Correspondent Daniloff was seized by KGB agents in Moscow on August 30. Reagan declared that the arrest could become a 'major obstacle' in US–Soviet relations and insisted that there would be no summit unless Daniloff was freed.[3] On September 19 1986, Eduard Shevardnadze – who was in Washington for meetings with George Shultz (that were scheduled before Daniloff's arrest) – gave the Secretary of State an unexpected letter from Gorbachev to Reagan. The letter suggested that Gorbachev and Reagan should 'personally involve' themselves in preparations for a summit meeting.[4]

Gorbachev's letter was in response to one sent by Reagan which Gorbachev received in the summer of 1986. Gorbachev saw 'no significant proposals in Reagan's message'.[5] The US administration hastily agreed to a summit on the condition that Daniloff be released beforehand. A day later, Zakharov was on a plane to Moscow.[6] In his memoirs *Turmoil and Triumph: My Years as Secretary of State*, George Shultz recalled that although President Reagan wanted the Reykjavik meeting to take place, the US used the Soviet desire for a meeting as additional pressure to 'bring the Daniloff case to a satisfactory conclusion'.[7]

Why Reykjavik Happened

The Motivations for the Summit

Time magazine asserted that the US motivation for a summit meeting was because Reagan wanted to 'wind up his presidency in a blaze of glory as the leader who restored US military and economic might to a point at which he could negotiate a favourable arms control deal'.[8] Gorbachev in his *Memoirs* placed Reagan's acceptance of the summit meeting down to the 'tempting opportunity to go down in history as the "President of peace" – and the elections were drawing nearer'.[9] *Time* further added that progress had to be made in the following year before the US became preoccupied with the 1988 presidential campaign.[10] The immediate Soviet motivation for talks was accounted for by the Soviet uncertainty whether Reagan's successor would be willing to make an arms deal. Gorbachev himself was eager for some kind of arms deal, as he feared the potential political backlash; a heavy propaganda defeat at home if he failed to go to a summit.[11]

A day before the summit began, a *New York Times* editorial 'More Than Theatre in Iceland' stated that a summit meeting would be good for Reagan's own popularity, as well as the election of November 4 1986. One Reagan aide referred to Reykjavik as 'our October surprise for the Democrats'. Ultimately, the best reason to go was the hope of making progress on arms control.[12] Republican Edward J. Markey (Mass.), as well as the Democrats, accused Reagan of agreeing to the quickly arranged summit in the hope of improving Republican prospects for retaining control of the Senate in the November 4 Congressional elections.[13]

The SDI Discussions in Congress

In his memoirs, George Shultz described the circumstances surrounding the Reykjavik meeting which had 'come about so suddenly'. Amongst them was the fact that 'Republican prospects in some key Senate contests did not look good' and that the mid-term elections were underway. Another factor was that the Democrat controlled House of Representatives was attempting to force a sharp curtailment of nuclear testing.[14] This would have had significant repercussions for it could stop the SDI. Reagan's surprise decision to meet with Gorbachev in Iceland could be reconciled with his ultimate desire to implement the SDI, by preventing House efforts to impose a ban on most nuclear weapons tests.

The proposed House provision was that all but the smallest nuclear weapons tests would be banned. The talks, however, came to a standstill after Reagan announced on September 30 1986 the Iceland meeting. Reagan wanted to overturn the legislation which the House passed. Consequently, John M. Poindexter, urged Les Aspin that the House conferees drop all of their arms control provisions to avoid undermining the President's bargaining position in Reykjavik.[15]

After the announcement of the 'pre-summit' meeting, the Senate conferees adopted a harder approach against the House provisions. They warned that by imposing any kind of restrictions on US weapons testing or production that the House approved, Congress would undermine the President's bargaining position against the Russians.[16] Reagan's insistence on a total surrender by the House (a phrase coined by Majority Whip Thomas S. Foley, (Washington))[17] places Reagan's motivation for the Reykjavik summit as ending the challenge to his political pre-eminence. This total surrender by the House was a domestic issue linked to foreign policy (the Iceland meeting). Domestic politics featured in foreign policy decision making. Perhaps by demonstrating the importance of the SDI at the summit Reagan could convince Congress the importance of funding the project. The Senate had accepted a substantial cut in SDI funding that had been voted for by the Armed Services Committee in order to protect the SDI from a political savaging.[18]

SDI Funding in Congress

From the initiative of Democrat Sam Nunn, (Georgia), and Republican William S. Cohen, (Maine), SDI research and development funding was cut from the requested $5.3 billion to $3.9 billion. Senate however sustained that figure, and rejected two further amendments to cut SDI further.[19] On August 5 1986, by a 50–49 vote, the Senate tabled the amendment by Democrat Senator J. Bennett Johnson (La.), which would have cut SDI funding to $3.24 billion.[20] (Several months earlier, in late May, Senator Bennett rounded up 48 Senators to support his call for giving SDI funding only enough of an increase in fiscal year 1987 to cover the cost of inflation and a 'real growth' of 3 per cent.)[21]

Another amendment the Senate rejected was by Democrats J. James Exon (Neb.) cutting Reagan's funding request to $3.56 billion.[22] SDI critics claimed victory, declaring that the narrow vote, as well as the Armed Services panel's cut, was indicative of the Congressional unhappiness about the dramatic spending increases which the President sought.[23] Reagan knew that Soviet arms control proposals were conditional upon the SDI. By attending the Reykjavik summit the President acknowledged that any outcome could only further raise the 'already high political profile of SDI', thereby circumventing SDI's political difficulties in Congress. Reagan's unexpected acceptance of a summit can be reconciled with this argument, for the timing was crucial. In August and September 1986, Reagan's funding requests were scrutinized in Congress. Reagan's motivation to go to a summit in order to ease SDI's political difficulties in Congress (as well as improve Republican electoral prospects) is further evidenced by a speech he made after the Reykjavik summit and the campaigning which he did.

On October 15 1986, Reagan told a Baltimore audience that it would be a tragedy 'if those on Capitol Hill opposed to SDI are allowed to hand over to the Soviet Union free of charge what we refused to hand over across the bargaining table'. The President made support for SDI a 'prominent theme of campaign appearances on behalf of Republican Senate candidates in Maryland and North Dakota'.[24]

The INF Background

Although the Soviets walked out of the Geneva arms negotiations (and did not return until sixteen months later) because of the US installation of Pershing II in Western Europe, the significance of these weapons, the cruise missiles and the Soviet SS-20s was not strategic, but political. They were less important as weapons but political symbols, and even in that capacity had outlived their usefulness.[25] The Pershing II, cruise missile and Soviet SS-20s no longer played a central role in either the US or Soviet nuclear strategy. The initial Soviet SS-20 installation was to scare West Europe and undermine the US alliance. This Soviet aim failed. Instead, the allied governments allowed the US missiles to counter the Soviet weapons. The original purpose of the American deployment was to persuade the Soviets to scrap most of their SS-20s.[26] An agreement on the INF, therefore, appeared conducive to both superpowers. Weeks before the Reykjavik summit was announced, there were press reports of progress towards an INF agreement.[27]

The Soviet Desire for an Arms Control Accord

Politically, the US and Soviet desire for a summit can be understood as coming at a time when it was necessary to divert attention from both their domestic difficulties. This was especially so in the Soviet Union, where the new regime of Gorbachev presided over the transition in Soviet policy, after recognising the inadequacies of the old system. At the 27th Party Congress (Twenty-Seventh Congress of the Soviet Communist Party), February 25 to March 6 1986, Gorbachev referred to the US as 'that great country'. He contended that 'it is in fact impossible to win the arms race, just as it is impossible to win a nuclear war itself. Therefore it is essential above all to considerably reduce the level of military confrontation'.[28]

Earlier, on January 15 1986, Gorbachev's nuclear disarmament programme proposed the elimination of all nuclear weapons worldwide by the year 2000.[29] His INF proposal included the exception of British and French nuclear missiles, which was a fundamental Soviet shift, and was, in essence, the acceptance of Reagan's 1981 'zero option'. However, this was conditional upon the abandonment of the SDI,[30] which Gorbachev failed to obtain at the Geneva summit in 1985.

The Soviet backlash to the Geneva summit, which included public criticism from the military, ensured that Gorbachev stalled for six months on setting a date for the next US–Soviet summit meeting, whilst, simultaneously seeking a guarantee that he would not come away from it empty handed.[31] A *Congressional Quarterly Weekly Report* article, of October 4 1986, asserted that the 'Soviet officials refused to schedule the US meeting until there was evidence that the two heads of government would be able to nail down some significant arms control accord'.[32]

At the end of the summer of 1986, despite all the setbacks which had occurred, Gorbachev's impatience resulted in him proposing a 'preliminary meeting'.[33] *The New York Times* suggested that Gorbachev's desire for a summit was linked to his desire to be seen as a peacemaker in the eyes of the world, to calm fears about his leadership, and, ultimately, to make progress on strategic arms control.[34]

Soviet and East European Affairs Specialist (Chief Soviet Policy Official) on the National Security Council staff, Richard Pipes, believed that this desire for arms control was a way of enabling Moscow to 'preserve the Stalinist system intact and continue its expansion while giving the appearance of good will'.[35] However, *The New York Times* journalist Bernard Gwertzman stated that 'the Russians made the point that the prime purpose of the Iceland talks is to provide impulses for accords on arms that could be signed when Mr Gorbachev visits the United States'.[36]

Summit Expectations

The possibility of a summit was raised by both superpowers at the opening of the 41st session of the United Nations General Assembly. Simultaneously, in Geneva, American and Soviet arms control negotiators were close to reaching an agreement whereby the Soviets would drop their condition that an INF agreement be linked to agreements involving space-based offensive weapons (SDI) and long-range strategic arms (START).[37] To the US, this more realistic premise for talks would only be an incentive to go to a summit. A further incentive was Eduard Shevardnadze's disclosure that Moscow had dropped the inclusion of the British and French nuclear arsenals condition in the INF talks.[38] Clearly, INF offered the greatest prospect for any agreement on nuclear agenda.[39]

A substantive agreement, however, was not expected from the summit, according to administration officials. They informed reporters (days before the Reykjavik summit began) that what was hoped for was an 'impulse' from Reagan and Gorbachev that would accelerate the conclusion of the formal agreements taking place in the ongoing Geneva arms reduction talks.[40] President Reagan cautioned Americans not to expect too much saying that 'Iceland is a base camp before the summit'.[41]

At a news conference, Deputy Chief of the Central Committee's Propaganda Department, Nikolai V. Shishlin, said that the main objective for the Reykjavik meeting from the Soviet standpoint was to 'turn on a green light for a full-scale summit meeting' in the US. At Reykjavik, however, Mikhail Gorbachev was prepared 'to do all in his power to bring about reasonable compromises' in his meeting with President Reagan.[42] The director of the Institute of World Economy and International Relations, Yevgeny M. Primakov, stated that:

> The Soviet Union believes the major task is to reach agreement on cessation of the arms race. Regional conflicts are also of great importance. The agenda for the summit is wide open for discussion of any problems.[43]

After the Daniloff–Zakharov affair, the Soviet Union announced that it would withdraw some troops from Afghanistan. The pullout was expected several days after the Reykjavik summit was scheduled to end.[44]

Reagan said of his hopes for the Reykjavik meeting:

In fact we have serious problems with the Soviet Union on a great many issues, and success is not guaranteed. But, if Mr Gorbachev comes to Iceland in a truly cooperative spirit, I think we can make some progress. We go to Reykjavik for peace. We go to this meeting for freedom. And we go in hope.[45]

Upon arrival in Reykjavik, Gorbachev expressed hope that the talks would:

remove the threat of nuclear war ... which would allow us to tackle thoroughly the problems of disarmament and to move to the goal that we have set for ourselves, that is, the final elimination of nuclear weapons by the year 2000.[46]

Gorbachev affirmed that the Soviet Union was prepared to 'look for solutions of the burning problems that concern peoples all over the world'.[47]

What Exactly Happened at Reykjavik

The Summit Begins

Reykjavik was the most of astounding summit meeting of the 1980s. It was also the least planned. Had the agreements not fallen through because of Reagan's failure to give up the SDI – (the crucial factor upon which Soviet concessions were based) – Reykjavik would have been marked as the most radical reduction in military capabilities ever achieved. Although the Reykjavik summit was not to be prenegotiated, the US, according to George Shultz, was prepared for the summit, for it had a big book of clarified US positions 'on every conceivable proposal' and the 'president's talking points were available to each person on the delegation'.[48]

Reagan's big three advisers were George Shultz, John Poindexter and Donald T. Regan. The President's inner core of policy advisers would be with him most of the time. Caspar Weinberger was not invited to the talks but was on a trip to Asia. He was represented in Reykjavik by Richard Perle, but not in Reagan's core concentric circle of advisers.[49] Each member of the delegation, however, was not permitted to talk to the press. On Saturday October 11 1986, the summit began with the two leaders meeting alone, except for two interpreters and two note takers. On being joined by Shultz and Eduard Shevardnadze, Gorbachev began his proposals, all of which moved towards US positions.

Gorbachev's proposals on strategic weapons, intermediate-range arms (INF in Europe), space weapons and defence, and nuclear testing were sweeping. Finishing the presentation, Gorbachev handed the President a directive entitled 'Directives For the Foreign Ministers of the USSR and the USA Concerning the Drafting of Agreements on Nuclear Disarmament'. It stated that the two leaders 'having bought the position of the two countries considerably closer together at their working meeting at Reykjavik' agreed to issue directives to the foreign ministers to 'prepare the text of accords and agreements to be signed in Washington' during Gorbachev's visit to the US.[50] Gorbachev told Reagan that he would not set a date for the US summit (which would witness the signing of accords and agreements) unless there were high prospects of signing a major arms control deal.[51] It was perceived that Gorbachev used this absence of a firm date as 'additional leverage' on President Reagan at Reykjavik.[52]

Strategic Arms: Strategic Offensive Nuclear Forces

Gorbachev proposed that strategic offensive weapons be cut by 50 per cent (taking into account the historically established specificities of the structures of each side's strategic forces). These arms comprised land-based and sea-based missiles, including bombers and the heavy ICBMs which worried the US the most. This was a major cut for the first time in big Soviet heavy missiles which had been one of the most important US objectives. The reduction was later agreed to 50 per cent.[53] According to Mikhail Gorbachev the Soviet offer was not intended as a one-sided offer. This is because the US were supposed to reduce by 50 per cent their major striking force; nuclear submarines and strategic bombers where they had the advantage.[54]

The US and Soviet Union agreed to limit their nuclear launchers, missile warheads and bombers to 1,600. The number of warheads would be limited to 6,000. The Soviet Union gave in on the issue of a 'common limit' of bombs and missile warheads, the latter which the US found more threatening. Similarly, the Soviet Union moved towards another American position, by agreeing the ceiling of 6,000 would not cover sea-launched cruise missiles. Both superpowers agreed to work towards a separate agreement on this.[55]

Speaking after the summit, Gorbachev contended that the Soviet proposals eliminated several major stumbling blocks to agreement. Moscow's willingness to set aside its long standing insistence that reductions in strategic weapons include reductions in American bombers, as well as nuclear-capable tactical aircraft stationed both in and around Europe, was indicative of this.[56] Gorbachev in his *Memoirs* wrote 'Our far-reaching proposals seemed to have caught President Reagan off guard'. He added that the President appeared confused 'although we had suggested something the United States had always wanted to do': radically cut Soviet intercontinental ballistic missiles.[57]

Medium-Range Missiles

On INF (intermediate-range missiles), Gorbachev proposed the total elimination of all Soviet and American missiles in Europe. Gorbachev dropped his long-standing demand that British and French weapons be included in an INF agreement (or frozen at existing levels). This was a major concession, for the British and French systems were increasing in numbers and quality.[58] Gorbachev accepted the US definition of strategic weapons which was range rather than presumed target. Previously, the Soviet definition had included US INF missiles deployed in Europe, but excluded Soviet missiles deployed in the Soviet Union which were aimed at Europe and Asia. His proposal of a freeze on the deployment of short-range INF systems, despite knowing that the US deployed none, was not to the advantage of the US.[59]

Gorbachev maintained that his proposals amounted to 'President Reagan's own zero option proposal of 1981', although Gorbachev did not want to include intermediate-range nuclear systems in Asia, but only Europe. However, Gorbachev directly stated that 'as soon as it is practically possible, separate talks will be started on Soviet and American medium-range systems in Asia'.[60] The Soviets, according to Gorbachev, would be allowed to keep 100 warheads on the medium-range missiles stationed in Asia, whilst the Americans would keep theirs within the US. This was part of the global image of 100 warheads. The Soviets conceded to the US that the medium-range agreement would last until replaced.[61]

After the summit, Gorbachev revealed that he was surprised by Reagan's initial reluctance to accept the proposal for the elimination of intermediate-range missiles because Reagan had made a similar suggestion in 1981. Gorbachev said to Reagan of this 'I don't understand how you can abandon your own child'.[62] Gorbachev later stated that he believed that the US refusal to accept its own 'zero option' was 'probably less for fear of a negative reaction from their European allies than because they were reluctant to harm the American arms industry'.[63]

According to Shultz, the US delegation was surprised that Gorbachev's proposals were 'heading dramatically in our direction'. To quote Paul Nitze: 'This is the best Soviet proposal we have received in twenty-five years'. Richard Perle believed that the Soviet acceptance of the 'zero option' in Europe was a great concession. However, the Soviets could simply dispatch the missiles to Asia and shift them back to Europe later.[64]

The US–Soviet dialogue intensified with the setting up of two working groups; one on arms control, and the other on human rights, bilateral and regional issues. The arms control group was headed by the Administration's top arms control adviser, Paul H. Nitze. The human rights group was chaired by Assistant Secretary of State for European and Canadian Affairs, Rozanne L. Ridgway. Their Soviet counterparts were the Soviet negotiators in Geneva arms talks; Victor P. Karpov and Alexander A. Bessmertnykh, respectively.[65]

The arms control group – with specific reference to the START negotiations – was informed by Shultz to 'Get SDI deployment worked into the equation so that continuing reductions in offensive weapons are clearly the result of a continuing SDI programme'.[66] Shultz affirmed that the total elimination of all ballistic missiles was crucial because the more was reduced, the less need there was for a full SDI; if there was a total reduction there was no need for argument about the SDI. He further added that although Gorbachev would expect credit for the proposals he was making, 'His proposals are the result of five years of pressure from us'.[67] Shultz believed that bargaining from strength had paid off, and more significantly, that the SDI was 'in a powerful way, propelling the Soviet concessions'. He wrote in his memoirs that he believed that this would happen as soon as the Soviets heard Reagan's SDI announcement in March 1983, for the Soviets overestimated the US technological capacity.[68]

On the issue of nuclear testing, Gorbachev broke the impasse and conceded to the US position. Gorbachev dropped his demand for an immediate secession of all nuclear tests. Instead, he accepted Reagan's proposal to begin a phased accord, starting by reducing the 'number and yield' of the explosive force of the tests (provisional to eventual cessation), and verifying the existing treaties of 1974 and 1976.[69] This was sought by the Russians. Gorbachev made the talks 'a condition for the elaboration of an agreement on strategic arms'. An accord on the banning of anti-satellite systems was needed. Such accords were necessary to limit and reduce nuclear arms, prevent an arms race in space – and stop the one on earth – and 'strengthen strategic stability and universal security'.[70]

Non-Arms Issues

Although when the summit began Reagan immediately pointed out to Gorbachev the importance of human rights and regional issues, human rights according to US officials, played a secondary role in the meetings.[71] At a news conference, Shultz announced that:

> The issue of human rights was brought up on a number of occasions and some very significant material was passed to the Soviet Union, which they accepted, and stated not only our views, but, in detail, things about Jewish emigration, the number of people who have signified their desire to leave, lists of people, things of that kind.[72]

Although the issue of Jewish emigration suffered a setback because of the inability to reach an arms control agreement, there was an agreed statement on emigration and on reuniting separated families.[73] Progress was encouraged on several potential areas of superpower cooperation. This included non-proliferation of chemical and nuclear weapons, thermonuclear fusion, peaceful space cooperation and risk reduction centres.[74]

 The ABM Treaty: Limitation of Anti-Ballistic Missile Systems

The ABM Treaty and space weapons were the most contentious issues at the Reykjavik summit. To Gorbachev every agreement made was conditional to the US abandonment of the SDI, which Gorbachev hoped to achieve by forcing a newer interpretation of the ABM Treaty, which he proposed the US and Soviet Union would observe 'strictly and in full'.[75] According to Gorbachev 'the Americans had always viewed verification procedures as the most important factor'.[76] The Soviet position was thus: to begin dismantling nuclear weapons, inspection and verification had to be intensified to prevent either side from 'attaining military superiority'.[77] Consequently, existing arms control and verification mechanisms had to be reinforced. This included the ABM Treaty. Reinforcing the ABM Treaty was logical. As both sides committed themselves to a non-withdrawal period from the treaty of ten years, nuclear arsenals would be dismantled.[78]

The Soviets had previously demanded a fifteen-year to twenty-year period of non-withdrawal from the 1972 ABM Treaty which was of indefinite duration (with six months notice of withdrawal). At Reykjavik, however, Gorbachev made a 'compromise' – proposing a mandatory non-withdrawal period of 'not less than ten years'. This would be followed by 'a period of negotiations'.[79] Reagan had originally proposed a seven-and-a-half year notice of withdrawal from the treaty. Gorbachev no longer demanded that SDI research be banned. This was a significant concession. However, he insisted that it be confined to the 'laboratory', and that all anti-ballistic missile defence tests in space be banned. This prohibited the SDI.[80]

This was unacceptable to President Reagan who proposed that research on a missile defence system continue, for, success with the SDI would 'make the elimination of nuclear weapons possible'. To Reagan, SDI research was necessary on grounds of defending the American people against the horror of a nuclear weapons attack against which there was no defence.[81] Reagan declared that representatives of the Soviet Union would be present at the SDI tests. If the tests were successful, then the US would be obligated to share SDI technology with the Soviet Union. Reagan wanted both countries to eliminate 50 per cent of their missiles. Once all ballistic missiles (nuclear weapons) were eliminated, both the US and Soviet Union would deploy the SDI simultaneously.[82]

Gorbachev refused to believe that the US would share SDI technology with the Soviet Union, for it did not even share its 'oil drilling equipment or even milk-processing factories'. Responding to Gorbachev's accusation that the US would 'take the arms race into space', and could launch a first-strike from there, Reagan replied that this would be 'impossible' as the US was 'willing to eliminate all ballistic missiles before SDI is deployed'.[83] The President affirmed that the US would 'abide by the ABM Treaty and agree not to deploy the system unilaterally for ten years'.[84]

Gorbachev made the point that if all ballistic missiles were to be eliminated within ten years, then there would be no need for the SDI. To this, Reagan and Shultz responded that defences were needed in case of cheating, accidents or attacks by third countries, for 'Who knows what kind of madman might come a long after we're gone?'[85] Speaking after the Reykjavik summit, Reagan attested that the SDI was an 'insurance policy' to guarantee that the Soviets kept the commitments they made at Reykjavik. The SDI was America's 'security guarantee'.[86] At his news conference, Shultz simply confirmed that the SDI was essential to ensure Soviet compliance with reductions in offensive forces.[87]

The US proposal, known as the Linhard idea, on the second day of the summit comprised the following provisions; neither side would withdraw from the ABM Treaty for five years; there would be a 50 per cent reduction in strategic nuclear arsenals (ICBMs, submarine-launched missiles, long-range bombers). Both sides at the end of the first five-year period would renew their pledge not to withdraw from the ABM Treaty, whilst beginning the second five-year period dismantling all the remaining offensive ballistic missiles. (These including ICBMs, INF ballistic missiles and shorter-range nuclear missiles.) During the entire ten-year period, both sides would be entitled to conduct SDI research, development and testing as permitted by the 1972 ABM Treaty. After ten years both sides would be free to deploy defences.[88]

Although the Soviets and Americans agreed on a 50 per cent cut in all missile warheads and launchers by the end of the first five years, disagreement focused on the scope of the allowable research and testing during the ten-year observation of the ABM Treaty. Disagreement also focused on what, if any, SDI defences would be permitted after the ten years.[89] Also, there was a difference between the revised Soviet proposal and the US proposal in the second five-year period; the Soviets referred to 'strategic offensive arms' whilst the US referred to the 'offensive ballistic missiles'.[90] Gorbachev again rejected the revised US proposals unless it incorporated a ban on SDI testing outside the laboratory. Reagan refused and the talks ended.[91] Reagan wrote in his diary that night:

> He wanted language that would have killed SDI. The price was high but I wouldn't sell and that's how the day ended. All our people thought I'd done exactly right. I'd pledged I wouldn't give away SDI and I didn't, but that means no deal on any of the arms reductions. He tried to act jovial but I was mad and showed it. Well, the ball is now in his court and I'm convinced he'll come around when he sees how the world is reacting.[92]

Reagan was 'very disappointed' and 'very angry'.[93] At Reykjavik, he saw his hopes for a nuclear-free world soar briefly and then fall during one of the 'longest, most disappointing – and ultimately angriest' days of his presidency.[94] To quote Gorbachev: 'Success was a mere step away, but SDI proved an insurmountable stumbling block'.[95] Gorbachev told Anatoly Sergeevich Chernyayev:

> Despite the absence of concrete agreement, the results of Reykjavik have exceeded expectations. The Americans have begun to roll back. Reykjavik is a success for the peace process.[96]

According to Anatoly Dobrynin, at Reykjavik, Gorbachev 'decided that he could and would work with Reagan'.[97]

Years later it revealed by Alexander Aleksandrovich Bessmertnykh, that the Soviet demands on the SDI were introduced 'into the follow up system of working up the documents' by the General Staff of the Soviet Union.[98] Initially, the Soviet President gave the idea of 50 per cent cuts in all parts of the strategic triad. Later, when the plan went to the General Staff, the conditions regarding the laboratory interpretation of the SDI were introduced.[99] Gorbachev believed that without the US commitment to limit the SDI the 'Soviet Union would not be able to go that deep into the reductions'.[100] Anatoly Dobrynin stated that initially, Gorbachev – like his advisers – believed that it was 'time to stop being afraid of SDI', as the system could be easily defeated and was not necessarily an impediment to arms control.[101] However:

> under the influence of our military–industrial complex, Gorbachev gradually began to revert to his insistence on Reagan's withdrawal from SDI as the condition for the success of a new summit on disarmament.[102]

Personal advisor on foreign affairs to Gorbachev in 1986–1991, Anatoly Sergeevich Chernyaev, recalled that 'Gorbachev at that time believed we could end the cold war mostly or exclusively through a process of disarmament'.[103]

The Reaction to Reykjavik

Reykjavik failed because of the SDI. All arms reduction (and non-arms) agreements reached by Reagan and Gorbachev at Reykjavik, foundered because Reagan refused to abandon his dream for space-based defences against ballistic missile attacks. To Gorbachev, every agreement reducing arms was dependent on America's willingness to abandon SDI. At a news conference, Gorbachev attributed the failure of the summit to American intransigence on this issue.[104] The Soviets had bought to Reykjavik a whole package of major proposals and had made 'very serious, unprecedented concessions and compromises'. In contrast, 'the Americans came to this meeting empty-handed, with an entire set of mothballed proposals'.[105]

On the issue of strategic weapons and medium-range weapons, the US responses were 'not adequate' or relevant. Regarding their position on the ABM Treaty, the US and Soviet Union 'were missing a historic chance. Never had our positions been so close together'.[106] Gorbachev declared that:

> Being literally within one, two or three steps from reaching a decision, or decisions, that could have become historic for our entire nuclear missile era, these steps we were unable to take. So there was no turning point in world history ... although it was possible.[107]

Gorbachev continued that:

> After Reykjavik, the SDI has become an even more sore spot in everybody's eyes, as a thorn, as a stumbling block, which does not allow us to find a way out of the threat that hangs over the heads of mankind.[108]

Reykjavik was nevertheless 'an important event' and 'was useful'. It created the potential 'for a step forward once United States adopts a realistic position' and reassesses their thinking. Reykjavik, above all, convinced the Soviet Union of the need for a 'constructive, realistic, approach to the political situation and we're full of energy and determination'.[109] This need for further dialogue was highlighted by President Reagan who appealed to the Soviets 'not to miss the opportunity' for eliminating nuclear weapons, for it was 'within our grasp'.[110] Reagan accused Gorbachev of failing to achieve this at Reykjavik because of Gorbachev's insistence on 'killing' the SDI.[111]

Reagan asserted that 'We came to Iceland to advance the cause of peace, and though we put on the table the most far-reaching arms control proposal in history, the General Secretary rejected it'.[112] Nevertheless, Reagan recognized that the US and the Soviet Union were closer than ever before to reaching an agreement on the elimination of all nuclear weapons. He stated that he was 'still optimistic that a way will be found', as the US invitation for further meetings continued to stand.[113] Reagan attributed the Soviet attendance at the Reykjavik summit as a result of his SDI proposal, for SDI 'is what brought the Soviets back to arms control talks'.[114] In his news conference, Shultz stated the importance of the SDI:

It has been clear for a long time and it was certainly clear today and particularly this afternoon, the importance the Soviet leader attaches to the Strategic Defense Initiative. And I think it was quite apparent that at least a key reason why it was possible to reach such sweeping potential agreements was the very fact of SDI's vigorous presence.[115]

The SDI would be needed to insure Soviet compliance with the agreements.[116]

By not giving up the SDI, Reagan refused to compromise the security of the US and the allies, and freedom; which the space-based defence shield offered hope for. After the Reykjavik summit failed, Shultz stated that 'we are deeply disappointed at this outcome'.[117] However, he highlighted the 'extremely important potential agreements' reached, including reducing strategic arms by 50 per cent, and the deal with intermediate-range missiles.[118] Gorbachev in his *Memoirs* described Shultz's readjustment upon his return to the US. Shultz's characterization of Reykjavik as a 'breakthrough' was due to his reading of Gorbachev's speech and the worldwide reaction to it.[119] Shevardnadze believed it was perhaps 'a good thing that the meeting in Reykjavik ended as it did'.[120] The two leaders attempted to 'make a quick, long-distance gain'. A rapprochement frightened many people.[121]

The Press Reaction

The press labelled the summit a 'failure'. *The New York Times* editorial of October 13 1986, 'Derailment at Reykjavik', stated that 'Not only did the talks fail to bring substantive progress; they failed to set a date for the real summit that this one was supposed to prepare for'.[122] In a more positive tone, the French press, especially Socialist daily *Le Matin,* regarded the summit as a public relations coup for Gorbachev. The Soviets had broken the news blackout which the US had requested; Gorbachev had briefed the press first and accused Reagan first of rejecting historic Soviet proposals.[123] *Tass* political analyst Aleksei Grigoryev wrote that 'Hope gave way to disappointment'.[124]

The London newspaper *The Daily Telegraph*, stated that 'Time is needed to make a proper assessment of what took place and what emerged or failed to do so'. Analysing whether 'The Icelandic Saga' was a 'good thing or a disaster', *The Times* reported that 'The answer is far from clear'.[125] What was clear, however, was following the disappointment on Reagan and Shultz's faces, which the press focused on as indicative evidence of the failure of Reykjavik, a massive 'damage control operation' was embarked upon by the Reagan administration to enhance a positive image of the Reykjavik talks.

One of the most extensive public relations efforts of Reagan's Presidency, the objective of the media blitz was formed less than 24 hours after the President's return from Reykjavik. The aim was to portray the summit as not being the failure that it was perceived to have been, but as achieving remarkable progress which would lead to arms control agreements later on. Also, the goal was to increase public support for the SDI. Contrary to newspaper and television reports that portrayed Reagan's adherence to the SDI as the primary cause for the collapse of the agreement, that explanation was 'simplistic and false'.[126] The President had no choice but to uphold the SDI. The SDI was one of the chief reasons the Soviets went to the summit and would come back. It was the key to a nuclear-free world. Finally, Gorbachev was the one who blocked reductions in nuclear weapons by insisting on SDI confinement to the laboratory.[127]

John Poindexter (who rarely gave interviews) conducted an 80-minute press briefing on Air Force One, and held an extended news conference at the White House. Similarly, Shultz for two days invited himself to be interviewed by *The Washington Post, The Wall Street Journal, The New York Times* and *CBS Morning News*. President Reagan had 23 sessions with the media. The campaign was launched by White House Chief of Staff, Donald T. Regan who said 'we wanted our side to get the story out', and Larry Speakes.[128]

Public Opinion

The Reagan administration's 'media blitz' had 'transformed what looked like a defeat in Iceland into a triumph on the home front' for public opinion strongly supported President Reagan after the Reykjavik summit. According to a *US News and World Report–CNN* poll, Reagan's popularity rating leapt to 68 per cent, which was ten points higher than a similar poll in late August.[129] In another article 'Is There life after Iceland?', (in the same *US News and World Report* issue) the statistic was a 64 per cent approval of President Reagan's handling of US–Soviet relations. Twenty-five per cent disapproved.[130]

Sixty-six per cent endorsed Reagan's refusal to compromise SDI at Reykjavik, while 21 per cent believed that Reagan should have traded the space-based defence system for a reduction in nuclear arms on both sides and 13 per cent of respondents did not know.[131] In a comparable *Time* poll, 69 per cent of people believed that Reagan made the right decision whilst 14 per cent blamed Reagan for the failure to reach an agreement. Forty-five per cent blamed Gorbachev, and 25 per cent blamed both. Reagan was trusted by 63 per cent of Americans as more committed to reach an arms control agreement than Gorbachev (who polled nine per cent). Fifty-three per cent of respondents in October had 'a lot' of confidence in Reagan to negotiate an agreement (compared to only 28 per cent in July).[132]

That a deal could still be made during Reagan's term in office, to reduce nuclear weapons, was the opinion of 62 per cent of people questioned in the *Time* poll. Only nine per cent of people in the *CNN* poll believed that Reykjavik hurt the prospect for an arms agreement. In October 1986, 64 per cent of respondents in the *Time* poll favoured SDI deployment, compared to 59 per cent in November the previous year. In October, 26 per cent opposed it while 54 per cent favoured development of SDI regardless of what happened in arms control negotiations and 27 per cent wanted it to be used as a bargaining chip.[133]

The Congressional Reaction

The Congressional reaction to the failure to reach an arms control agreement at Reykjavik was mixed and along partisan lines, with Republicans (generally proponents of the SDI) supporting Reagan for avoiding the 'Soviet trap' of giving the SDI up for Soviet arms cuts.[134] Conservative Republican Jack Kemp claimed that he was relieved that the President did not abandon the SDI, whilst Republican Senator Richard G. Lugar stated that Reagan acted in the proper way to 'preserve the defence of our country'.[135] Senator Bob Dole of Kansas issued a statement accusing the Soviets of trying to 'blackmail' the President into burying the SDI.[136]

Some Democrats blamed Reagan for refusing to give up the SDI and missing the historic opportunity to eliminate nuclear weapons. According to them, the SDI should have been used as a bargaining chip. An advocator of such a strategy was Senator Claiborne Pell who stated that the obvious compromise was 'a deep reduction in strategic offensive weapons in exchange for an equivalent limitation to the Strategic Defense Initiative'.[137] Similarly, Democrat Senator Gary Hart criticized the administration as more interested in building 'star wars' than seeking 'meaningful' arms control. According to him, the SDI should have been used as the bargaining chip which the administration so often alleged they would use, but did not.[138]

The *US News and World Report* asserted that although there were some critics of Reagan (mainly Democratic candidates Edward Garvey and Bob Elgar who wanted to catch up with the Republicans in the November 4 1986 election), these were 'scattered exceptions'.[139] Most Democrats (whilst relieved that the summit was not successful and would not impair their electoral prospects on November 4) avoided directly criticizing the President for the failure of Reykjavik. Democrat House Majority Leader Jim Wright put it succinctly: 'In times of crisis, we need to stand by the Commander in Chief'.[140] Most arms control advocates who had opposed the SDI were relieved that they had agreed, on October 10 1986, to have the House drop its efforts to force Reagan to adopt certain arms control policies on nuclear testing and SALT II which banned all but the smallest nuclear test explosions. Their efforts ensured that Reagan did not have a scapegoat for the failure of Reykjavik.[141]

Although 'In one weekend, Gorbachev did more for SDI than anyone except Ronald Reagan', House Armed Services Committee Chairman Les Aspin predicted that SDI funding was in trouble.[142] The Reykjavik summit had raised SDI's political profile. The summit's outcome showed that the administration's major priority was to 'protect SDI'. Whilst some senators, such as Frank R. Lautenberg, expressed hope for further US–Soviet negotiations,[143] both Republican and Democrat Congressional leaders agreed that the outcome of the Reykjavik summit would 'lead to greater pressure from Capitol Hill next year for progress in arms control negotiations with the Soviet Union'. Congressional leaders said that the US administration would face more questions and deeper scrutiny on SDI proposals.[144]

After the Reykjavik summit, the Democrat controlled House of Representatives approved a $292 billion (£206 billion) compromise defence bill for fiscal 1987, which slowed the growth of Reagan's military build-up for its second successive year. This included a cut in SDI funding.[145] There was talk among some House members of cutting the appropriation further because of the failure of the Reykjavik summit. Reagan consequently appealed to voters not to elect 'liberals' in Congress who would 'chop up' the SDI. Curtailing SDI's funding would reduce SDI's effectiveness as a bargaining chip.[146] Regarding the issue of the SDI as a bargaining chip, William Graham contended that Paul Nitze proposed that the US bargain away the SDI in late 1986–1987, but 'I and Ronald Reagan did not think that was a good idea'.[147]

The Allies' Reaction

The immediate reaction of the allies to the summit was one of 'considerable confusion in Western Europe' over what had actually happened at Reykjavik, and why the talks had collapsed without setting a date for a future summit. The public reaction of world politicians was disappointment that the summit ended in stalemate, yet hope that future progress on arms control could be made. Privately, prominent European arms control analysts expressed relief that Reykjavik had not resulted in an ill-conceived agreement limiting intermediate-range weapons. Especially so as it could have been reached without prior consultation with the allies.[148]

This was publicly articulated in France by former Defence Ministry Adviser Francois Heisbourg. Privately, it was stated in Rome, Italy.[149] Europe was not only surprised that the US could propose and negotiate changes in Western security which directly affected Europe without any prior consultation with the allies, but they were:

> perhaps even more disturbed by the sudden realization that the American negotiators apparently proceeded at Reykjavik without the slightest understanding of the basis of the system of Western security.[150]

Privately, several European allies complained to the US for failing to consult them on its proposals. NATO's Supreme Allied Commander in Europe, General Bernard Rogers, complained in a written letter a week before the summit to Caspar Weinberger, that he and his NATO commanders had not been consulted about the military effect of the US proposed INF 'zero option' in Europe. Eliminating the weapons would leave the allies vulnerable to the superior non-nuclear conventional Soviet forces.[151]

The Times reported four days after the end of the summit that NATO commanders had still not been informed of the details of the proposals, which would have involved Cruise, Pershing II and the Russian SS-20s. The US proposal of the 'zero option' had taken NATO officers and General Rogers by surprise. General Rogers complained that he was not sufficiently consulted. He should have been one of the first people to have been informed, not one of the last.[152]

In contrast, *The New York Times* reported that NATO was briefed by Shultz in Brussels on October 13 1986, and substantiated the Secretary of State's assessment that Reykjavik was 'a tremendous success'. Privately, however, bitter disappointment was voiced over the failure to reach agreement. One diplomat attested that 'it's a grim Monday at NATO for a lot of people'. British Minister of

State, Timothy Renton, described the summit as 'one step more along the laborious road to arms control'.[153]

At Reykjavik, the US casually proposed to eliminate the missiles stationed in Europe after there had been so much political debate and turmoil in European governments to get the missiles deployed.[154] Margaret Thatcher had disliked the original INF 'zero option' because she believed that the missiles offered a counter to an attack by the Warsaw Pact.[155] In her memoirs, Thatcher stated that she had 'always had mixed feelings about the INF "zero option"':

> On the one hand, it was a great success to have forced the Soviets to withdraw their SS-20 missiles by deploying our Cruise and Pershing. But, on the other, the removal of our intermediate-range land-based missiles would have two undesirable effects.[156]

It threatened the 'decoupling of Europe from NATO'. Secondly, she wrote, 'the INF "zero option" also cast doubt on – though as I has always argued it did not in fact undermine – the NATO strategy of "flexible response"'.[157]

The US failure to sacrifice the European missiles for a strategic arms cut only clarified to the allies Reagan's commitment to his SDI programme. Helmut Kohl, claimed that had the President given in on SDI, Moscow would have had no reason to make the concessions.[158] Bonn daily newspaper *Die Welt* contended that 'The US will not give up its SDI card, and that is precisely why the disarmament dialogue will continue'. Dominique Moisi, of the French Institute for International Relations, affirmed that 'SDI has been the prime motor for negotiations since the Euromissiles crisis'.[159] Although public opinion had been hostile towards the SDI, since Reykjavik the SDI had won some supporters.

Le Quotidien de Paris asserted that Gorbachev's intransigence on SDI prevented the withdrawal of NATO Euromissiles which would have risked 'decoupling the defence of the US from that of Europe'.[160] Failure to reach agreement did not diminish the importance of the summit which, according to French Prime Minister Jacques Chirac, was a step in the right direction towards significant progress on limiting nuclear arms. The West German Government's chief spokesman Friedhelm Ost stated that 'The door to another summit was closed by neither side'. Chancellor Kohl said that the progress would have been unthinkable two or three years ago.[161]

Kohl's parliamentary foreign policy spokesman Voelker Ruehe elucidated that the talks were a 'setback' for disarmament. The opposition – Deputy leader of the Social Democrats, Horst Ehmke contended that the failure of the summit was 'a black Sunday for humanity'. He contended that an arms control accord would be years away and publicly accused Reagan of missing a chance for real peace because of 'the dream of an invincible America'.[162] The Inter-Church Peace Council (the coordinating group for the anti-nuclear movement) in the Netherlands who had played a prominent role in the campaign against NATO's INF deployment, believed that 'a historical chance' for peace was missed.[163]

Margaret Thatcher felt 'intense relief' that Reagan's proposal of eliminating strategic ballistic missiles altogether was withdrawn, as they would have 'effectively killed off the Trident missile, forcing us to acquire a different system if we were to keep an independent nuclear deterrent'.[164] According to her, 'We must not allow a second Reykjavik to happen'.[165] Caspar Weinberger said that the Western European allies had no reason to complain about the failure to reach agreement at Reykjavik. NATO's General Secretary Lord Carrington issued a statement that 'possibilities for significant progress had emerged'.[166]

The Reaction of the US Administration and Arms Experts

To quote James Schlesinger: 'Reykjavik represented a near disaster from which we were fortunate to escape'. Former President Richard Nixon stated that 'No summit since Yalta has threatened Western interests so much as the two days at Reykjavik'.[167] The summit, according to Schlesinger, Alexander M. Haig (Secretary of State, 1981–1982) and Democratic Senator from Georgia, Sam Nunn, was 'ill-prepared'.[168] There was no prior consultation about the proposals with the Joint Chiefs of Staff, the Congress or the allies.[169]

It was stated that the summit was 'quite badly executed with spur-of-the moment despair'.[170] The Joint Chiefs were:

> not asked to study the implications of the President's proposal for a total elimination within ten years of all ballistic missiles, let alone to consider the elimination of all strategic arms.[171]

This American proposal to eliminate all ballistic missiles itself, however, was not a spur of the moment policy, but a concrete proposal to be achieved by 1996. It was unfeasible as it rejected the deterrence doctrine (which had kept the peace since World War II for twenty-five years) and Reagan's promulgation of the Scowcroft Commission report. Abandoning traditional deterrence, according to Haig, would have the consequence of 'making the world less safe in the long run'. The American proposal meant the abandonment of two of the three elements of nuclear triad which upheld America's military position.[172] Caspar Weinberger was against the Gorbachev–Reagan vision at Reykjavik to eliminate all nuclear missiles.[173]

According to Under Secretary of State during the Lyndon B. Johnson administration, George Ball, and Senator Nunn the danger of Reagan's proposal to eliminate nuclear arms was that it would increase the possibility of a conventional war. It would cause NATO great alarm for it would give the Soviet Union, with its larger conventional forces, an advantage.[174] Chairman of the London-based International Institute for Strategic Studies, Michael Palliser, stated that it was impossible for the President to have given up the SDI and accepted the Soviet proposals.[175]

Cyrus Vance, and Paul Warnke, both asserted that the President should have accepted the deal regarding the SDI. This was similarly echoed by George Ball who felt 'a real opportunity was missed in Reykjavik. SDI is not only a fantasy, it is a fraud'. It escalated the arms race and made arms control more difficult to achieve.[176] Robert McFarlane told Director of Soviet Affairs on the National Security Council Staff in 1983–87, Jack F. Matlock Jr., that he was appalled that Reagan turned down Gorbachev's offer at Reykjavik. He affirmed that:

> What Gorbachev offered at Reykjavik was exactly what I was aiming for. Once we
> had an agreement on reductions, ten years [of delaying on SDI testing] was fine. It
> was crazy to turn that down.[177]

Although Sidney Drell favoured Reagan accepting the 'terrific deal', he believed
that 'There is still so far to go and so many technologies to develop in SDI'.
According to his analysis, Reagan's acceptance of curtailing the SDI by adhering
to a strict interpretation of the ABM Treaty – in exchange for an agreement to
reduce weapons – would not have damaged the programme in any way.[178]

In contrast, former chief scientist at the SDI Organization, Defense
Department, Gerold Yonas, and former member of the National Security Council
under Reagan, Richard Pipes, believed that confining the SDI to a strict ABM
interpretation (which in practical terms meant confining SDI to research in the
laboratory) would have had devastating effects. Such was the view from scientists
and Pentagon officials. Yonas believed that it would have crippled the programme
for 'There are major experiments planned for SDI ... and some of them cannot be
done in the lab'. Pipes asserted that the Soviet proposal was 'not a good proposal
for us. The Soviet offer to allow research in the laboratory is meaningless'.[179]

Critics of field tests who included Gerard C. Smith (chief negotiator of the
1972 ABM Treaty) believed that field tests were more political than technical, for
they were intended to impress the public and Congress.[180] Robert McNamara,
(Secretary of Defense under Presidents Kennedy and Johnson) noted that 'The
Soviets did not propose that we sacrifice SDI. They proposed to limit the
program'.[181] McNamara and Gerard C. Smith believed that an accommodation
could be possible.[182] Richard Perle believed that the Soviets were 'uncomfortable
with the prospect of eliminating all ballistic missiles' and consequently responded
by raising the demands on the SDI, 'a demand that ... made it impossible for the
President to accept'.[183] According to Perle, the Soviet Union 'needed a device for
causing the negotiations to fail at that moment', however, not on the issue of
eliminating all ballistic missiles as it was perceived that that would have had a
negative effect on world opinion. Critics of the US position asserted that the US
agreement to a ten-year commitment to the ABM Treaty, conditional to the
elimination of all missiles, was the same tactic.[184]

Insisting that a reduction of offensive weapons be conditional upon
restricting SDI research, the Soviets found a way to make the collapse of the talks
appear the US fault. It is asserted that this is indicative of the fact that the Soviets
were not as frightened of the SDI as suggested, despite the considerable American
advantage in high technology areas. The Soviets had their own SDI around
Moscow and were advanced in ballistic missile research.[185] More plausible is the
contention that the Soviets feared the US SDI and wished to maintain their
monopoly over strategic defences. Experts claimed that the Soviets had conducted
tests in space of the type they wanted banned in the ABM Treaty. The Soviets had
proposed at Reykjavik that such anti-missile weapons tests should be banned for a
period of ten years. This lends credence to those who believe that the Soviets
feared the US SDI.[186]

James Schlesinger stated that the SDI 'was treated and continues to be treated as if it were already a reality ... instead of a collection of technical experiments and distance hopes'.[187] Reagan's failure to compromise over the SDI saved the US from entering into agreements from which it would have had to subsequently withdraw. Viewed in this context, the SDI made an 'invaluable contribution to Western security', by 'preserving the elements of nuclear deterrence from our own recklessness at Reykjavik'.[188]

Caspar Weinberger declared that he was disappointed by the collapse of the Reykjavik talks. Although the proposals offered would have 'achieved a very substantial reduction', the President was 'entirely correct in not being willing to give up strategic defense in response to Soviet promises on these reductions'. Reagan had 'complete and eternal credit' for not giving up the SDI, contrary to the Soviets 'principal' intentions so they could 'keep their monopoly on it'.[189]

The New York Times questioned how a meeting designed to give impetus to the arms talks had suddenly erupted to a 'full-fledged bargaining session'. The newspaper questioned the feasibility of the elimination of nuclear weapons. The newspaper asked how the US administration would maintain security for the US and the allies without nuclear weapons when the Soviets had conventional military superiority.[190] Gorbachev perceived the SDI as an 'attempt to impose a new and prohibitively expensive arms race on the Soviet Union'.[191]

The Significance of Reykjavik

The significance of the Reykjavik summit was not immediately apparent to observers. The potential of what might have been achieved made the summit even more remarkable than the fact it had taken place. This was a striking achievement following all that had happened in the year which had led to a deterioration in relations between the US and the Soviet Union. According to an American official 'the point is, that the desire on both sides to improve relations was strong enough to surmount the difficulties'.[192] To reach tentative agreements on most arms and non-arms issues, especially the agreement to eliminate nuclear weapons, was amazing.

At Reykjavik, both leaders made great strides towards resolving their differences. Gorbachev made the greatest concessions. Reagan and Gorbachev's desire to continue with their efforts was the greatest achievement of Reykjavik, as the door to negotiation remained open. Although both sides accused each other for being responsible for the failure to reach agreement 'both sides were at the same time careful not to charge one another with bad faith'. For the most notorious anti-Communist President in US history to call upon the Soviets 'not to turn back' in their desire to 'achieve some truly historic breakthroughs' was significant.[193]

Addressing his Executive Branch Employees, on October 14 1986, Reagan stated that 'The Reykjavik meeting may have set the stage for a major advance in the US–Soviet relationship'.[194] Reagan elucidated that the significance of the Reykjavik meeting: 'Is not that we didn't sign agreements at the end. The significance is that we got as close as we did. The progress that we made would have been inconceivable just a few months ago'.[195] John Poindexter said that the understandings between Reagan and Gorbachev would be starting points for further arms control bargaining. Yevgeny Velikhov asserted that he was very optimistic that agreements would be reached on arms control.[196]

The INF Treaty, which was signed during the Washington summit 1987, was essentially the same agreement reached at Reykjavik. According to Margaret Thatcher, the significance of the Reykjavik summit was enormous, though this was not realized at the time. President Reagan's refusal to trade away the SDI was 'crucial to the victory over communism'. The implication was that the Cold War ended at Reykjavik and the Americans had won. According to Thatcher the Soviets 'had lost the game and I have no doubt that they knew it'. The Soviets realized that they could not compete with the superior US technology, and many of the concessions they made 'proved impossible for them to retrieve'.[197] George Shultz saw Reykjavik as significant. The summit demonstrated that contentious issues could be resolved; and bureaucratic stalemate could be broken.[198] Reykjavik, according to Stanley Hoffman, demonstrated the 'promise of a somewhat better nuclear world, and the delusion of a world beyond nuclear weapons'.[199]

Gorbachev believed that Reykjavik had been 'a kind of intellectual breakthrough'. In his 1987 book *Perestroika: New Thinking For Our Country and The World*, Gorbachev wrote that 'Reykjavik marked a turning point in world history'. He further added that:

> It tangibly demonstrated that the world situation could be improved ... At Reykjavik we became convinced that our course was correct and that a new and constructive way of political thinking was essential. [200]

In Reagan's memoirs, published in 1990, Reykjavik was referred to as 'a major turning point in the quest for a safe and secure world'.[201] To quote Shultz, 'Ten years from now, people will record the Reykjavik Summit meeting as having accomplished more than any previous summit'.[202] Eduard Shevardnadze affirmed that the Reykjavik meeting 'had enormous significance and exerted a strong influence on our perceptions of the dimensions of what was possible in Soviet–American relations and in world politics'.[203] According to Anatoly Dobrynin, Gorbachev perceived Reykjavik as 'worthwhile after all'.

> First, it showed the world that the Soviet leadership was really prepared for serious discussion of disarmament; second, Reagan unexpectedly demonstrated his readiness to negotiate nuclear arms reduction; third, America's NATO partners in Europe would be critical of Reagan's insistence on continuing SDI at all costs.[204]

In his 1997 *Memoirs*, Gorbachev described the press conference he attended after the Reykjavik meeting broke up. When he came into the room he felt:

> emotional even shaken. These people standing in front of me seemed to represent mankind waiting for its fate to be decided. At this moment I realised the true meaning of Reykjavik and knew what further course we had to follow.[205]

The audience reacted to Gorbachev's phrase 'In spite of all its drama, Reykjavik is not a failure – it is a breakthrough, which allowed us for the first time to look over the horizon', with 'thunderous applause'. Gorbachev expressed the hope that Reykjavik would 'be followed by further progress'.[206] To him:

> Reykjavik showed that an agreement was possible and the new Soviet Union was not into propaganda but wanted genuine disarmament … Reykjavik strengthened our conviction that we had chosen the right course.[207]

In 1998, Edwin Meese III commented that:

> the most important and significant factor in the end of the Cold War, other than the introduction of the SDI, was the fact that President Reagan did not give SDI up at Reykjavik in exchange for Soviet concessions.[208]

Meese III claimed that the SDI was the single most important factor in ending the Cold War.[209] According to William (Bill) Lee, that the SDI broke up the Reykjavik meeting was 'one of the best piece of evidence of demonstrating the importance of SDI'.[210] Lee explained that Reagan was not only prepared to accept Soviet concessions but was prepared to go further to get rid of nuclear weapons. Gorbachev's failure to obtain Reagan's abandonment of the SDI led to the failure of Reykjavik.[211]

Carolyn McGiffert Ekedahl and Melvin A. Goodman argued that the Reykjavik talks 'created the foundation for a series of significant agreements over the next five years and in the long run must be viewed as a major success'.[212] They state that 'It broke the bureaucratic logjam in both capitals, allowing Shultz and Shevardnadze greater freedom to negotiate'.[213] Shevardnadze and Shultz perceived Reykjavik as 'the most remarkable summit ever held'.[214] Writing in *Foreign Affairs*, in 2000, David Greenberg contends that 'in retrospect, the talks were an important step – not because Reagan drove a hard bargain on SDI but, to the contrary, because he proved willing to compromise on so much else'.[215] Greenberg writes that 'The real news of Reykjavik, buried under the headline of the last-minute collapse, was that the two nations were not so far apart'.[216]

Synopsis

Reykjavik was the most significant and least planned meeting of the 1980s. The agreements had fallen through due to Reagan's failure to give up the SDI. The Soviets offered concessions for SDI abandonment. Had the SDI not been an obstacle, the summit would have signified the most radical reduction in military capabilities ever achieved. Gorbachev's INF proposal (regarding medium-range missiles) was an acceptance of Reagan's 1981 'zero option'. However, it was conditional upon the abandonment of the SDI, which Gorbachev failed to achieve. He also failed to achieve this at the 1985 Geneva summit.

The ABM Treaty was the most contentious issue discussed at Reykjavik. To Gorbachev, every agreement made was conditional upon US SDI abandonment. Gorbachev hoped to achieve this by forcing a newer and stricter interpretation of the 1972 ABM Treaty. Gorbachev previously demanded that SDI research be banned. At Reykjavik he no longer demanded this. Instead, he insisted that the SDI research be confined to the laboratory; all anti-ballistic missile defence tests in space would be banned. These conditions prohibited the SDI. To Reagan, this was unacceptable for the SDI could eliminate nuclear weapons and protect against nuclear war.

The most notorious and controversial tentative agreement made (but not signed) at Reykjavik was the proposal to eliminate all nuclear weapons. This demonstrated just how far Reagan and Gorbachev had come and how impulsively the issues were being discussed. To make such an agreement in the first place was significant: a major achievement in mutual trust.

Reykjavik was built upon the previous 1985 Geneva summit, which broke the ice between the two superpowers. Reykjavik built the success for future US–Soviet summits. The improved superpower relationship was evident at Reykjavik. So too was the stalemate regarding the SDI and the failure to reach agreement, provisional upon Reagan's abandonment of this space-based defence shield. Notwithstanding, for the two superpowers to agree on issues was remarkable. Reykjavik was a success: the most remarkable summit ever held. The role of the SDI was significant at Reykjavik. It precluded agreements being signed and was the paramount reason for the failure of the summit.

Notes

[1]   For the Geneva summit, see the following: Garthoff, Raymond L., *The Great Transition: American–Soviet Relations and the End of the Cold War*, Washington, D.C., The Brookings Institution, 1994, pp. 197-251.; Gorbachev, Mikhail, *Perestroika: New Thinking For Our Country and the World*, New York, Harper and Row, 1987, pp. 226-227.; Regan, Donald T., *For The Record: From Wall Street to Washington*, London, Hutchinson, 1988, pp. 265, 293-318, 325, 329.; Shultz, George P., *Turmoil and Triumph: My Years as Secretary of State*, New York, Charles Scribner's Sons, 1993, pp. 597-607.; Thatcher, Margaret, *The Downing Street Years*, London, Harper Collins, 1993, p. 470.; Ekedahl, Carolyn McGiffert and Melvin A. Goodman, *The Wars of Eduard Shevardnadze*, London, Hurst, 1997, pp. 107-108.; Dobrynin, Anatoly, *In Confidence: Moscow's Ambassador to America's Six Cold War Presidents 1962–86*, New York, Random House, 1995, pp. 592-593.; 'The Summit: What it's All About', *NYT*, November 18 1985, pp. A6, A7.; Weinraub, Bernard, 'US and Moscow Are Said To Agree On Future Talks: Leaders Will Meet Today', *NYT*, November 19 1985, pp. A1, A13 Col. 5.; Gelb, Leslie H., 'The Summit: A Prologue?', *NYT*, November 19 1985, pp. A1, A13 Col. 2.; Schmemann, Serge, 'Gorbachev, in Geneva Asks For End to the Arms Race', *NYT*, November 19 1985, p. A12.; 'Text of Gorbachev Statement After His Arrival in Geneva', *NYT*, November 19 1985, p. A12.; Apple, Jr., R.W., 'Reagan Confers With Gorbachev in Geneva Parley: Sessions Total 4 Hours', *NYT*, November 20 1985, pp. A1, A20 Col. 5.; Weinraub, Bernard, 'Reagan Continues Private Meetings

With Gorbachev: Joint Appearance Today', *NYT*, November 21 1985, pp. A1, A16 Col. 3.; Apple, Jr., R.W., 'The Tete-a-Tetes at the Summit: A Drawn Curtain of Uncertainty', *NYT*, November 21 1985, pp. A1, A17 Col. 5.; Morris, Edmund, 'Saving The World', *The Sunday Times*, September 26 1999, pp. 1-2.; According to Anatoly Dobrynin, the Geneva summit was the beginning of the end of the Cold War. Dobrynin, *In Confidence*, p. 564.; Gorbachev publicly described the meeting in Geneva as 'necessary and useful'. Dobrynin, *In Confidence*, p. 593.; That 'Later Reagan himself marked Geneva as the greatest moment of his presidency', see FitzGerald, Frances, *Way Out There in the Blue: Reagan, Star Wars and the End of the Cold War*, New York, Simon and Schuster, 2000, p. 313.; For SDI and the Geneva summit, see the following: Talbott, Strobe, *The Master of the Game: Paul Nitze and the Nuclear Peace*, New York, Vintage Books, 1989, pp. 285-288.; Dobrynin, *In Confidence*, pp. 586-591.; 'Where "Star Wars" Fits in', *NYT*, November 18 1985, p. A7.; Sanger, David E., 'Director of "Star Wars" Predicting a Speed-Up When Meeting Ends', *NYT*, November 21 1985, p. A16.

[2] Church, George L., Reported by Johanna McGeary with Shultz and Strobe Talbott/Washington, 'Summit Hopes: Arms-Control Expectations Create Pressure to Solve the Daniloff Affair', *Time*, No. 40, October 6 1986, p. 6.

[3] Oberdorfer, Don, *The Turn: How the Cold War Came to an End. The United States and the Soviet Union, 1983–1990*. London, Jonathan Cape, 1991, p. 177.; Chaze, William L. with Peter Ross Range, Maureen Santini, Dennis Mullin and Kenneth T. Walsh in Washington and Jeff Trimble and Douglas Stanglin in Moscow, 'Now For the End Game: Nicholas Daniloff is Out of Prison. The Question is: How Long Will He Remain a Hostage?', *USNWR*, September 22 1986, pp. 14-18.; Chaze, William L. with James M. Hildreth, Dennis Mullin, Maureem Santini, Miriam Horn and Kenneth Walsh in Washington and Jeff Trimble in Moscow, 'Trying to Repair the Damage', *USNWR*, September 29 1986, pp. 22-25.; Bialer, Seweryn, 'A Test of Soviet Intentions', *USNWR*, September 29 1986, p. 27.; Huntley, Steve with Maureen Santini, Kenneth T. Walsh and Charles Fenyvesi, 'Who Got The Best of the Deal? Sharp Debate Rages Over How the Daniloff Affair Ended', *USNWR*, October 13 1986, p. 18.; Towell, Pat, 'Reagan, Gorbachev Set Surprise "Pre-Summit"', *CQWR*, Vol. 44, No. 4, October 4 1986, p. 2359.; For the Daniloff arrest, see Reagan, Ronald, *An American Life*, London, Hutchinson, 1990, p. 666.

[4] 'The Iceland Summit', *NYT*, October 10 1986, p. A13.

[5] Gorbachev, Mikhail, *Memoirs*, London, Bantam Books, 1997, p. 534.; Reagan writing in his memoirs, *An American Life*, stated that he believed that Gorbachev's letter, aside from inviting Reagan to an 'impromptu summit', indicated that Gorbachev had little interest in the arms control they had devoted such effort to in July. Reagan, *An American Life*, p. 669.

[6] 'The Iceland Summit', *NYT*, p. A13.; For the 'tug of war' over Daniloff, as excerpted from Reagan's diary, see Reagan, Ronald, *An American Life*, pp. 673-674.; Eduard Shevardnadze, maintained that the Reykjavik summit 'would never have taken place' if the US and Soviets had not resolved the 'Daniloff affair'. Shevardnadze, Eduard, *The Future Belongs to Freedom*, New York, The Free Press, p. 88.; For the Daniloff Affair, see Ekedahl and Goodman, *The Wars of Eduard Shevardnadze*, pp. 110-111.

[7] Shultz, *Turmoil and Triumph*, p. 750.

[8] Church, 'Summit Hopes', *Time*, p. 7.

[9] Gorbachev, *Memoirs*, p. 536.; For the Caspar Weinberger memorandum to Reagan, before the Geneva Summit, where Weinberger recommended that the President reject any steps towards disarmament, see Dobrynin, *In Confidence*, p. 586.

[10] Church, 'Summit Hopes', *Time*, pp. 7-8.

11 Ibid., p. 8.

12 Editorial, 'More Than Theater in Iceland', *NYT*, October 10 1986, p. A38.

13 Towell, 'Reagan, Gorbachev', *CQWR*, p. 2359.

14 Shultz, *Turmoil and Triumph*, p. 753.

15 Towell, Pat, '"Pre-Summit" Snags Hill Arms Control Efforts', *CQWR*, Vol. 44, No. 40, October 4 1986, p. 2336.

16 Ibid.

17 Ibid., p. 2337.

18 Felton, John, '"High-Water Mark" for "Star Wars" … While Senate Blunts Most Arms Challenges', *CQWR*, Vol. 44, No. 32, August 9 1986, p. 1787.

19 Ibid.; For Congress's cut in SDI funding see also Chaze, William L. with John W. Mashek, Gloria Borger, James M. Hildreth, Melissa Healy, Kenneth T. Walsh and Dennis Mullin, 'The Blitz That Made Reagan a Winner: How the White House Team Transformed What Looked Like a Defeat in Iceland into a Triumph on the Home Front', *USNWR*, October 27 1986, p. 26.

20 Felton, '"High-Water Mark" for "Star Wars"', *CQWR*, p. 1787.

21 Towell, Pat, 'Funds for "Star Wars" Program Held to $3.4 Billion by Panel', *CQWR*, Vol. 44, No. 38, September 20 1986, p. 2244.

22 Felton, '"High-Water Mark" for "Star Wars"', *CQWR*, p. 1787.

23 Ibid, pp. 1787-1788.

24 Reagan quote and information from Towell, Pat, 'In the Wake of the Summit: Proposals, Politics', *CQWR*, Vol. 44, No. 42, October 18 1986, p. 2589.

25 Church, 'Summit Hopes', *Time*, p. 8.

26 Ibid.

27 Towell, 'In the Wake of the Summit', *CQWR*, p. 2589.

28 Oberdorfer, *The Turn*, p. 160.

29 For Gorbachev's January 15 1986 announcement of the elimination of all nuclear weapons by the year 2000, see Shevardnadze, *The Future Belongs to Freedom*, pp. 48-49.

30 Oberdorfer, *The Turn*, pp. 156-157.

31 Ibid, pp. 157, 155.; To quote Shevardnadze, the idea for the Reykjavik summit 'arose in the hiatus that had occurred in Soviet–American relations after the meeting in Geneva, when the two sides announced that nuclear war should never be unleashed and that there are no victors in such a war'. Shevardnadze, *The Future Belongs to Freedom*, p. 88.

32 Towell, 'Reagan, Gorbachev Set Surprise "Pre-Summit"', *CQWR*, p. 2360.

33 Oberdorfer, *The Turn*, p. 155.

34 Editorial, 'More Than Theater in Iceland', *NYT*, p. A38.

35 Pipes, Richard, 'Why Hurry Into a Weapons Accord?', *NYT*, October 10 1986, p. A39.

36 Gwertzman, Bernard, 'US Stressing Human Rights and Regional Issues', *NYT*, October 12 1986, p. A12.

37 Church, 'Summit Hopes', *Time*, p. 7.; For President Reagan's speech to the United Nations, see 'President Reagan's Sept. 22 UN Address', *CQWR* Vol. 44, No. 39, September 27 1986, pp. 2303-2305.

38 Church, 'Summit Hopes', *Time*, p. 8.; See also Duffy, Brian with Dennis Mullin, James M. Hildreth and Robert Kaylor in Washington and Jeff Trimble in Moscow, 'Big Issues at a Small Summit', *USNWR*, October 13 1986, p. 15.

39 Towell, 'Reagan, Gorbachev Set Surprise "Pre-Summit"', *CQWR*, p. 2360.

40 Towell, 'In the Wake of the Summit', *CQWR*, p. 2589.

41 'The Iceland Summit', *NYT*, October 10 1986, p. A13.

42 All information from Weinraub, Bernard, 'President Arrives for Iceland Talks', *NYT*, October 10 1986, p. 1.; and Taubman, Philip, 'Gorbachev is Described as Set for Compromise', *NYT*, October 10 1986, p. A12.

43 Taubman, 'Gorbachev is Described as Set for Compromise', *NYT*, p. A12.

44 'The Iceland Summit', *NYT*, p. A13.

45 Weinraub, 'President Arrives for Iceland Talks', *NYT*, p. A12.

46 Gwertzman, Bernard, 'Reagan in a Shift on Nuclear Tests on Eve of Talks', *NYT*, October 11 1986, p. 1.; Weinraub, Bernard, 'Gorbachev, in Iceland, Cites Hope of Ending War Threat', *NYT*, October 11 1986, p. 5.

47 Weinraub, 'Gorbachev, in Iceland, Cites Hope of Ending War Threat', *NYT*, p. 5.

48 Shultz, *Turmoil and Triumph*, p. 752.

49 Gwertzman, Bernard, '"Core" Advisers 3 or 4 on Each Side, Stay Close to Reagan and Gorbachev', *NYT*, October 12 1986, p. 10.

50 Shultz, *Turmoil and Triumph*, p. 757.; Oberdorfer, *The Turn*, pp. 190-191.

51 Weinraub, Bernard, 'Work Units Set Up: Soviet Links Scheduling of Summit to Gains on Weapons Control', *NYT*, October 12 1986, p. 1.

52 Gelb, Leslie, H., 'A Quest for Compromise: Areas of Agreement Appear to Take Shape as Summit Leaders Seek Concrete Results', *NYT*, October 12 1986, p. 12.

53 Shultz, *Turmoil and Triumph*, pp. 758-759.

54 Gorbachev, *Memoirs*, p. 538.

55 Weinraub, Bernard, 'How Grim Ending in Iceland Followed Hard-Won Gains', *NYT*, October 14 1986, p. A11.; Gordon, Michael R., 'US Officials Look to Geneva Talks, but Critics are Skeptical on Prospects', *NYT*, October 14 1986, p. A11.

56 Taubman, Philip, 'Gorbachev Angrily Accuses Reagan of Scuttling an Accord at Reykjavik', *NYT*, October 13 1986, p. A8.; For Gorbachev's account of the START discussions, see Gorbachev, Mikhail, *Memoirs*, pp. 537-538.

57 Gorbachev, *Memoirs*, p. 538.

58 Shultz, *Turmoil and Triumph*, pp. 758-759.

59 Ibid.

60 Ibid.; Oberdorfer, *The Turn*, p. 191.

61 Gordon, Michael R., 'US Officials Look to Geneva Talks, but Critics are Skeptical on Prospects', *NYT*, p. A11.; 'Arms Control: What Might Have Been', *NYT*, October 14 1986, p. A11.; See also Gwertzman, Bernard, 'No US Summit Date: Effect on Ties Unclear – Understandings Cited on Certain Issues', *NYT*, October 13 1986, p. A8.

62 Taubman, 'Gorbachev Angrily Accuses Reagan of Scuttling an Accord at Reykjavik', *NYT*, p. A8.

63 Gorbachev, *Memoirs*, p. 539.

64 Shultz, *Turmoil and Triumph,*, pp. 760-761.; For the press briefing, on October 13, by John M. Poindexter which highlighted the conclusions reached at Reykjavik, see Towell, 'In the Wake of the Summit: Proposals, Politics', *CQWR*, pp. 2589-2590.

65 Weinraub, 'Work Units Set Up', *NYT*, p. 1.; Gelb, 'A Quest for Compromise: Areas of Agreement Appear to Take Shape', *NYT*, p. 1.; See 'Key Advisers on the Principal Issues', *NYT*, October 12 1986, p. 10.

66 Shultz, *Turmoil and Triumph*, p. 764.

67 Ibid., p. 765.

68 Ibid., p. 770.

69 Gelb, Leslie H., 'Sticking Points in Iceland: "Historic" Gains on Arms Cuts Were Near, But Talks Foundered on 'Star Wars' Issue', *NYT*, October 13 1986, p. A9 Col. 3.

70 'To The Foreign Ministers of the USSR and the USA Concerning the Draft of Agreements on Nuclear Disarmament', Reprinted in Oberdorfer, *The Turn*, p. 446.

71 Weinraub, Bernard, 'Arms Issues Overshadowed Question of Rights in Soviet', *NYT*, October 13 1986, p. A9.
72 Ibid.; 'Excerpts From Comments by Shultz at the News Conference in Reykjavik', *NYT*, October 13 1986, p. A9.
73 Weinraub, 'Arms Issues Overshadowed Question of Rights in Soviet', *NYT*, p. A9.
74 'Arms Control: What Might Have Been', *NYT*, October 14 1986, p. A11.; For the other issues involved at the Reykjavik summit and an analysis of the INF proposals, see Duffy, Brian, 'Big Issues at a Small Summit', *USNWR*, pp. 14-17.
75 See Towell, 'In the Wake of the Summit', *CQWR*, p. 2590.; Reagan, *An American Life*, pp. 676-679.; Shultz, *Turmoil*, pp. 759-761, 768-772.; Gelb, 'Sticking Points in Iceland', *NYT*, pp. A1, A9.
76 Gorbachev, *Memoirs*, p. 539.
77 Ibid.
78 Ibid.
79 Towell, 'In the Wake of the Summit', *CQWR*, p. 2590.; Reagan, *An American Life*, pp. 676-679.; Shultz, *Turmoil*, pp. 759-761, 768-772.; Gelb, 'Sticking Points in Iceland', *NYT*, pp. A1, A9.
80 Towell, 'In the Wake of the Summit', *CQWR*, p. 2590.; Reagan, *An American Life*, pp. 676-679.; Shultz, *Turmoil*, pp. 759-761, 768-772.; Gelb, 'Sticking Points in Iceland', *NYT*, pp. A1, A9.
81 Shultz, *Turmoil*, p. 760.
82 Reagan, *An American Life*, p. 676.
83 Shultz, *Turmoil*, p. 761.
84 Reagan, *An American Life*, p. 676.
85 Gwertzman, 'No US Summit Date: Effect on Ties Unclear', *NYT*, p. A8.; Reagan, *An American Life*, pp. 678.; That the SDI 'could serve as a safety valve against cheating – or attacks by lunatics who managed to get their hands on a nuclear missile', see Reagan, *An American Life*, p. 608.
86 Reagan, *An American Life*, pp. 677-678.; Boyd, Gerald M., 'Defends His Stand: President Won't Give Up "Star Wars" But Says Pacts are Possible', *NYT*, October 14 1986, p. A10.
87 Gelb, 'Sticking Points in Iceland', *NYT*, p. A9.; 'Excerpts From Comments by Shultz at the News Conference in Reykjavik', *NYT*, p. A9.
88 All information from Towell, 'In the Wake of the Summit', *CQWR*, p. 2590.; Shultz, *Turmoil*, p. 769.; Sultz Speech reprinted in Oberdorfer, *The Turn*, p. 446.
89 Gelb, 'Sticking Points in Iceland', *NYT*, p. A9.
90 Shultz, *Turmoil*, p. 770.
91 Towell, 'In the Wake of the Summit', *CQWR*, p. 2590.; see also Shultz, *Turmoil*, pp. 771-773.
92 Reagan, *An American Life*, p. 679.; For the Reagan–Gorbachev SDI encounter at Reykjavik, see ibid., pp. 675-679.; For the Reykjavik summit, see the following: Shevardnadze, *The Future Belongs to Freedom*, pp. 88-89.; Dobrynin, *In Confidence*, pp. 619- 622.; Thatcher, *The Downing Street Years*, pp. 470-471.; Ekedahl and Goodman, *The Wars of Eduard Shevardnadze*, pp. 111-112.
93 Reagan, *An American Life*, p. 679.
94 Ibid., p. 675.
95 Gorbachev, *Memoirs*, pp. 539-540.
96 Anatoly Chernyayev quote stated in Jackson, William D., 'Soviet Reassessment of Ronald Reagan, 1985–1988', *Political Science Quarterly*, Vol. 113, No. 4, Winter 1998–99, pp. 632-633.

[97] Dobrynin, *In Confidence*, p. 610.; Jackson, 'Soviet Reassessment of Ronald Reagan', p. 633.; William D. Jackson states that to Gorbachev the Reykjavik summit was 'a sophisticated element in his peace campaign designed to increase political pressure on the Reagan administration to alter its policies towards the Soviet Union and to build international support for his own policy rather than as an opportunity for serious negotiations'. Jackson, 'Soviet Reassessment of Ronald Reagan', p. 632.; For an assessment of Reykjavik within the context of Gorbachev's policy, see Jackson, 'Soviet Reassessment of Ronald Reagan', pp. 629-634.

[98] Wohlforth, William C., (ed.), *Witnesses to the End of the Cold War*, Baltimore, The John Hopkins University Press, 1996, p. 168.

[99] Ibid.

[100] Bessmertnykh quote in ibid., p. 168.

[101] Dobrynin, *In Confidence*, p. 667.

[102] Ibid., p. 620.

[103] Wohlforth, (ed), *Witnesses*, p. 166.; For the role of the SDI at the Reykjavik summit, see Regan, *For the Record*, pp. 348-355.; Talbott, *Master of the Game*, pp. 317-318.; For the Reykjavik summit, see Regan, *For the Record*, pp. 29, 313-314, 336-355.

[104] Gelb, 'Sticking Points in Iceland', *NYT*, p. A1.; Gwertman, 'No US Summit Date', *NYT*, p. A1.; Schmemann, Serge, 'Moscow is Critical: Says Washington Wasted Historic Opportunity for Weapons Cuts', *NYT*, October 14 1986, p. A1.; Schmemann, Serge, 'Russian is Critical: Says President Lacked Will on Arms to Make a "Turn in History"', *NYT*, October 15 1986, p. A1.; Anatoly Dobrynin states that 'As an eyewitness at Reykjavik, I feel Gorbachev was no less responsible than Reagan for its failure because he held SDI hostage for the success of the meeting'. Dobrynin, *In Confidence*, p. 622.; According to Dobrynin, Gorbachev was 'very angry with Reagan's stubbornness on SDI, which he considered the major reason for the failure of the meeting'. Dobrynin, *In Confidence*, p. 622.; Gorbachev wanted to stop the SDI and convince international opinion that it was blocking the START and INF agreements. Ekedahl and Goodman, *The Wars of Eduard Shevardnadze*, p. 112.

[105] All information from 'Remarks by Reagan and Gorbachev After Reykjavik Talks', *NYT*, October 13 1986, p. A10.

[106] Ibid.

[107] 'Excerpts From Speech by Gorbachev About Iceland Meeting', *NYT*, October 15 1986, p. A12.

[108] Ibid.

[109] Ibid.

[110] Boyd, Gerald M., 'President Hopeful: Citing Gains on Arms, He Asks Moscow Not to "Miss Opportunity"', *NYT*, October 15 1986, p. A1.

[111] Boyd, Gerald M., 'Defends His Stand: President Won't Give Up "Star Wars" But Says Pacts Are Possible', *NYT*, October 14 1986, p. A1.

[112] 'Remarks by Reagan and Gorbachev After Reykjavik Talks', *NYT*, p. A10.; Gwertzman, 'Effect on Ties Unclear', *NYT*, p. A1.

[113] For President Reagan's account of the Reykjavik meeting, see 'Transcript of President Reagan's Broadcast On Talks With Gorbachev in Iceland', *NYT*, October 14 1986, p. A10.; For Gorbachev's televised account of the Reykjavik meeting in which he highlighted Soviet proposals, and elaborated on the ABM debate, see 'Excerpts From Speech by Gorbachev About Iceland Meeting', *NYT*, p. A10.; See also 'Remarks by Reagan and Gorbachev After Reykjavik Talks', *NYT*, p. A10.

114 Boyd, 'President Won't Give Up "Star Wars" But Says Pacts Are Possible', *NYT*, p. A1.; 'Transcript of President's Broadcast On Talks With Gorbachev in Iceland', *NYT*, p. A10.
115 'Excerpts From Comments by Shultz at the News Conference in Reykjavik', *NYT*, p. A9.
116 Ibid.
117 Ibid.; Boyd, 'President Won't Give Up "Star Wars"', *NYT*, p. A1.
118 'Excerpts From Comments by Shultz at the News Conference in Reykjavik', *NYT*, p. A9.
119 Gorbachev, *Memoirs*, p. 541.; Reykjavik was, according to Gorbachev, a 'kind of intellectual breakthrough'. Ekedahl and Goodman, *The Wars of Eduard Shevardnadze*, p. 114.; Anatoly Dobrynin argues that both Gorbachev and Reagan came away from the Reykjavik summit 'bitterly disappointed'. Dobrynin, *In Confidence*, p. 621.
120 Shevardnadze, *The Future Belongs to Freedom*, p. 89.
121 Ibid.
122 Editorial, 'Derailment at Reykjavik', *NYT*, October 13 1986, p. A18.
123 'Disappointment is Expressed in World Capitals Over Iceland Talks, But Also Hope', *NYT*, October 14 1986, p. A12.
124 Schmemann, 'Moscow is Critical: Says Washington Wasted Historic Opportunity for Weapons Cuts', *NYT*, p. A12.
125 'Disappointment is Expressed in World Capitals Over Iceland Talks', *NYT*, p. A12.; Binyon, Michael, 'The Icelandic Saga: Good Thing or a Disaster?', *The Times*, (London), October 18 1986, p. 5.
126 See Weinraub, Bernard, 'US Acts to Enhance Image After Talks', *NYT*, October 15 1986, p. A13.; Chaze, 'The Blitz That Made Reagan a Winner', *USNWR*, p. 25.; Church, George J., Reported by David Beckwith and Johanna McGeary/Washington, 'Forward Spin: Trying to Get Arms Control Back on Track', *Time*, No. 43, October 27 1986, p. 6.; 'Simplistic and False', words are by Patrick J. Buchanan, Director of White House Communications.
127 Church, 'Forward Spin', *Time*, p. 6.
128 Ibid.; Chaze, 'The Blitz That Made Reagan a Winner', *USNWR*, p. 25.
129 Chaze, 'The Blitz', *USNWR*, pp. 25-26.
130 Duffy, Brian with Dennis Mullin, Maureen Santini, Kenneth T. Walsh and Melissa Healy in Washington, Jeff Trimble in Moscow, Robin Knight in London and Douglas Stanglin in Bonn, 'Is There Life After Iceland?', *USNWR*, October 27 1986, pp. 18.
131 Ibid., pp. 16-18.
132 Church, 'Forward Spin', *Time*, p. 9.
133 Ibid.
134 Boyd, 'President Won't Give Up "Star Wars"', *NYT*, p. A10.; Herbers, John, 'View in Congress on Talks is Mixed: Reagan Criticized and Praised for Stand on "Star Wars"', *NYT*, October 13 1986, p. A1.
135 Herbers, 'View in Congress on Talks is Mixed', *NYT*, p. A8.
136 Roberts, Steven V., '"Star Wars" Battle Looms in Congress', *NYT*, October 15 1986, p. A14.
137 Herbers, 'View in Congress on Talks is Mixed', *NYT*, p. A8.
138 Ibid.
139 Chaze, 'The Blitz That Made Reagan a Winner', *USNWR*, pp. 25-26.
140 A *Time* poll examining whether the President was right to have accepted curtailment of the SDI for an arms deal revealed that support for Reagan cut across party and ideological lines. A majority of Democrats, as well as Republicans, believed that Reagan

should have turned down the package. Church, George J., 'Forward Spin', *Time*, p. 9.; For a *USNWR–CNN* poll which questioned voters on their opinions of Republican and Democrat fortunes in the November elections, following the Reykjavik summit, see Chaze, 'The Blitz', *USNWR*, p. 26.

141 Towell, 'In the Wake of the Summit', *CQWR*, pp. 2589-2590.
142 Chaze, 'The Blitz That Made Reagan A Winner', *USNWR*, pp. 25-26.
143 Herbers, 'View in Congress on Talks Is Mixed', *NYT*, p. A8.
144 Roberts, '"Star Wars" Battle Looms in Congress', *NYT*, p. A14.; Weinraub, Bernard, 'US Acts to Enhance Image After Talks', *NYT*, October 15 1986, p. A13.
145 Binyon, Michael, 'Threat to "chop" SDI Deined', *The Times* (London), October 16 1986, p. 9.; See Fuerbringer, Jonathan, 'Reagan Military Budget Gets Big Cut', *NYT*, October 15 1986, p. A20.
146 Boyd, Gerald M., 'President is Critical of "Liberals" Who May "Chop Up" "Star Wars": Sees Critics Playing into Gorbachev's Hands on Missile Defense Plans', *NYT*, October 16 1986, pp. A1, A10; For Congress's cut in SDI research, see Church, 'Forward Spin', *Time*, p. 8.; Chaze, 'The Blitz That Made Reagan a Winner', *USNWR*, p. 26.
147 Graham, *Interview*.
148 All information from 'Disappointment is Expressed in World Capitals Over Iceland Talks, But Also Hope', *NYT*, p. A12.
149 Ibid.
150 Schlesinger, James, 'Reykjavik and Revelations: A Turn of the Tide?', *Foreign Affairs*, 65, p. 435.
151 Duffy, 'Is There Life After Iceland?', *USNWR*, p. 18.; Davenport, Peter, 'Nato Commanders Angry at Being Kept in the Dark', *The Times*, (London), October 17 1986, p. 7.
152 Davenport, 'Nato Commanders', *The Times*, (London), p. 7.
153 Prial, Frank J., 'Shultz Briefs NATO Allies on Talks', *NYT*, October 14 1986, p. A12.
154 Schlesinger, 'Reykjavik and Revelations', p. 435.
155 Thatcher, *The Downing Street Years*, p. 472.
156 Ibid., p. 771.
157 Ibid.
158 'Disappointment is Expressed in World Capitals Over Iceland Talks', *NYT*, p. A12.; Davenport, 'Nato Commanders Angry', *The Times* (London), p. 7.
159 Painton, Frederick, Reported by William McWhirter/Bonn and B.J. Phillips/Paris, 'So Near and Yet So Far ... But Not So Bad, Say U.S. Allies of the Wreckage at Reykjavik', *Time*, October 27 1986, p. 16.
160 Ibid.
161 'Disappointment is Expressed in World Capitals', *NYT*, p. A12.; Davenport, 'Nato Commanders Angry', *The Times*, (London), p. 7.
162 Reuters, 'Bonn Sees Setback', *NYT*, October 13 1986, p. A8.; Painton, 'So Near and Yet So Far', *Time*, p. 16.
163 Painton, 'So Near and Yet So Far', *Time*, p. 16.
164 Thatcher, *Downing Street Years*, p. 472.
165 Thatcher quote stated in Gorbachev, Mikhail, *Memoirs*, p. 542.
166 Gordon, 'US Officials Look to Geneva Talks', *NYT*, p. A11.; Prial, 'Shultz Briefs NATO Allies on Talks', *NYT*, p. A12.
167 Schlesinger, 'Reykjavik and Revelations', p. 429.
168 Ibid, p. 428.; 'How Good Was the Deal?: Experts Debate the Pros and Cons of the Reykjavik Proposals', *Time*, October 27 1986, p. 14.; The words 'ill-prepared' are by Alexander Haig, in 'How Good Was the Deal', *Time*, p. 14.

[169] Stated by Gerard C. Smith in 'How Good Was the Deal', *Time*, p. 14.

[170] Schlesinger, 'Reykjavik and Revelations', p. 428.

[171] Quote by Sam Nunn, in 'How Good Was the Deal', *Time*, p. 14.; The NATO allies and the Joint Chiefs of Staff (JCS) were shocked by 'Reagan's willingness to give up nuclear deterrence without advance consultation and reacted bitterly to the idea of substantial cuts in the nuclear arsenal'. Admiral William Crowe, the Chief of the JCS was 'particularly angry with Reagan's proposal to eliminate all ballistic missiles before the turn of the century, a concept the joint chiefs had not been allowed to study'. Ekedahl and Goodman, *The Wars of Eduard Shevardnadze*, p. 114.; For Reagan's proposal to eliminate strategic ballistic missiles, see Thatcher, Margaret, *The Downing Street Years*, p. 471.

[172] Schlesinger, 'Reykjavik and Revelations', pp. 430-433.; 'How Good Was the Deal?', *Time*, p. 14.; See also Schlesinger, James, 'The Dangers of a Nuclear-Free World', *Time*, October 27 1986, p. 15.

[173] Reagan, *An American Life*, p. 685.; Ronald Reagan in his memoirs wrote that 'Cap Weinberger was strongly against the vision Gorbachev and I shared at Reykjavik calling for the elimination of all nuclear missiles'. Ibid.

[174] 'How Good Was the Deal?', *Time*, p. 14.; Duffy, 'Is There Life After Iceland?', *USNWR*, p. 18.; Chaze, 'The Blitz That Made Reagan a Winner', *USNWR*, p. 26.

[175] 'How Good Was the Deal?', *Time*, p. 14.

[176] Ibid, p. 13.

[177] This was revealed by Matlock at the Princeton University Conference, in late February 1993. Wohlforth, (ed), *Witnesses*, p. 58.

[178] 'How Good Was the Deal?', *Time*, p. 13.

[179] Ibid, p. 14.; Broad, William J., 'Experts Disagree On Space Test Ban: Same Assert a 10-Year Curb Wouldn't Hurt "Star Wars"', *NYT*, October 14 1986, p. A13 Col. 1.; However, Dr George Chapline, at the Lawrence Livermore National Laboratory, – the leading Federal facility for SDI research – believed that so many technical problems remained to be solved in the laboratory, that a ten year ban on testing in space would have no significant effect on SDI. In contrast, Dr Robert Jastrow, Dr Richard Garwin and Lieut. Gen. James A. Abrahamson (director of the Strategic Defense Initiative Organization), believed that testing in space should be imminent. Broad, 'Experts Disagree on Space Test Ban', *NYT*, p. A13 Col. 1; For a discussion on whether the ten year ABM restrictions that Gorbachev wanted would hurt the SDI, see Budiansky, Stephen with Stanley N. Wellborn, 'Is SDI a Poker-Chip – or the Pot?', *USNWR*, October 27 1986, pp. 19-23.; For the experts view that the Soviet Union had conducted tests in space of the type they wanted banned in the ABM Treaty, see Broad, William J., 'Experts Say Soviet Has Conducted Space Tests on Anti Missile Weapons', *NYT*, October 15 1986, p. A14.; For an analysis of the SDI and arms control, see Fossedal, Gregory A., 'For Star Wars and Arms Control, Too', *NYT*, October 14 1986, p. A35.; For an analysis of Reykjavik, see 'Reykjavik and Riddles', *NYT*, October 14 1986, p. A35.; For general information on the summit, see Hoffmann, Stanley, 'An Icelandic Saga', *The New York Review of Books*, Vol. XXXIII, No. 18, November 20 1986, pp. 15-16.; For the promotion of the SDI, see Apple, Jr., R.W., 'Senate Nominee Pushes "Star Wars" in Colorado', *NYT*, October 15 1986, p. A18.

[180] Wellborn, 'Is SDI a Poker-Chip – or the Pot?', *USNWR*, p. 21.

[181] 'How Good Was the Deal?', *Time*, p. 14.

[182] Ibid.

[183] Wellborn, 'Is SDI a Poker-Chip – or the Pot?', *USNWR*, p. 22.

[184] Gordon, Michael R., 'Official Describes Parley in Iceland: Details of Talks are Filled in by Perle of Defense Dept', *NYT*, October 15 1986, p. A14.

[185] Wellborn, 'Is SDI a Poker-Chip?', *USNWR*, pp. 22-23.; See also Stengel, Richard, Reported by David Alkman/Washington and James O. Jackson/Moscow, 'Was It All a Soviet Sting?', *Time*, October 27 1986, p. 11.

[186] Broad, 'Experts Say Soviet Has Conducted Space Tests on Anti Missile Weapons', *NYT*, p. A14.

[187] Schlesinger, 'Reykjavik and Revelations', p. 433.; Schlesinger, 'The Dangers of a Nuclear-Free World', *Time*, p. 15.

[188] Schlesinger, 'Reykjavik and Revelations', p. 434.; Schlesinger, 'The Dangers of a Nuclear-Free World', *Time*, p. 15.; See Talbott, Strobe, 'A Compromise May Yet Be Possible: The ABM Treaty Could Be the Key to a Superpower Trade-Off', *Time*, October 27 1986, p. 12.

[189] Gordon, 'US Officials Look to Geneva Talks', *NYT*, p. A11.; For the SDI–ABM discussion Reagan and Gorbachev had, and an analysis of the tentative agreements made, see Lamar, Jr., Jacob V., Reported by Barrett Seaman/Washington, 'When to Hold 'Em – and to Fold 'Em: Did the President Play His Cards Right at the Summit?', *Time*, October 27 1986, pp. 10-11.; For an analysis of the 'grand compromise': the curtailment of the SDI in exchange for reductions in Soviet missiles, see Talbott, 'A Compromise May Yet Be Possible', *Time*, p. 12.

[190] Gelb, Leslie H., 'Summit Puzzles Linger: Basic Questions About What Took Place at Reyjavik Talks are Still Unanswered', *NYT*, October 16 1986, p. A1.

[191] For Gorbachev's reaction to the SDI and the Reykjavik summit, see Schmenann, 'Russian is Critical', *NYT*, pp. A1, A13.

[192] Gelb, 'A Quest for Compromise', *NYT*, p. 12.

[193] Gelb, 'Sticking Points in Iceland', *NYT*, p. A1.; Boyd, 'President Hopeful: Citing Gains on Arms', *NYT*, p. A1.

[194] 'Excerpts From Reagan's Talk to Executive Branch Employees', *NYT*, October 15 1986, p. A13.

[195] Ibid.

[196] Boyd, 'Defends His Stand: President Won't Give Up "Star Wars"', *NYT*, p. A10 Col. 1.; 'Discord Erupts Over Row of Silence', *NYT*, October 13 1986, p. A8.

[197] Thatcher, *The Downing Street Years*, pp. 470-471.

[198] Shultz, *Turmoil*, pp. 779-780.

[199] Hoffman, 'An Icelandic Saga', *The New York Review of Books*, p. 15.

[200] Shultz, *Turmoil*, p. 996.; Oberdorfer, *The Turn*, pp. 183-184.; Gorbachev, Mikhail, *Perestroika: New Thinking For Our Country and the World*, New York, Harper and Row, 1987, p. 240.; For Gorbachev's views on Reykjavik, see Gorbachev, *Perestroika*, pp. 236-241.

[201] Oberdorfer, *The Turn*, p. 184.; Reagan, *An American Life*, p. 683.; For the US and Soviet officials' reaction to Reykjavik, revealed at the February 1993 Princeton University Conference, New Jersey, see Wohlforth, (ed), *Witnesses*, Chapter 6: 'The Riddle of Reykjavik', pp. 163-188.; Greenstein, Fred I., and William C. Wohlforth, (eds), 'Retrospective on the End of the Cold War', *Report of a Conference Sponsored by the John Foster Dulles Program for the Study of Leadership in International Affairs*, Center of International Studies, Monograph Series No. 6, Princeton University, 1994, Session 6: 'The Riddle of Reykjavik', pp. 39-43.; For more information about Reykjavik, see *The Annual Register: A Record of World Events 1986*, pp. 59, 60-63, 100-103, 354, 378, 382-384.

[202] Shultz, *Turmoil*, p. 996.

[203] Shevardnadze, *The Future Belongs to Freedom*, p. 89.
[204] Dobrynin, *In Confidence*, p. 622.
[205] Gorbachev, *Memoirs*, p. 541.
[206] Ibid.
[207] Ibid., pp. 541-542. For more on the Reykjavik summit, see Shultz, *Turmoil*, pp. 751-780.; Gorbachev, Mikhail, *Perestroika*, pp. 236-241.
[208] Meese III, *Interview*.
[209] Ibid.
[210] Lee, *Interview*.
[211] Ibid.
[212] Ekedahl and Goodman, *The Wars of Eduard Shevardnadze*, p. 111.; Reykjavik 'set a foundation for later success'. Ibid., p. 114.
[213] Ibid., p. 115.
[214] Ibid., p. 111.; The February 1993 Princeton University 'Retrospective on the End of the Cold War' conference heard, for the first time, that the break up of the Reykjavik summit might have been averted if Marshal Sergei Akhromeyev, who was the Chief of Staff of the Soviet armed forces, had allowed Gorbachev to present a compromise proposal. Wohlforth, (ed.), *Witnesses*, pp. 5-6.
[215] Greenberg, David, 'Review Essay: The Empire Strikes Out: Why Star Wars Did Not End The Cold War: A Review of FitzGerald, Frances, 'Way Out There in the Blue: Reagan, Star Wars and the End of the Cold War', New York, Simon and Schuster, 2000', *Foreign Affairs*, Vol. 79, No. 2, March/April 2000, p. 142.
[216] Ibid.

Chapter 4

US–Soviet Relations after the Reykjavik Summit

The Washington Summit: December 7–10 1987 and the INF Treaty

Introduction

Mikhail Gorbachev arrived in Washington on December 7 1987 for his third summit meeting with President Reagan. The centrepiece of the summit was to be the signing of the INF Treaty, on December 8 1987, at exactly 1.45pm. However, the summit meeting had earlier been endangered by Gorbachev's declaration that the pending INF agreement was not sufficient to justify a summit. The US had to be willing to discuss restricting its SDI programme.[1] Reagan believed that Gorbachev was 'ready to talk' at the Washington summit because the US had walked out on him at Reykjavik and 'gone ahead with the SDI program'.[2]

Gorbachev's SDI–INF Delink, and the SDI and the ABM Treaty

On February 28 1987, Gorbachev proposed the elimination of all Soviet and US intermediate-range nuclear forces (INF) in Europe.[3] However, unlike the previous condition at Reykjavik, – which led to the failure of the summit – there was no linkage between this proposal and the SDI. In other words, Gorbachev was 'willing to sign an INF accord independent of any progress on SDI'.[4] Gorbachev's new concession involved no strings attached to strategic forces (START) or British and French intermediate-range nuclear forces.[5] This had been a capitulation to the US demand ever since the Geneva summit in 1985 to eliminate US and Soviet INF missiles in Europe.[6] Gorbachev's proposal was an acceptance of Reagan's 'zero option' proposal, which critics argued was originally put forward because the US knew that the Soviets would reject it.[7] On April 13 and 14 1987, Gorbachev proposed a 'double zero' INF and SRINF (shorter-range INF) agreement. On July 23 1987, he proposed a global double zero, eliminating all INF and SRINF in Asia, America and Europe.[8] A couple of months earlier, addressing an international forum 'For a Nuclear Free World, For The Survival Of Humanity' on February 16 1987, Gorbachev declared that the Soviet Union was 'prepared to renounce its status as a nuclear (super) power and to rely on mutual international security'.[9]

Raymond Garthoff argues that Gorbachev decided that it was up to him to take the initiative in arms control as President Reagan failed to offer a new approach to strategic arms reduction.[10] A few weeks before the Washington summit, Gorbachev insisted on pre-summit concessions on the SDI. Gorbachev was still preoccupied with the SDI. This was evident by Eduard Shevardnadze's visit to Washington to work out the details of the INF agreement. In a letter which Shevardnadze delivered, in September 1987, from Gorbachev to Reagan, Gorbachev wrote that 'strategic offensive arms in space' were vital for the security of US–Soviet relations. Gorbachev no longer asked for limiting ABM research to the laboratory. Instead, he insisted on 'ensuring strict observance of the ABM Treaty'.[11] The new Soviet revised proposal was a restriction of the research and development of the SDI technologies, to testing in space/anywhere else conditional upon them being less powerful than agreed upon levels. (More powerful systems would be tested on laboratories on the ground.)[12]

Earlier, Gorbachev's insistence on the SDI restrictions was met with George Shultz walking out of the talks in Moscow, which surprised the Soviet leader. A US official revealed that, 'Our guys got up and walked out. They said, "if that's your precondition, goodbye"'.[13] Within days, Shevardnadze asked to come to Washington for talks. Reagan had earlier agreed to discuss the SDI with Gorbachev, but as part of a broad range of outstanding issues.[14]

Two days before the Washington summit began, Soviet aides revealed that they would put aside their differences with the US over the interpretation of the 1972 Anti-Ballistic Missile Treaty. This was in order to make progress towards reducing long-range nuclear arms. The decision, in essence, deferred another showdown over the SDI (which had in 1986 led to the breakdown of the Reykjavik summit). Officials revealed that the new Soviet approach was due to their recognition that Congress refused to let the US administration implement a broad interpretation of the ABM Treaty. Congress's stricter/narrower interpretation would 'severely limit the scope' of the SDI tests.[15]

Gorbachev had said that the ABM Treaty must be observed strictly if long-range arms (strategic weapons) were to be reduced. However, Reagan insisted on a new broad ABM interpretation that would allow unlimited testing of the new anti-missile systems. Subsequently, the Soviets had insisted that they would not be bound by any long-range arms reduction agreement reached, if the US broke out of the ABM Treaty.[16] A day before the summit began, *The New York Times* disclosed that the superpowers would discuss the period of 'non-withdrawal' from the ABM Treaty.[17] Soviet Foreign Ministry spokesman Gennadi I. Gerasimov revealed that a compromise might be reached. The Soviet Union had proposed a ten-year period of non-withdrawal. The US earlier had stated that the non-withdrawal agreement should end in 1994.[18]

The INF Treaty

Although Mikhail Gorbachev and President Reagan both wanted a START agreement to be reached,[19] the Washington summit's main achievement would be the signing of the INF Treaty. Discussions on Afghanistan, the Persian Gulf and human rights would play a secondary role.[20] If approved by the Senate, the INF Pact (Treaty between the United States of America and the Union of Soviet Socialist Republics on the Elimination of Their Intermediate-Range and Shorter-

Range Missiles) would require the destruction within three years of all 859 US and 1,752 Soviet missiles with ranges of 500 and 5,500 kilometres, and their nuclear warheads.[21] The number of nuclear warheads could not be directly calculated from the total, since they included missiles which were not deployed and those missiles which carried no warheads.[22]

The INF Treaty required the elimination within three years of all US and Soviet ground-launched missiles with ranges between 1,000 and 5,500 kilometres (approximately 600-3,300 miles). These missiles included the US Pershing II and ground-launched cruise missiles (GLCMs), and the Soviet SS-4, SS-5, SS-20 and SSCX-4 missiles.[23] The treaty required the elimination within 18 months of all ground-launched missiles with ranges between 500 and 1,000 kilometres. These missiles included the US Pershing IA and the Soviet SS-12 and SS-23.[24] The pact also permitted stationing inspection teams on each other's soil, with the right to conduct short notice inspections.[25]

Analysis of the INF Treaty

Richard Perle perceived the treaty's provisions for 'on-site inspection' of the Soviet missile facilities as inadequate. They would not permit on-site inspections of suspected treaty violations anywhere but the 128 Soviet designated sites.[26] *US News and World Report* described the treaty as 'at once a military irrelevance and the most sweeping arms-control agreement in modern history'.[27] The INF Treaty did set important precedents for future US–Soviet arms control agreements. It was important because Moscow accepted the principle of asymmetrical reductions, eliminating more weapons than the US to arrive at a parity.[28]

The number of nuclear warheads removed was in the US favour, since a large proportion of the scrapped Soviet weapons were triple-warhead SS-20s. (In contrast, all of the eliminated US missiles were single warhead Pershing II and ground-launched cruise missiles (GLCMs.))[29] It was the contention that the INF Treaty was in the US interest, since it required the Soviet to remove 'substantially more nuclear firepower' than the US, which was the Reagan administration's strongest argument for ratification of the Treaty.[30]

North Carolina Republican Jesse Helms argued that the 'apparent US advantage' (a 'ratio of 3.4 to 1') was a 'liability', for the nuclear explosives removed from the INF missiles could be 'rebolted' onto new missiles 'not covered' by the INF Treaty, and could be aimed at the US. This placed the US at a disproportionate disadvantage. Also, as Soviet warheads were 'more powerful' than the US nuclear explosives, the 'ratio of destructive power' would be 'even greater', and to the detriment of the US. According to Helms there was a 12-to-1 destructive power ratio 'in favour of the Soviets'.[31]

Although the Soviets would eliminate four weapons to every one American weapon, (the *US News and World Report* put this figure at 1,575 warheads on 680 launchers to 364 launchers with one warhead each) the numbers alone revealed little about the stability.[32] The INF Treaty would only have a modest impact on the US and Soviet overall nuclear arsenals, as it would not affect the longer-range intercontinental nuclear weapons.[33] Both sides retained thousands of battlefield warheads and strategic missiles. The military balance between the superpowers would be little changed.[34]

A veteran intelligence official in *Time* magazine revealed that:

> Not a single one of the SS-20s that Gorbachev will be giving up can hit the US, and not a single SS-25 is affected by an INF Treaty, so there's nothing to stop him from replacing every SS-20 he takes out of service with an SS-25 that can hit us easily.[35]

After the signing of the Treaty, Helms argued that even if the Soviets complied with the treaty, the agreement would leave them with significant military advantages. The Soviets had already begun to cheat by concealing hundreds of missiles that should be destroyed.[36] As the INF Treaty banned some conventional as well as nuclear weapons,[37] an objection voiced by conservative hardliners (including Republican Senators Steve Symms (Idaho) and Malcolm Wallop (Wyo.)) was that the treaty removed an important element of NATO's nuclear counterweight against the Warsaw Pact's numerical superiority in conventional forces. Verification of the treaty would also be problematic.[38]

Although Raymond Garthoff states that critics highlighted that the INF Treaty only affected approximately five per cent of the US and Soviet nuclear arsenals (50,000 warheads), he points to the significance of it. The significance of the INF Treaty was 'psychological, political and military–strategic'. It not only meant reductions of arms but the destruction of 'very recent and current arms'. It eliminated an entire class of missiles; those most likely to lead to an escalation to general nuclear war.[39] The INF Treaty was significant in that it was the first arms control deal that reduced the number of nuclear weapons, rather than limited their increase. Simply because Reagan (who had earlier opposed the US–Soviet arms agreement of the 1970s) had negotiated the treaty, it lends political legitimacy to future arms control discussions. The INF Treaty was the first arms treaty to be signed by both superpowers since 1979.[40]

A few days prior to the signing of the INF Treaty, a *Times–CBS* News Poll indicated that two-thirds of the public supported the proposed treaty.[41] Following the conclusion of the Washington summit, President Reagan, in his television address to the nation, revealed that the INF Treaty was 'accomplished with unprecedented consultation with our allies and friends ... This treaty has full allied support'.[42] Allied leaders who supported that INF Treaty included British Prime Minister Margaret Thatcher, West German Chancellor Helmut Kohl and Italian Premier Giovanni Goria.[43]

In Congress, Majority Whip Alan Cranston, (Democrat), from California and former US Secretary of State William Rogers, supported the INF Treaty. Republican Senator Larry Pressler opposed it. Republican Jack F. Kemp, of New York, claimed that the data provided by the Soviets on the missiles to be destroyed under the treaty was inconsistent.[44] Pete du Pont, Pat Roberston, Alexander Haig, Caspar Weinberger, Richard Nixon, Henry Kissinger, Brent Scowcroft and Senator Dan Quayle opposed the Treaty.[45]

Notwithstanding, after the signing of the agreement, a joint US–Soviet summit statement, released on December 10, stated that:

This treaty is historic, both for its objective – the complete elimination of an entire class of US and Soviet nuclear arms – and for the innovative character and scope of its verification provision. This mutual accomplishment makes a vital contribution to greater stability.[46]

To quote President Reagan, the INF Treaty was 'an historic treaty' which 'didn't simply codify the status quo or a new arms build up' and 'didn't simply talk of controlling an arms race'. The INF Treaty ensured that 'the language of arms control was replaced by arms reduction'.[47] Mikhail Gorbachev perceived it as 'the first step down the road leading to a nuclear free world',[48] and 'a historic milestone in the chronicle of man's eternal quest for a world without wars'.[49]

Communist Party newspaper *Izvestia* reviewed the treaty as 'Success for the President, Example for the Future'. Historian Roy A. Medvedev stated that 'Both propaganda and people's opinions will see it as a step forward'. A Soviet journalist claimed that he perceived the Soviet people as feeling 'real joy', for 'they were tired of the Cold War'. He further added that although the reductions in arsenals was only four per cent, the most important thing was, 'there will be more trust now'.[50] The East European governments supported the treaty, and favoured Gorbachev's role in it, to that of Reagan who was 'hesitant'. In Czechoslovakia, the treaty was described by Communist Party newspaper *Rude Pravo* as a 'historic step to a world without nuclear weapons'. Warsaw's General Jaruzelski statements echoed a similar theme.[51]

Both in East and West Germany approval of the treaty was mixed. In West Germany, the Free Democrats and opposition Social Democrats had welcomed the pact, but there was opposition to it from the right wing of the Christian Democratic Union. Conservatives feared that the elimination of weapons had left the Warsaw Pact with a conventional arms superiority.[52] The fear about the future of the NATO alliance exacerbated the fear of the West European governments that there would be public pressure to remove all nuclear weapons from Europe. In Italy and Spain, there were open celebrations regarding the INF agreement. France, however, had the most sceptical response.[53]

Francois Leotard, a member of Premier Jacques Chirac's coalition government, called the treaty 'dangerous for Europe's security'. French daily newspaper *Le Figaro* claimed that the Soviet missiles were 'obsolete' and could not reach the US, whilst the US could hit the Soviet Union.[54] China welcomed the official signing of the treaty, but pointed out that it did not eliminate the threat of nuclear war (or international tensions).[55] According to Eduard Shevardnadze:

> The INF Treaty was unquestionably advantageous both for the Soviet Union and for the United States, as well as all other countries. I continue to consider it a major contribution to our country's security.[56]

He added that although the US and Soviet intermediate missiles made up only four per cent of each country's nuclear arsenal:

the agreement to dismantle them spoke to the world about the possibility of actually getting rid of the most lethal weapons of war. It translated the idea of nuclear disarmament from the realm of dreams to concrete realization.[57]

In his memoirs, George Shultz recalled what Marshal Akhromeyev, of the Soviet Union, told him:

> My country is in trouble, and I am fighting alongside Mikhail Sergeyevich to save it. That is why we made such a lopsided deal on INF, and that is why we want to get along with you. We want to restructure ourselves and to be part of the modern world. We cannot continue to be isolated.[58]

Non-Arms Issues: The Other Issues at the Washington Summit

Aside from its arms control success, the Washington summit was criticized for being 'thin on tangible results'.[59] A joint communique, of eight pages in length, devoted only two and a half lines to human rights. Issued on December 10 1987, it noted that 'The leaders held a thorough and candid discussion of human rights and humanitarian questions and their place in the US–Soviet relationship'.[60] Hopes were earlier raised for human rights 'to become a prominent and contentious issue in the summit'.[61] According to President Reagan, there would be 'continuous dialogue' on the issue at 'the highest levels'.[62] Reagan conceded that he made 'very limited movement' with Gorbachev on human rights. Although 'a number of individual cases' were resolved, there was no broad agreement on the release of political prisoners, or the emigration of Soviet Jews.[63]

Bilateral issues   Some progress was made on issues directly affecting the US–Soviet relationship. An agreement was reached on the expansion of a joint US–Soviet direct air passenger service. The service would operate from New York to Moscow and would be run by Pan American Airways and Aeroflot. The US and Soviet Union renewed their 1973 US–Soviet World Ocean Agreement, to promote cooperation in oceanographic research. Further, an agreement was reached whereby each superpower would be allowed to monitor some of the other superpower's underground nuclear tests.[64] Intensified efforts to reach mutual agreements on commercial maritime issues, radio navigational systems and cooperation in transportation were called for by Reagan and Gorbachev. The leaders reflected on the success of the November 1985 Geneva agreement regarding people to people contacts and exchanges, and global climate, and environmental change. Cooperation among US and Soviet scientists was urged and mutually beneficial trade was encouraged.[65]

Afghanistan   Expectations were raised prior to the Washington summit that Gorbachev might use the occasion to announce a specific timetable for the withdrawal of Soviet troops from Afghanistan. Unfortunately, these expectations were not met. Gorbachev restated his willingness to withdraw his troops within a year, conditional upon the US and its allies terminating their aid to the Islamic rebels (guerrillas). Gorbachev also urged that an agreement be reached that the successor regime be non-aligned and be neutral.[66] President Reagan accepted the latter proposal, yet, insisted that the Soviet premier set a specific timetable for withdrawal, which included dates for its beginning and end. He also insisted on continuing to aid the anti-Soviet guerrillas until the Soviets began withdrawing their troops. The leaders failed to agree on the withdrawal terms. Both parties portrayed each other as unwilling to make a concession.[67]

Other regional issues   At the Washington summit, Gorbachev continued his opposition to the US led UN initiative to impose an arms embargo on Iran. Earlier, US officials had accused the Soviets of 'protecting' Iran by delaying action on the resolution. Regarding another issue, after the Reagan–Gorbachev meeting, on December 11 1987, Reagan had the 'impression' that the Soviet Union might withdraw some of its people and weapons from Nicaragua and he asked the Soviets to stop the shipment of military weapons to Nicaragua.[68] Academic discussion on this issue tends to conclude that Soviet involvement there was minimal. Reagan had contested this view.

Despite the urgency of resolving the regional issues, in his news conference on December 10 1987, Gorbachev announced that 'I can't say that we made much headway in the discussion of these problems'. President Reagan appeared more optimistic that the two powers could have 'real cooperation' in resolving the conflicts.[69] Their joint communique noted that the leaders discussed Afghanistan, the Iran–Iraq War, the Middle East, Southern Africa, Central America and Cambodia. It stated that serious differences remained, but it was agreed that discussions were vital to settle the conflicts, and 'help the parties to regional conflicts find peaceful solutions that advance their independence, freedom and security'.[70]

Analysis of the Washington Summit

To quote Ronald Reagan, the Washington summit 'was a clear success; we made progress in each item in our four-part agenda'. He further added that 'there is a reason for hope and optimism'.[71] Mikhail Gorbachev called the summit meeting 'a major event in world politics'.[72] The summit meeting had opened 'a new phase in US–Soviet relations'. Due to a 'deepening political dialogue', although differences remained they were no longer insurmountable.[73] President Reagan stated that the summit had 'lit the sky with hope for all people of good will'. Whilst Gorbachev elaborated that the Soviet Union and US were 'closer to the common goal of strengthening international security', he said that there was 'still much work to be done'.[74] Margaret Thatcher in her memoirs contended that the summit was a 'success'.[75]

Caspar Weinberger believed that the 'arms control treaty' was 'very good', although he was concerned that people overestimated the improved US–Soviet superpower relationship. He believed that the Soviet Union still sought world domination, evident not least by the large number of overseas bases they acquired.[76] The *US News and World Report* evaluated that there was no real breakthrough in strategic arms talks, no progress on regional conflicts (despite hope that the Soviets would announce their timetable of withdrawal from Afghanistan) and no common ground reached on human rights.[77]

After the Soviets left Washington, Reagan wrote in his diary: 'They've departed and I think the whole thing was the best summit we've ever had with the Soviet Union'.[78] According to William D. Jackson, the summit marked a 'significant' turning point in Moscow's perception of the Reagan administration. As the diplomatic relations improved, 'Gorbachev relied decreasingly on the strategy of seeking to mobilize world opinion against the Reagan administration'. Gorbachev had 'greater confidence' that the US would move away 'from the harsh anti-Soviet policies of its first term in favour of a policy of increased cooperation with Moscow'.[79]

The SDI and the Interpretation of the ABM Treaty

Regarding the contentious issues of the SDI and the ABM Treaty;[80] the Soviet position was that they wanted the US to observe the ABM Treaty, whilst the Americans wanted the Soviets to concede the right to allow anti-missile system (SDI) deployment. After the end of the summit, the Americans claimed that the Soviets had conceded that the ABM Treaty should be strictly observed. In contrast, senior administration arms control officials claimed that the US and Soviet Union had merely deferred the issue of how to interpret the ABM Treaty.[81] *The New York Times* affirmed that the main achievement of the Washington summit (aside from the signing of the INF Treaty, and better personal relations between the leaders) was the decision not to allow the SDI to stand in the way of the negotiations. The SDI had been responsible for the previous failure of the Reykjavik summit.[82]

The New York Times claimed that this time, Reagan and Gorbachev 'side-stepped' their disagreement. They did not try to resolve the critical issue of what SDI testing was allowed under the 1972 Anti-Ballistic Missile Treaty. Instead, they temporarily deferred the resolution.[83] This was done by using intentionally ambiguous instructions.[84] By agreeing to disagree, the US and Soviet Union hoped for progress on the strategic arms treaty.[85] For Gorbachev, deferral of the SDI issue was a major concession. It was recognized as such by Reagan's advisors. However, one advisor said that the Soviets had not retreated from their arguments that a strategic offensive arms (START) agreement must be linked on an understanding of SDI research and development.[86] President Reagan called the discussion about the SDI a victory for his position.[87]

The interpretation of the 1972 Anti-Ballistic Missile Treaty was imperative to determining the permissible scope of the SDI testing. (To put it succinctly: the Soviets insisted on a strict interpretation which would limit the scope of SDI tests; the US insisted on a 'broad' interpretation, allowing unlimited testing.) The Soviets agreed to drafting an agreement on strategic arms which would not prevent SDI testing, because they recognized Congress's restriction of any SDI tests other than those allowed by the narrow interpretation of the ABM Treaty, which Moscow favoured.[88] This was an 'agreement to disagree' which 'should allow for progress on the strategic arms treaty'.[89]

In the final communique, it was stated that:

> Taking into account the preparation of the Treaty on Strategic Offensive Arms, the leaders of the two countries also instructed their delegations in Geneva to work out an agreement that would commit the sides to observe the ABM [Anti Ballistic Missile] Treaty, as signed in 1972, while conducting their research, development and testing as required, which are permitted by the ABM Treaty, and not to withdraw from the ABM Treaty, for a specified period of time.[90]

In principal, the joint statement merely said that the two sides should observe the ABM Treaty. The communique did not address what testing the treaty allowed.[91] The US did not get the specific reference to testing in space which they wanted to get. They also dropped the demand that the communique issued should state the legitimacy of anti-missile system (SDI) deployment.[92] The US and Soviet Union agreed to hold talks on 'strategic stability'; – what should happen after the period of non-withdrawal from the treaty elapsed.[93] If the US and Soviet Union could not agree on what would happen, then both countries would have the right to, as Gorbachev stated in his news conference, determine their own 'mode of action'.[94]

According to the US, the vague language of the US–Soviet joint statement (relating to the observation of the ABM Treaty) appeared to legitimize the right of either side to carry out anti-missile tests 'as required'.[95] That 'each side will be free to decide its course of action' appeared to permit US SDI development, after the period of adherence to the ABM Treaty expired. However, it also appeared to legitimate Soviet counter-measures against anti-missile defences.[96] The statement did not contradict the US 'broad interpretation' of the ABM Treaty. It did not undermine the Soviet claim that tests in space were not 'permitted by the ABM Treaty'.[97]

The Long-Range Arms Discussions (Strategic Arms) = START

Although the interpretation of the ABM Treaty, and what limit to have on the actual number of warheads (on the ballistic missiles which the ABM Treaty itself aimed to limit) were issues left undecided at the summit, a great deal of progress had, nevertheless, been made. In the long-range arms (strategic arms) discussions held, both countries made concessions. The Soviets agreed to the US demand that conventionally armed cruise missiles on aircraft should be outside the jurisdiction of the START treaty which the US and Soviet Union hoped to negotiate.

The US conceded to the Soviets that the new START (long-range arms) Treaty should have a 'ceiling' on cruise missiles aboard ships and submarines. This limit on sea-launched cruise missiles (SLCMs) was a precedent, and was significant, as the missiles were weapons where the US had an advantage. However, Reagan insisted that the limits on SLCMs remain outside the overall START ceiling. The Soviets conceded to the US that sea-based cruise missiles be limited to certain types.[98]

The progress reached on the sublimits were tentative terms which were reached at Reykjavik the year before. Both sides agreed to limit warheads permitted on both land-based and sea-based ballistic missiles to a figure of 4,900. (The Soviets had wanted the figure to be 5,100; the Americans had wanted 4,800). The US had decided to limit the Trident submarines deployed, and the Soviets had agreed not to encode any electronic signals during missile tests. Both sides agreed to work out rules for counting the number of warheads.[99] However, the talks produced no breakthrough.

Why Gorbachev Delinked the SDI to the INF Treaty and the START Discussions

Prior to the Washington summit, the Russians rejected any START deal unless the US agreed to limit the SDI under the terms of the 1972 ABM Treaty, which restricted all anti-ballistic missile (ABM) systems. Just before the Washington summit began, the Soviets implied that there would be a significant change in their position. Gorbachev demonstrated this new Soviet negotiating position in Washington; the negotiations could proceed on START, and the US and Soviet Union would leave the SDI aside.[100] Why Gorbachev changed course; delinking the SDI to the INF agreement (as well as the ongoing START negotiations which were yet to produce an agreement) is an issue of contention. In evaluating the motivations underlying Gorbachev's change in policy, it is necessary to recognize the historiographical debates regarding the Soviet concessions.

In a slight variant from the 'bargaining from strength' argument, some commentators (like Jonathan Haslam), have argued that it was the specific threat of the SDI which convinced the Soviets to make the concessions on the INF.[101] It is argued by Thomas Risse-Kappen that this argument is unconvincing, as it does not explain why the Soviets shifted their position regarding the SDI–INF linkage twice (during 1985 and 1987). According to Risse-Kappen, the Soviet concessions regarding the SDI are not sufficient to explain both the Soviet policy in 1985, (insisting that the INF agreement would only be reached if progress was made in prohibiting ballistic missile defences), and their subsequent, February 28 1987, decision to drop the SDI and INF linkage.[102]

Although Risse-Kappen is correct in stating that Haslam's contention fails to account for the change in the Soviet policy, Risse-Kappen's argument fails to acknowledge several factors. The Soviets prior to the summit were still pressing the US to restrict its SDI programme by setting presummit conditions.[103] Furthermore, after the Soviet INF concession was made (the delink of SDI to INF), and just before the signing of the INF Treaty, Gorbachev admitted in an interview in the US, (with the NBC TV company) that the Soviet Union was engaged in basic research related to those aspects covered by the SDI in the US, and that it was doing practically everything that the US was doing. A few weeks later (during the Washington summit which witnessed the signing of the INF Treaty on December 8 1987) Gorbachev reiterated that the Soviet Union had its own research programme into ballistic missile defence.[104] He said that they would not deploy the system, although they could overwhelm any US deployment.

Viewed in this context, the Soviet concession on INF does not discredit the contention that the threat of the SDI made them concede. Similarly, it does not discredit the contention that it did not, nor does it serve to indicate that they stopped regarding the SDI as a threat, for they were developing their own Strategic Defence Initiative. Above all, Gorbachev's public acknowledgement of this undermines the very premise of the argument of those who believe that the SDI had no real effect on the Soviet Union. It also undermines the position of those who argue that the Soviets decided on an asymmetrical (or anti-symmetrical) rather than a matching response to the US policy.[105]

Even after the agreement in principle of the INF 'zero option' (in September 1987), seeking a 50 per cent cut in strategic weapons Gorbachev still tried to bring the SDI into the discussions, but left it to one side when the US refused.[106] The Soviet change of policy regarding the SDI, INF and START linkages goes beyond an explanation which simply states that the Soviets feared the SDI and conceded to the US. The explanations for the change in policy are ones which can account for the fact that the Soviets were concerned enough about the SDI to make it a prominent theme of discussion with the US (even after their delinkage decision) yet, can also account for why the Soviets were able to delink the INF and START negotiations to the SDI.

The most fundamental explanation for the new Soviet policy is that 'having tried and failed at the previous two Summit meetings' to get President Reagan to abandon the SDI, 'Gorbachev has evidently dropped the attempt at head-on confrontation' and had advocated a new approach. According to *The New York Times* journalist David K. Shipler, 'since last September, the Russians have signalled a shift of tactics on "Star Wars"'. Gorbachev's new tactics appeared to be negotiating arms reductions whilst 'trying to agree on a period which both sides would pledge to observe the 1972 Anti-Ballistic Missile Treaty'.[107] (The Soviet Union had proposed ten years whilst the US advocated seven.)

It was by trying to strengthen this ABM Treaty, (by pressing for a stricter adherence of both the US and Soviet Union to it) that Gorbachev hoped to get rid of the SDI. A senior US official said that the Soviets 'have become much more ambiguous' regarding the US SDI. 'They seldom mention SDI at all; instead they talk about strengthening the [1972] ABM Treaty'.[108] *The New York Times* similarly stated that the Soviet Union:

> may also have calculated that it will be more successful in pressing its demand for strict adherence to the ABM Treaty after greater momentum develops toward a Treaty to reduce long range arms.[109]

Gorbachev was aided in his hope of SDI abandonment by the US Congress which had restricted the SDI programme. Soviet officials revealed that their new approach 'is a recognition of the refusal by Congress to let the Reagan Administration go beyond the strict interpretation of the ABM Treaty for the time being'. This strict interpretation would severely limit the scope of the SDI tests.[110] It was this recognition of Congress's prohibition on any tests 'except those permitted under the narrow interpretation of the treaty' that made the Russians agree to a statement on strategic arms which would not prevent SDI testing.[111] The (medium-range) missiles destroyed in the INF Treaty would not be used in the SDI tests. Gorbachev's signing of the INF Treaty, therefore, appears a way of destroying the SDI.[112]

Regarding the START agreement, Gorbachev concluded that stressing linkage between SDI and START would only result in Reagan insisting to build the SDI and foregoing an imminent START agreement. Gorbachev's new policy was to 'conclude a START agreement separately and let the American political process kill SDI for him'.[113] According to the *US News and World Report:*

> The fate of SDI is exactly where Gorbachev wants it – under constraints imposed by Reagan's opponents in Congress for at least a year, and in uncertain limbo beyond that.[114]

There were Democratic gains in the Congressional elections, and Reagan was also weakened in 1987 by the Iran–Contra revelations. Congress had forced Reagan to sign a defence spending bill decreasing funds for the SDI and requiring Reagan to 'go slow on SDI until nearly the end of his term'.[115]

Gorbachev recognized that the next President would be less 'enthralled' by the SDI than Reagan,[116] whose own rhetoric on SDI appeared to some to be less committed than before.[117] As an issue the SDI appeared 'an idea whose time has come and gone'.[118] The Soviets could only conclude that time would take care of it further. Gorbachev clearly needed to conclude an INF/START agreement for personal political reasons. Both he and Reagan faced opposition at home. Gorbachev's need for international prestige could only provide him with legitimacy, in a country beset by domestic difficulties.

The Soviets could also have concluded that the risks in SDI research and testing were less significant than Moscow first supposed. The Soviets revealed that they had little faith in the US building a 'true space shield'. In the event of any US SDI deployment, Moscow could 'quickly build thousands of new offensive weapons to overwhelm it'.[119] Even the US recognized that the Soviets could deploy an ABM system 'much quicker' than the US could.[120] The Soviet Union had a history of ballistic missile defence research and had its own SDI research programme.[121] Gorbachev himself admitted that the Russians were building an anti-missile defence system in his interview with NBC's Tom Brokaw.[122]

American officials believed that Gorbachev's revelations would mean discussions on the issue would progress 'more smoothly'.[123] Margaret Thatcher suggested that Gorbachev's admission in the NBC News interview meant that the door was opened to a compromise on the SDI. She contended that it was 'a quite significant step, which makes further arrangements of the kind of I've indicated possible'.[124] To many, Gorbachev's new approach was a sign of diplomatic flexibility.[125]

However, Gorbachev, in his December 10 1987 news conference, stated that he said:

> that we were not addressing ourselves, or working on our defensive system. I said that we were engaging in fundamental research which in the various specific areas

encompass problems which in the United States are within the limits of SDI. That I said, but I said we were resolutely opposed to SDI.[126]

Gorbachev further added that 'We shall not build up an SDI in our own country, and that is what we are urging the US Administration to do'.[127] Soviet officials had revealed that Gorbachev had not abandoned the goal of preventing the deployment of the SDI, but decided that the 'issue was now moot because budget cuts and technological problems were limiting Mr Reagan's development program'.[128] The conclusion of a START Treaty, according to Richard Perle, would mean the death of the SDI. He argued that the Soviets would withdraw from the treaty if the US went ahead with the SDI. Congress would not go 'beyond SDI research' if the alternative was a suspension of the START Treaty.[129]

Mike Bowker believes that the Soviet Union thought that the SDI deployment would be unlikely. By 1987 both superpowers recognized that difficulties existed in the SDI. Two strong SDI supporters left their respective US office; Caspar Weinberger (November 1987), and head of the SDIO (Strategic Defense Initiative Organization), James Abrahamson (1988). Reagan had suffered from the Iran–Contra revelations and Congress was unlikely to fund the SDI at a time when the budget deficit was increasing. Secondly, the scientific and defence community in Moscow decided that the USSR could tolerate an active SDI system.[130]

SDI: Budget Cuts and Technical Problems

A poll, taken by Richard Wirthlin, revealed that 56 per cent of the people in the US supported the INF Treaty and the SDI. However, when the US public heard Gorbachev's interview with NBC's Tom Brokaw (and his admittance that the Soviet Union was working on its own SDI) support for the SDI in the US increased to 71 per cent of the population.[131] Prior to the Washington summit, President Reagan reiterated his refusal to trade away SDI for an arms deal, for it would be 'too high a price to pay for any agreement'. Speaking to workers, on November 24 1987, at a plant in Denver, operated by one SDI contractor, Reagan declared, 'You are not working to build a bargaining chip'.[132] A few weeks earlier, in his address to the United Nations (UN), Reagan stated that the 'SDI has greatly enhanced the prospects for real arms reduction'.[133] After such reductions were reached, with the signing of the INF, Reagan maintained that 'I made it clear that our SDI program will continue, and that when we have a defense ready to deploy – we will do so'.[134]

The SDI was beset by funding cuts and technical problems. Much of Congress's disbelief in the programme ran from 'technical misgivings'. Chemical laser project 'Zenith Star' had never produced a laser beam. The laser generator itself over the last two years had problems, including budget cuts. The energy source needed to generate the laser would be too heavy, large and expensive to lift into orbit. Chemical lasers based on the ground had wavelengths that were too long to effectively penetrate the earth's atmosphere. The free electron laser was more promising, but problems included its weight and focus of the beam.[135] Theodore Postol, of the Stanford Center for International Security and Arms Control, stated that the 'biggest problem' facing the SDI was that 'nobody knows how to discriminate real objects from false ones. It is the Achilles' heel of the program'.[136]

The SDI and ABM Debate in Congress

On October 6 1985, the Reagan administration announced its broad interpretation of the ABM Treaty, arguing that it allowed for more realistic tests of the SDI than experts had earlier thought were permitted. Protests from Congress and the allies resulted in the administration revealing 'a week later' that it would test the SDI under the narrow (more restrictive) reading of the treaty, although the new broad US interpretation was legally correct.[137] In late January, early February 1987, Senate debated the meaning of the 1972 ABM Treaty, with specific reference to what implications this had for the SDI. A group of Republican conservatives – a 'gang of five' argued that the SDI would be politically doomed unless the Reagan administration demonstrated that a partial defence could be deployed within the following five years. This group consisted of Senators Dan Quayle (Ind.), Malcolm Wallop (Wyo.) and Pete Wilson (Calif.), and Republicans Jack F. Kemp (N.Y.) and Jim Courter (N.J.).[138]

In response, Caspar Weinberger decided that a limited defence of the SDI should be deployed by 1994. The SDI should focus on 'realistic testing'. Whilst Weinberger had been opposed to a partial defence shield, he continued to insist that the SDI would protect the US population, not just missile silos and military targets. Caspar Weinberger attributed his new course for accelerated deployment to the successful technical breakthroughs in anti-missile weapons in late 1986. Critics argued that this was due to political expediency, not technological breakthroughs.[139]

Chairman of the Senate Armed Services Committee Sam Nunn's series of speeches, March 11–13 1987, denounced the claims of the administration to legally test anti-missile weapons in space (SDI) without violating the 1972 ABM Treaty. Democrat Senator Albert Gore Jnr's (Tenn.) proposed deal (in February 1987) with officials was 'bad news' to SDI. Gore proposed that the Senate granting of the $5.8 billion which the President requested for the SDI (in fiscal year 1988) be conditional upon Reagan abiding to the narrow (or traditional) interpretation of the 1972 Treaty.[140] On September 17 1987, the Senate voted for a narrow interpretation of the ABM Treaty. This was a defeat for the Reagan administration.

The Legality of the ABM Treaty's Provision for SDI Testing

The legality of SDI testing was questioned by Articles 2, 5 and Agreed Statement D of the 1972 US–Soviet Treaty limiting anti-ballistic missile (ABM) systems.[141] Article 2 defined an ABM system as 'a system to counter ballistic missiles or their elements in flight trajectory currently consisting of' radars, interceptor missiles and missile launchers for these interceptors.[142] The traditional or 'narrow' interpretation of the treaty, it was argued, stated that the ABM system 'covered all current and future anti-missile systems'.[143] Article 5 committed the two countries 'not to develop, test or deploy ABM systems or components which are sea-based, air-based, space-based or mobile-land based'.[144] The narrow interpretation ban on space-based systems therefore appeared 'all-inclusive'.[145] This did not permit SDI testing. Articles 2 and 5 of the ABM Treaty, therefore, prevented SDI testing.

However, Agreed Statement D reads that 'in order to ensure fulfilment of the obligation not to deploy ABM systems and their components' except for the very limited deployments permitted by the treaty:

> in the event ABM systems based on other physical principles ... are created in the future, specific limitations on such systems and their components would be subject to discussion.[146]

The Agreed Statement D provision of the ABM Treaty permitted amendment to the treaty by mutual agreement. Agreed Statement D gave the right to amend the treaty in the future, and could, if the US and Soviet Union mutually agreed, give the right to test the SDI. (Legally, therefore, the narrow interpretation of the ABM Treaty stated the rights of the two countries to work out the details of how limits of the 1970s ABM systems would apply to future systems.[147] This narrow interpretation of the ABM Treaty legally permitted the right, if the US and Soviet Union agreed, to test the SDI.)

The US administration promoted a new interpretation of the ABM Treaty (in October 1985) developed by Abraham D. Sofaer, the State Department's Senior Lawyer. He argued that the treaty's use of the terms 'ABM System' and 'component' were in contexts that referred only to the 1972-style equipment. Sofaer argued that if the restrictions were intended to cover future anti-missile systems, there would have been no need for Agreed Statement D in the ABM Treaty.[148]

Sofaer further documented that the negotiations leading to the signing of the 1972 Treaty, showed that the 'Soviet officials expressly rejected the efforts of US negotiators to have the treaty ban future types of ABM defenses'.[149] Sofaer even argued that the Senate's own 1972 debates on the ABM Treaty supported the contention that new space-based weapons could be tested. Sofaer's arguments for the new 'permissive' interpretation of the treaty were branded 'not credible' by Senator Sam Nunn. According to Nunn, Sofaer had 'distorted' facts. Nunn stated that the Nixon administration officials had affirmed that the deployment of lasers were permitted, but as long as they were fixed on land.[150]

Nunn argued that:

1)   The 1972 Treaty prohibited 'any' deployment or 'testing of space-based defences';
2)   The US and Soviet Union's actions 'since 1972' have 'been consistent' with such an agreement;
3)   The Senate acknowledged such an interpretation in October 1972 during the ratification discussions.[151]

Nunn's assessment was challenged by Richard Perle, on March 12 1987. Perle, (who was behind the reinterpretation of the ABM Treaty), argued that the issues involved in the current debate had received little attention in 1972. Nixon officials had misinterpreted the 1972 pact, for 'the statements they made did not reflect the treaty and the negotiating record'.[152] The few Senators during the Nixon administration who focused on the debate (in 1972) were misinformed by the Nixon administration officials, who unknowingly had deceived the Senate by exaggerating the effectiveness of gaining Soviet concessions.[153]

At the joint hearing, on March 26 1987, of the two Senate Committees, Perle insisted that in 1972 the Senate had not concentrated on the ABM Treaty or its implications. Even the hearings were poorly attended: 'There were questions in hearings – poorly attended hearings – but there was virtually no debate on the floor of the United States Senate'.[154] Republican Jesse Helms (N.C.) of the Foreign Relations panel supported Perle's argument, 'The Senators simply didn't understand what the Treaty was all about'.[155] The Reagan administration argued that this absence of formal Senate action in 1972 (with its belief in the narrow interpretation of the 1972 Treaty) did not bind the Reagan administration in 1987.[156]

It was argued by Sofaer and the Reagan administration that many statements made by the officials (during the 1972 Senate's consideration of the ABM Treaty) support the Reagan administration's lenient interpretation of it. Perle also produced evidence that the ABM Treaty allowed SDI testing. He cited an internal government document that supported the broad interpretation of the treaty.[157] Admiral Thomas Moore, (then Chairman of the Joint Chiefs of Staff) wrote in the document (which was contemporary with the ABM Treaty) that the 1972 Treaty permitted the testing of future ABM systems. Apparently this had been acknowledged all along, provided that the weapons were ground-based and in fixed sites.[158]

Perle further argued that prior to President Reagan's SDI speech in 1983, 'Soviet comments all pointed to the validity of the broad interpretation' of the ABM Treaty. Such Soviet statements and the actual Soviet research and development programme itself, according to Perle, refuted Nunn's assertion that the Soviet Union's actions since 1972 were consistent with the ABM Treaty of 1972.[159] During negotiations that led to the 1972 Treaty itself:

> Despite the desire on the part of our negotiators to conclude a treaty prohibiting the development and testing of certain new defensive technologies, the Soviets failed to accept the proposals.[160]

Perle further added that 'In the end, we withdrew from the negotiating table language that would clearly have obligated the Soviets to the narrow interpretation'.[161] As the 1972 Treaty did not bind the Soviets (who carried on with their own research and development into space-based anti-missile defences), neither could it bind the US government (in 1987).[162]

If the treaty (if incorrectly interpreted by a previous administration to the Senate) could allow the other party to the agreement to carry out its own actions, surely it could not legitimately bind the US President to it. If the Senate was misinformed about the treaty, the Reagan administration was (in 1987) not bound by an interpretation which it declared mistaken.[163] Also at the hearing, held on March 26 1987, it was stated that the debate over the ABM was a waste of energy. Republican Gordon J. Humphrey (N.H.) – a Judiciary Committee Member – argued that Reagan should withdraw from the treaty and 'ask the American people to support withdrawal'. According to Humphrey, 'The President is losing the opportunity to rally the American people to the side of SDI'.[164]

The SDI Funding Debate in Congress

On April 2 1987, the House Armed Services Subcommittee on Research and Development urged a \$2 billion cut in President Reagan's request of \$5.2 billion for the SDI for fiscal year 1988.[165] The SDI further suffered setbacks when the panel recommended that Congress impose legal restrictions on the testing of anti-missile systems, as established by the 1972 ABM Treaty. Specifically, the subcommittee banned the use of funds to develop the new anti-missile space-based weapons (KKV) deemed deployable in 1994. The 'Kinetic Kill Vehicle' (KKV) – a rocket which could home in on heat generated by Soviet missiles and destroy them on collision – would have been important in the near-term SDI deployment.[166]

The Reagan administration had agreed to conduct SDI research under the narrow interpretation of the ABM Treaty.[167] In October 1985, the Reagan administration had announced the ABM Treaty's traditional interpretation was mistaken. According to it, the testing of space-based ABM weapons was allowed; deployment however, was not.[168] In late 1986, Caspar Weinberger, and other officials, and Congressional SDI proponents, including Republican Senator Dan Quayle (Indiana), pushed for early SDI deployment using KKVs which could be tested under the broad interpretation of the ABM Treaty. The new proposal was 'hundreds of orbiting "garage" satellites', with each 'garage' carrying 'several KKVs' and other heat detection satellites.[169] Critics of the SDI which included Nunn and Republican Senator William S. Cohen (Maine), in the week of March 30 1987 argued that KKV was 'based on physical principles' that were well known in 1972 when the ABM Treaty was signed. Therefore, they could not be tested.[170]

In contrast, Quayle argued that the 'physical principle' of the KKV was different from those systems in 1972. This meant they could be tested under the new permissive interpretation of the ABM Treaty.[171] In April, House Armed Services Subcommittee rejected 'three amendments that would have made less drastic cuts' to the SDI programme. Republican Senators Malcolm Wallop (Wyo.) and Jim Courter (N.J.) announced that they would propose amendments to the 'fiscal 1988 defence authorisation bill', in order to incite a public demand 'for an anti-missile defence'.[172] Although the House ordered the SDI to 'skip over' the development of a 'phase-one' defence (using the anti-missile technologies which were nearly completed), it voted that the Pentagon concentrate on developing lasers as well as other exotic weapons which would offer a potentially more effective anti-missile shield.[173]

On May 5 1987, by a vote of 12–8, the Senate Armed Services Committee voted to give Congress power over the Reagan administration's plans to accelerate the testing and deployment of the SDI. The provision was co-authored by Democrats Carl Levin (Mich.) and Sam Nunn (Ga.).[174] On May 12 1987, the House members, in a vote of 219–199, voted to reduce Reagan's fiscal 1988 request for SDI funding by more than 45 per cent to $3.1 billion. In the initial version of HR1748, the Armed Services Committee had reduced the administration funding request of $5.7 billion for the SDI to $3.8 billion. On May 5 1987, this had further been reduced to $3.6 billion.[175]

On May 12 1987, the House debated four amendments regarding the SDI funding levels. It rejected an amendment by Republican Joel Hefley (Colo.) by 129–286, which would have increased funding to $4 billion. In contrast, it rejected Republican John G. Rowland's (Conn.) amendment to slightly decrease funds. The House rejected, by a vote of 105–307, an amendment by Democrat Ronald V. Dellums (Calif.) that would have 'dismantled' the SDI programme in its current state. It voted 219–199 in favour of an amendment forwarded by Democrat Charles E. Bennett (Flo.) that curtailed SDI funding to $3.12 billion.[176]

Regarding the SDI programme's pace and scope, the House, on May 12 1987, rejected an amendment that would have barred tests of the 'space-based kinetic kill vehicle (SBKKV)'. The House rejected amendments by two SDI proponents to force deployment of a limited defence.[177] One was by Republican Jack F. Kemp (N.Y.) (defeated 121–302) which would have ordered the Pentagon to deploy a system in 1993. The other was by Republican Jim Courter (N.J.) (defeated 121–297) that would have ordered the Defense Department to prepare to deploy an accidental nuclear missile launch system which protected against the accidental launch of nuclear missiles.[178]

Nunn warned that unless the administration gave assurance that Congress would play an important role in deciding whether or not to withdraw from the narrow (traditional) interpretation of the ABM Treaty, there would be greater cuts in SDI funding.[179] On September 17 1987, the Senate barred tests of space-based anti-missile weapons without prior approval by Congress. This prevented the Reagan administration enacting a new interpretation of the 1972 ABM Treaty. This would slow down the administration's SDI programme.[180] House–Senate conferees later insisted that all tests conformed to the traditional narrow interpretation of the 1972 Treaty.

A motion by Republican John W. Warner (Va.) was defeated 58–38, which aimed to delete from the annual defence authorization bill (S1174) the provision limiting SDI testing. Warner had contended that the Levin–Nunn motion would deprive the administration of means to extract Soviet concessions in the arms control negotiations.[181] The Senate Armed Services Committee, whilst admitting that SDI was a powerful diplomatic lever for obtaining Soviet arms control concessions, stated that:

> Negotiating leverage is sometimes a perishable commodity ... we should be prepared to consider adjustments to the pace and scope of SDI if the Soviet Union agrees to significant, stabilizing and verifiable reductions.[182]

Caspar Weinberger's Resignation: November 23 1987

Caspar Weinberger resigned in late 1987. On November 17 1987, there was a Pentagon ceremony at which he stepped down as Defense Secretary.[183] At the ceremony, Weinberger criticized Congress for permitting US military power in the 1970s to be weakened. He also criticized opponents of the SDI. Weinberger said that to trade away that defence 'is one of the most dangerous ideas ever to infect our political discourse'.[184] Ronald Reagan reaffirmed that he would not make the SDI negotiable with the Soviet Union. Reagan said that the US would not 'repeat the mistakes of the last decade'. He announced that 'We will not unilaterally disarm in this one area or any area – S.D.I. holds out the hope of a world free from the fear of ballistic missiles'.[185] At the ceremony, the Army, Navy and Air Force each presented Caspar Weinberger with their highest decoration for civilian service. President Reagan awarded him the Presidential Medal of Freedom with Distinction.[186]

The Moscow Summit: May 29–June 2 1988

The Senate Resolution of INF Ratification

On May 23 1988, George Shultz urged Congress to vote on the INF Treaty,[187] in time for the Moscow summit, May 29–June 2 1988. The main achievement of the summit was the visit to Moscow of the most ardent anti-Communist President in US history. Although a START accord was not reached, the summit witnessed the signing (by the two leaders) of the ratification documents of the INF Treaty, which was signed in Washington a few months earlier.[188]

Although ratification (the formal acceptance of a treaty by a government) is a power of the President, the Constitution requires that such a procedure must be undertaken with the approval of two-thirds of the Senators in the US Congress. The Senate votes on a resolution approving ratification by the President. It does not vote on the text of the treaty.[189] Such a resolution was the speculation of much debate in the US. Prolonging the INF issue could have impaired the START discussions.[190]

The debate in Congress was not one which was predicated on the meaning (or text) of the INF Treaty. It was because of a dispute (in 1987) between Senate Democrats, and, on the other side, the Senate Republicans and the Reagan administration. It concerned the Reagan administration's 1985 proposal to reinterpret the 1972 ABM Treaty[191] which it claimed allowed more leeway than had previously been assumed, to test ABM weapons in space.[192] The most contentious issues involving the terms of the INF Treaty was whether the INF Treaty banned futuristic weapons. These were weapons designed to destroy targets with lasers/electrical beams/by collision but by non-explosive means.[193]

The Reagan administration certified that the INF Treaty stood on its own merits and should be approved with no amendments/strings attached.[194] The Senate Foreign Relations panel noted that Soviet compliance with any START Treaty would be more difficult to monitor than with the INF Treaty. The INF Treaty banned all weapons of specified types, whilst START would merely limit the number of weapons allowed of certain types.[195] On May 27 1988, the Senate approved the INF Treaty, just in time for the Moscow summit. The 93–5 vote was an endorsement for the INF Treaty to be formally ratified during President Reagan's trip to Moscow. All amendments requiring negotiations of the treaty with the Soviets were rejected by the Senate.[196]

The SDI Debate in Congress

Congressional support for the SDI was 'at a low ebb' around the time, January 19 1988, when Sam Nunn (Democrat–Ga.) urged the US to 'seriously consider' developing a limited defence against the nuclear missiles launched by accident.[197] Nunn's proposal for such a defence, or 'insurance policy', would fall within the jurisdiction of the ABM Treaty, or require minor amendments. The 1972 Treaty allowed the deployment of 100 ABM interceptors near Grand Forks, (N.D.). For the long term, Nunn argued that the SDI should be orientated towards developing advances weapons like laser-armed satellites for larger attacks.[198]

On May 13 1988, the Senate rejected an amendment proposed by Republican Senator Malcolm Wallop (Wyo.) which required $100 million to begin deployment of a limited defence, to guard against '"accidental" missile launches'.[199] An amendment by Democrat Carl Levin (Mich.) was tabled (killed) the same day which aimed to reduce SDI funding. Two days earlier, an amendment to the annual defence authorization bill, by Democrat J. Bennett Johnston (La.), was rejected. The amendment proposed an alternative approach to cutting SDI funding.[200] The House, on May 11 1988, passed a bill authorising defence spending for fiscal year 1989 which would cut SDI funding to $3.5 billion. Reagan had requested $4.9 billion for the SDI, whilst the Armed Services Committee approved $4.1 billion.[201]

The House voted 239–176 to adopt an amendment by Democrat John M. Spratt requiring that the accidental launch protection system (ALPS) (which was 'phase one' of the deployable SDI system) be designed to comply with the traditional interpretation of the ABM Treaty. The alternative Kemp amendment proposed was rejected 167–249.[202] The *US News and World Report*, June 13 1988, reported that the SDI was fading as an issue. Congress had 'sharply curbed SDI testing' and 'the Soviets apparently have decided that time will take care of their objections to Star Wars'.[203]

The Lead Up to the Moscow Summit

Since the Washington summit, the US and Soviet Union made no progress in resolving the dispute regarding the permitted scope of SDI testing under the 1972 ABM Treaty. Arms control experts revealed that research on the programme would be far slower than the administration hoped due to technical, budgetary, legal and political reasons. Consequently, the programme would conform to the traditional 'narrow' interpretation of the ABM Treaty.[204]

Pentagon officials revealed that work on space-based interceptors would be delayed due to an effort to save money and sort out technical problems. Congress continued its demand that the SDI be confined to the strict interpretation of the 1972 Treaty. This demand was the Soviet prerequisite for any reductions made in strategic offensive arms. President Reagan (on his way to the Moscow summit) was adamant to resist such a limitation on SDI testing in space.[205]

Prior to the summit, White House aides 'played down the chances for dramatic progress on substantive issues'. There was the failure of US and Soviet negotiations to complete work on a START Treaty, reducing strategic missiles. Nevertheless, Raymond Garthoff stated of the Moscow summit 'The Summit is primarily important as an illustration of the fact that both sides now accept the need for continuing diplomatic dialogue'.[206]

The dispute over how much SDI testing was permitted was still the principal obstacle to the START Treaty. US ideas, regarding how to resolve the (SDI) testing issue, failed to provide a breakthrough.[207] Lieutenant General Colin L. Powell revealed that the US was adhering to its position that space tests were permissible under the broad interpretation of the 1972 ABM Treaty.[208]

Arms Control and Long-Range Nuclear Arms = START = Strategic Arms

Although a START Treaty was not signed at the Moscow summit, two minor arms accords were reached on May 31 1988. One was an agreement requiring the US and Soviet Union to provide advanced notice of ballistic missiles launches (albeit from land-based or sea-based ICBMs). The notice would have to include the date and area of launch, as well as the area of impact.[209] This American proposal had originally been included in the draft American text of the START Treaty reducing nuclear arms. It was separated from it in early May to accelerate potential agreements made in Moscow.[210] The American proposal to provide notice of all ballistic missile launches was expanded upon by the Soviets, to cover aircraft and naval operations. The Soviet counter-proposal was wide-ranging, and created problems for agreement.[211]

The Soviet provision of the plan included the establishment of zones which prevented each side from carrying out naval (anti-submarine warfare operations) and aircraft operations near the other's territory.[212] Rozanne L. Ridgway reported that the agreement could not be reached because of the vast expansion of the treaty by the Russians. The Russians consequently dropped their demands.[213] The Soviets wanted both sides to notify each other of dispatches of large numbers of bombers. Notification of launchers of cruise missiles fired from planes and ships had to be given. The US had not proposed the notification of bombers and cruise missiles which were areas of US advantage. The US proposed the notification of ballistic missiles which was a Soviet advantage.[214]

The other arms accord reached, on May 31 1988, was an agreement providing for experiments in verification techniques at US and Soviet nuclear test sites. An agreed equipment would be held in the summer to measure underground nuclear tests in both countries. The equipment would determine verification requirements for the 1974 Threshold Test Ban Treaty, which was unratified.

Further agreements which would allow ratification of the 1974 Treaty and an unratified 1976 Treaty (which established limits on the size of peaceful underground nuclear explosions) would be worked on.[215]

The START Negotiations

Before the Moscow summit, the main outlines of a strategic arms treaty (nuclear weapons with ranges greater than 3,400 miles) were worked out. This included the combined ceilings on warheads and cruise missiles, limits on warheads and cruise missiles, limits on warheads on ballistic missiles and verification procedures.[216] In their joint communique, the Soviet and Americans restated their goal of a treaty limiting each country to 1,600 strategic offensive delivery systems and 6,000 warheads.[217]

The US and Soviet Union could not agree on the issue of sea-launched cruise missiles from both ships and submarines, and on how much SDI testing was allowed. The two issues became the two main obstacles to a strategic arms (START) treaty.[218] The Soviets held firm on their demands for strict SDI testing; the Americans offered no compromises.[219] Both leaders (as in previous summits) agreed to disagree on the testing of SDI systems, postponing decisions before a new treaty could be signed. On June 1 1988, Gorbachev repeated his opposition to the SDI: 'It doesn't meet normal logic to reduce strategic offensive arms on land and to build a bridge for such arms into outer space'.[220]

'Common ground' on verifying limits on mobile missiles and on long-range missiles launched from airplanes was reached.[221] On mobile missiles, the two sides reached general agreement on the US proposal of confining ground-based missiles (mobile land-based ballistic missiles) to special deployment areas. The missiles could be moved for maintenance, training and military exercises – but with prior approval. However, differences existed regarding the issues of verification; the size of the deployment areas and the forms of identification for the missiles.[222] On air-launched cruise missiles fired from bombers, 'considerable progress' was registered on distinguishing such missiles that carry nuclear warheads, from air-launched cruise missiles that carried conventional arms.[223] However, there was no agreement on how to count the permitted number of such missiles on each side.[224]

Non-Arms Issues

Human rights   Before the Moscow summit, Reagan stated that he would make human rights 'agenda item No. 1' at the meeting.[225] Reagan used every occasion to criticize the Soviets for their violations of human rights, including their refusal to allow Jews to emigrate.[226] After Gorbachev's criticism of Reagan's rhetoric, the President contended that although progress had been made in recent years under Gorbachev, the Soviet Union still fell short of international standards of freedom as dictated by the 1975 Helsinki accords.[227] However, Reagan contended that any 'lapses' were caused by government 'bureaucracy' not by the conscious official government policies of leaders like Gorbachev.[228]

Gorbachev stated that his country wanted contacts, but he did not like 'sermonizing'.[229] The Communist Party newspaper *Pravda* devoted its summit articles to charges of human rights violations in the US.[230] In Congress, Reagan was criticized for attributing human rights problems in the Soviet Union to the bureaucratic inertia.[231] Reagan stated, regarding his comment, 'Maybe it was a bad choice of words'. He furthered, 'I think it is a defect of the whole system'. Wanting to avoid blaming Gorbachev personally, Reagan added, 'You can't place the blame on any individual'.[232] Reagan was criticized by the Soviet leader as attempting to score points 'through such propaganda ploys' as Reagan's meeting with dissidents.[233]

Bilateral issues Several agreements on bilateral issues were concluded at the summit. Existing cultural exchanges for students, artists and teachers would be expanded, and mutual fishing relations were extended. There would be an increased cooperation in transportation science and technology, and improved cooperation in maritime search and rescue. There would be operational coordination in long-range radio-navigation systems.[234] A 1973 agreement for cooperation on peaceful uses of nuclear energy was extended.

Regarding Civil Space Cooperation, the two countries agreed to a new initiative to examine ways for cooperation in outer space. A joint mission to the moon and Mars would be considered.[235] Regarding people to people contacts, in his talks to Soviet artists and students, Reagan, on May 31 1988, stated 'It's time to remove the barriers that keep people apart. I am proposing an increased exchange program of high school students between our countries'.[236] The Soviet students felt that the SDI was holding up an arms treaty.[237] White House Officials, however, acknowledged that the seven agreements signed, including the student exchanges and fishing rights, meant very little.[238]

Regional issues The US and Soviet Union also discussed a wide range of regional issues, including the Middle East, Iran–Iraq War, Central America, Southern Africa and the Korean peninsula. It was acknowledged that they disagreed on the causes of the regional tensions, and the ways to overcome them. However, they agreed 'that these differences need not be an obstacle to constructive interaction between the USSR and the US'.[239] Gorbachev reiterated his declaration, (made six months earlier) that the Soviet Union would withdraw its troops from Afghanistan.[240] The US pressed for a withdrawal of Soviet troops, and the Soviet Union demanded an end to US support of the Mujahedin. The issue was resolved by an international agreement (The Geneva Accords) on April 14 1988, which provided for Soviet withdrawal.[241]

Disputes, however, remained on how the agreement would be carried out. The US complained that the Soviets continued to arm the Kabul regime and maintained that if this continued, the US would continue aiding the Mujahedin. The Soviets, in return, stated that Pakistan and the US by supplying the insurgents had violated the April 14 1988 agreement.[242] To Gorbachev, the significance of the Afghanistan settlement:

went far beyond its regional implications. It was the first time that the Soviet Union and the United States, together with the conflicting parties, had signed an agreement which paved the way for a political solution to the conflict.[243]

Some progress was made in resolving the Angolan Civil War and the independence of South West Africa. The Soviet Union refused to endorse the US led UN embargo on Iran.[244] US officials, however, were pleased at discussions on the Middle East, where the Soviets appeared to be showing more flexibility.[245] Reagan, on arrival to the Soviet Union, revealed that the first troop withdrawals had begun from Afghanistan.[246]

Analysis of the Moscow Summit

President Reagan, on June 1 1988, affirmed that the Moscow summit had 'accomplished a good deal of important work'. His contacts with the Soviet people were 'deeply moving' and 'a great deal' of credit for changes in the Soviet Union were due to Gorbachev.[247] According to Reagan, the Soviet Union was no longer an evil empire.[248] In his news conference on June 1, Gorbachev stated that the world's problems could not be resolved by military means. They had to be resolved politically. He continued that the Soviets felt some good chances 'to impair some good dynamics' was missed.[249] Gorbachev believed that the SDI was an obstacle to START. The SDI meant destabilization. According to Gorbachev logic did not dictate reducing strategic offensive arms on land and building 'a bridge for such arms into outer space'. He did not believe the SDI to be a purely defensive weapon, as the Americans claimed it would be. Soviet–US relations were, nevertheless, on a 'healthy track'.[250]

On 30 May 1988, Gorbachev emphasized that 'international security' was 'a condition for the survival of mankind'. President Reagan said that both countries had achieved 'a good beginning'.[251] Gorbachev later complained that US–Soviet dialogue had 'not been easy'. It was moving more slowly than what was required 'by the real situation, both in our two countries and in the whole world'. Nevertheless, it was like a train that was switching from dangerous tracks to safer ones.[252] Gorbachev concluded that both countries had every reason to regard the summit and Reagan's visit 'as a useful contribution to the development of dialogue between the Soviet Union and the United States'.[253] *The New York Times* front page of June 3 1988 stated that, 'Gorbachev Used Reagan's Visit to Bolster His Position Before Big Party Conference'.[254]

Reagan believed that the Moscow summit 'showed great promise and the response of the Soviet people was heartening'.[255] The press still urged caution and prudence, yet perceived that the US–Soviet tension was receding.[256] Reagan continued to insist that the SDI was 'my idea' and that it was for defensive purposes. He again affirmed that the idea would be made available worldwide to guard countries against a madman coming along and making nuclear missiles.[257] Although White House Officials stated that the summit had produced 'peanuts' in the way of practical agreements, it was a success because it continued to stabilize the relationship between the US and Soviet Union. The White House was disappointed over the Russian failure to broadcast President Reagan's speech at the Moscow State University.[258]

Gorbachev had said that the summit talks had been marked by 'missed opportunities' for progress due to Reagan's hesitation in the talks. A senior US official had said of Gorbachev: 'He may have missed a few opportunities, but we didn't miss any'.[259] Gorbachev said that Reagan's refusal to agree to the joint statement which declared 'peaceful coexistence' to be the goal of both countries, signified Reagan's reluctance to make changes in their traditional superpower competition.[260] Reagan said the term had 'ambiguities to it'. His aides feared such language would bar the US from pressing human rights and other issues.[261] Both Reagan and Gorbachev declared that the Moscow summit (as the previous summit) helped improve relations between the two countries. Gorbachev contended that the meetings had, 'dealt a blow at the foundations of the Cold War'.[262]

In Eastern Europe, there was enthusiasm at the results of the Moscow summit. There was also some apprehension about President Reagan and an accusation in Czechoslovak Party newspaper *Rude Pravo* that the West had used opposition groups in the Eastern bloc to foment social unrest. The paper stated that the US blocked further progress in Moscow.[263] Although there was little coverage of the summit in Rumania, in Poland and Hungary there were frequent reports. *Rzeczpospolita*, the Polish Government newspaper stated that the work achieved 'means that Soviet–American relations are stabilizing, moving onto a straight path, free of sharp and dangerous bends that hold the world breathless'.[264] However, *Trybuna Ludu*, (Poland's Communist Party newspaper) claimed that Reagan's behaviour demonstrated that 'there is much of the old way of thinking about United States doctrines and principles of unilateral benefits that politics should produce'. The paper credited the Soviets with initiating progress.[265] China avoided any editorial comments about the summit. Chinese Foreign Minister Qian Qichen acknowledged that dialogue was better than confrontation. He said he expected 'no significant breakthrough' from the talks. Later he described the Soviet–American arms balance as insufficient to maintain international stability. However, the world's opinion was generally favourable to the summit.[266]

Congressional Quarterly Weekly Report of June 4 1988, pointed out that the Moscow summit was 'an upbeat, if largely unproductive summit meeting'.[267] *US News and World Report*, June 13 1988, evaluated the summit as producing:

> little in the way of concrete results, but it met the urgent political needs of both, ratified new stability in great power behaviour and sent a message to every capital in the world that history was in the making.[268]

For Reagan, the Moscow summit was perhaps the most memorable summit because 'for the first time I also got to meet and shake hands with ordinary Soviet people'.[269]

Gorbachev's United Nations Speech: December 7 1988

Gorbachev's Speech

On December 7 1988, addressing the United Nations General Assembly, Mikhail Gorbachev gave a groundbreaking foreign policy speech.[270] In it, he announced an unprecedented number of unilateral Soviet proposals and concessions. Gorbachev emphasized the concept of an interdependent world and common security. He called for a greater UN role in world affairs (including the Soviet role in the UN), and promised to guarantee human rights in the Soviet Union. Gorbachev announced a ceasefire in Afghanistan to take effect as of January 1 1989. He proposed a solution to the war in the Middle East with the assistance of the UN Security Council.[271] Gorbachev's speech signalled the end of ideological conflict.

The unilateral arms cutbacks that Gorbachev announced were historic. They had significant implications and signaled a change in Soviet foreign policy. Gorbachev disbanded the Warsaw Pact. There would also be a reduction of Soviet forces in the Asian part of the Soviet Union. Soviet armed forces would be reduced by 500,000 men over two years. To quote Gorbachev: 'The number of conventional armaments will also be substantially reduced. This will be done unilaterally'.[272] Fifty-thousand men and 5,000 tanks in East Germany, Czechoslovakia and Hungary would be withdrawn. Six out of 15 tank divisions would be disbanded in these countries. In Eastern Europe, Soviet units would be reorganized to become 'clearly defensive'.[273] The Soviet troop withdrawal from East Europe was symbolic. It signified the end of the 'Brezhnev Doctrine'.[274] Now, as some commentators put it, the 'Sinatra Doctrine' was embraced; countries would be able to 'go it their way'.[275]

Soviet armed forces 'stationed in the European part of the Soviet Union' and in the 'territories of our European allies' would be reduced 'by 10,000 tanks, 8,500 artillery systems, and 800 combat aircraft'. Gorbachev stated that the Soviet Union would:

> maintain our country's defense capability at a level of reasonable and reliable sufficiency so that no one might be tempted to encroach on the security of the Soviet Union and our allies.[276]

Gorbachev announced that he wanted a 50 per cent reduction in strategic offensive arms, whilst preserving the ABM Treaty. Gorbachev emphasized that he hoped for continued relations with America, which he referred to as 'this great country'. Gorbachev hoped to continue dialogue with President-elect George Bush in a spirit of 'good will'. Gorbachev wanted the US and Soviet Union to join in a 'common goal' to 'put an end to an era of wars, confrontation and regional conflicts, to aggressions against nature, to the terror of hunger and poverty as well as to political terrorism'. This was an aim which the US and Soviet Union could only reach together.[277]

In his memoirs, Gorbachev recalled that 'The Politburo agreed to the initial concepts and suggestions that were to be included in the final draft of the speech.

Incidently, there were no objections of principle'.[278] He dismissed rumours of Marshal Akhromeyev's alleged opposition to the disarmament proposal. According to Gorbachev, the Marshal had prepared for this. [279]

Reaction to Gorbachev's Speech

In reaction to Gorbachev's United Nations speech, President Reagan stated that if 'the Soviet unilateral troop reduction ... is carried out speedily and in full, history would regard it as important, significant'. George Shultz earlier had called Gorbachev's announcement a 'significant step in the right direction', though he added that it would still leave 'a very significant asymmetry' in forces in favour of Moscow.[280] Chairman of the Joint Chiefs of Staff, Admiral William J. Crowe agreed that the plan 'falls far short of redressing the conventional balance between our two nations, or in Europe'.[281]

In his essay, 'A Virtue of Necessity' in *The New York Times*, December 8 1988, William Safire noted that Gorbachev:

> did not say that his unilateral reductions would lower the Warsaw Pact tank advantage from the present 3.1 to 1 to a mere 2.5 to 1, and artillery from 3.3 to 1 to "only" 2.4 to 1. Soviet conventional dominance is still overwhelming; It's a Long Way to Symmetrary (sic).[282]

Safire noted that Gorbachev's immediate goal was to 'buy time for recovery without profound change in his system by downplaying direct superpower competition'. This action was 'a temporary retreat caused by economic necessity.[283] Journalist Bill Keller also claimed that Gorbachev's underlying motive in 'demilitarizing international relations' was to reduce the military drain on the troubled Soviet domestic economy. This was evidenced by his announcement that two or three weapons and plants would be converted to civilian use.[284]

The New York Times editorial of December 8 1988: 'Gambler, Showman, Statesman', referred to Gorbachev's ideas as: 'Breathtaking. Risky. Bold. Naive. Diversionary. Heroic'.[285] Ralph Earle II and Elliot L. Richardson called Gorbachev's proposal to withdraw troops and tanks as 'a welcome step toward the ultimate goal of drastically reducing the risk of war in Europe'. Apart from reducing 'East–West tensions considerably', Gorbachev's approach would 'encourage the renewal of serious negotiations on conventional weapons'.[286] Margaret Thatcher 'warmly welcomed' Gorbachev's troop reduction.[287] Manfred Woerner, NATO Secretary General, maintained that if the cuts proposed were carried out, 'it is a very significant step that we emphatically welcome'. Friedhelm Ost, a spokesman for West German Chancellor Helmut Kohl, said that Mr Kohl perceived the plan as 'a good chance to reach conventional weapons stability in Europe'.[288]

Gorbachev stated that the Soviet military cuts would be 'unilateral'. He later told reporters 'we do hope that the US and the Europeans will also take some steps'.[289] The NATO allies responded, on December 8, with what *Congressional*

Quarterly Weekly Report, December 10 1988, called 'an even more sweeping cutback proposal of their own'.[290] Gorbachev's military force reductions coincided with the departure of Chief of the Soviet General Staff, Marshal Sergei F. Akhromeyev, for reasons of health. Earlier in July, the General stated his opposition to any unilateral Soviet reductions.[291]

On CBS's 'This Morning' programme, former Secretary of State Henry A. Kissinger questioned 'what type of tank is being destroyed? ... Is this a modernisation program in which the old tanks are being destroyed, or is it the useful tanks?'.[292] *Congressional Quarterly Weekly Report* revealed that 'of an estimated 53,000 tanks in the Soviet army, more than 60 percent are obsolescent'. Senate Democrat Whip Alan Cranston (Calif.) declared that Gorbachev had declared 'an end to the cold war, an end to the arms race'.[293]

Regarding the Soviet withdrawal from Afghanistan, 'Gorbachev did not say directly whether the Soviet Union would adhere to the February 15 withdrawal date'. Republican Senator Gordon J. Humphrey (N.H.) alleged that the Soviets would 'renege' on their promise to withdraw. Others believed that the measure was an effort to save face because the Soviets were losing to the Mujahedin.[294] Lieutenant General Brent Scowcroft, tipped to be President-elect George Bush's National Security Advisor, criticized President Reagan's vision of the SDI as a nationwide defence shield, and Reagan's broad interpretation of the ABM Treaty. Up until this point, George Bush 'avoided any public departure from the Reagan line on either START or SDI'.[295]

Governor's Island, New York Harbour: The New York Summit: December 7 1988

After delivering his United Nations speech, Mikhail Gorbachev took a ferry to Governor's Island in New York Harbour. He joined both outgoing President Ronald Reagan and his successor George Bush for a two-and-a-half hour meeting. The New York summit was to be the fifth summit and 'dramatized the steady warming trend in Soviet–American relations'.[296] President Reagan paid a sentimental farewell to Gorbachev and gave the leader a picture of the two of them walking at the 1985 Geneva summit meeting. Reagan signed the picture with the inscription: 'We have walked a long way together to clear a path for peace'. Reagan urged Bush and Gorbachev to continue the improved relations.[297]

Gorbachev referred to the meeting as 'very good'. It was 'a very open meeting' with 'a good atmosphere'. The major theme, Gorbachev said, was 'continuity'. President Reagan's spokesman Marlin Fitzwater said that Gorbachev and Reagan had discussed Southern Africa, the American call for a global ban of chemical weapons, the Anti-Ballistic Missile Treaty and unrest in the Soviet Republics of Armenia and Azerbaijan. The Reagan administration enthusiastically welcomed Gorbachev's announcement of Soviet troop withdrawal from East Europe.[298] In his news conference on Governor's Island, George Shultz stated that progress was made regarding discussions on Southern Africa and the Middle East. However, a lot of negotiations remained on issues.[299] Gorbachev's sudden return home followed a severe earthquake and violent ethnic unrest in the Caucasus mountain region.[300]

Gorbachev recalled that 'All in all, I had a good impression of this meeting on Governor's Island'.[301] Reagan wrote in his diary about the New York summit: 'The meeting was a tremendous success. A better attitude than at any of our previous meetings. Gorbachev sounded as if he saw us as partners making a better world'.[302] Reagan added that the first phase of the START Treaty, which was later signed by Bush and Gorbachev, was 'based on the principles Gorbachev, George Shultz, Eduard Shevardnadze, and I worked out in 1986 in that room overlooking the sea in Reykjavik'.[303]

Synopsis

At the Washington summit, the INF agreement was reached because Gorbachev no longer insisted that agreements were conditional upon Reagan abandoning the SDI. Gorbachev's SDI–INF (and START) delink resulted in the INF Treaty being signed, but produced no START agreement. The reason why Gorbachev delinked the SDI from the talks is an issue of debate. Most prominently, it was the result of his recognition that the SDI was being curtailed by the US Congress. It was here that the fate of the SDI seemed destined to be decided, not at the US–Soviet summits which had on two previous occasions failed to provide for an abandonment of the system.

Previous to the Washington summit, (on September 17 1987) the Senate voted for the narrow interpretation of the ABM Treaty. This was a defeat for the Reagan administration. A month later, the administration announced that it would test the SDI under the narrow interpretation of the 1972 ABM Treaty, although its new broad interpretation was correct. This was due to Agreed Statement D which allowed both countries, with mutual consent, to amend the ABM Treaty in the future. (The narrow interpretation of the treaty permitted further discussions and potentially provided leverage to SDI testing, if mutually agreed.)

The discussions of the SDI in Congress demonstrated the importance of the SDI. This is further evidenced by Gorbachev initially making the SDI a precondition for the Washington meeting. Gorbachev hoped to defeat the SDI by forcing a strict adherence to the ABM Treaty. He no longer restricted the SDI to the laboratory. His new method was again intended to force abandonment of the programme.

It is due to the fact that the Soviets recognized that Congress forced a narrow interpretation of the ABM Treaty, that the Soviet change of policy regarding their INF and SDI linkages was made possible. The Soviet policy in 1985 was one of SDI and INF linkage; by insisting that the signing of the INF agreement would be made possible in exchange for the prohibition of ballistic missile defences. The February 28 1987 policy was one of delinking this condition. Congressional budget cuts for the SDI, and the technological problems with it also accounted for Gorbachev's SDI–INF (and START) delink.

One of the main achievements of the Washington summit was not to let the SDI stand in the way of the negotiations. Using ambiguous wording, the US and Soviets 'side-stepped' their disagreement as to what testing of the SDI was allowed under the 1972 ABM Treaty. The joint communique committed the superpowers to adhere to the ABM Treaty. It did not clarify what SDI testing was permitted.

This improved superpower relationship was evident at the Moscow summit. Its significance was the visit to Moscow of President Reagan. To him, Moscow was the most important summit because of his contact with ordinary Soviet people. The Moscow summit was the summit which ratified the INF Treaty (which had earlier been signed in Washington.) The resolution of the ratification of the INF Treaty had been marked by much speculation in Congress, due to the fact that debate centred on the reinterpretation of the 1972 ABM Treaty with reference to SDI testing in space. The issue was whether the INF Treaty banned futuristic weapons. The treaty was approved by the Senate in May 1988.

Congress had curbed SDI spending. Research on the SDI would be slowed due to technical, budgetary, legal and political reasons. Consequently, the SDI would conform to the narrow ABM Treaty interpretation. However, the Soviets continued to insist that the SDI be confined to this narrow ABM Treaty interpretation in exchange for strategic offensive arms reductions. It was this dispute – how much SDI testing was allowed – which was the obstacle to the START Treaty. Despite Gorbachev's SDI–INF and START 'delink', his position was the same regarding the SDI: he wanted to stop it. At the Moscow summit, Reagan continued to resist limitations on SDI testing in space, and both leaders agreed to disagree on the issue, as they had previously done so at the Washington summit. Gorbachev, on June 1 1988, continued his opposition against SDI. He did not believe it to be a defensive weapon and believed it an obstacle to START.

Despite the SDI, US–Soviet relations were improving. The summit was a success as to Reagan, the Soviet Union was no longer an 'evil empire'. Such a statement reflected the general accomplishment in US–Soviet relations and the Moscow summit itself. This improved superpower relationship (and the consequent stability which emerged) outweighed the practical agreements reached in Moscow, which had been criticized by some as not achieving as much as had been hoped. The US–Soviet summits had been described by Gorbachev as dealing a 'blow' at the 'foundations of the cold war'. Many perceived Gorbachev's December 7 1988 UN speech as signifying the end of this Cold War. To those who perceived the origins of the Cold War as due to the Soviet stationing of troops in East Europe after the Second World War, Gorbachev's speech signified the end of this Cold War. The New York summit was about continuity: the continuity of stability in improved relations between the US and Soviet Union.

The SDI played an important role in the Washington and Moscow summits. It was the precondition for Soviet concessions and was the factor that precluded a START agreement. This factor and the US–Soviet disputes regarding the SDI demonstrate the importance of the issue. If the SDI were not important, it would not have been the issue of such concern. The SDI was not the only discussion at the summits. It was the paramount one which precluded agreements, though not on all issues. It was important, but it does not explain everything.

Notes

1   By Kohan, John, Reported by Ricardo Chavira, with Shultz and James O. Jackson/Moscow, 'Snuffing a Summit: Gorbachev Makes Star Wars the Obstacle to a Meeting With Reagan', *Time*, Vol. 130, No. 18, November 2 1987, p. 42.

2   Reagan, Ronald, *An American Life*, London, Hutchinson, 1990, p. 684.

3   Garthoff, Raymond L., *The Great Transition: American–Soviet Relations and the End of the Cold War*, Washington, D.C., The Brookings Institution, 1994, p. 305.

4   Kohan, 'Snuffing a Summit', *Time*, p. 42.

5   Garthoff, *Great Transition*, p. 305.

6   Ibid.

7   Towell, Pat, 'INF Pact to Sweeten Reagan–Gorbachev Summit', *CQWR*, Vol. 45, No. 48, November 28 1987, p. 2927.

8   Garthoff, *Great*, pp. 312, 314.

9   Quotation by Garthoff, in ibid., p. 304.

10 Garthoff, *Great*, p. 305.

11 Ibid., pp. 318-319.; Reagan, *An American Life*, p. 689.: For the letter that Gorbachev wrote to Reagan, see Reagan, *An American Life*, pp. 687-691.

12 Kohan, 'Snuffing a Summit', *Time*, p. 42.

13 By Budiansky, Stephen and Henry Trewhitt with Peter Ross Range and Maureen Santini, 'On to the Summit, as Star Wars Waits', *USNWR*, Vol. 103, No. 19, November 9 1987, p. 13.

14 Ibid.

15 All information from Gordon, Michael R., '"Star Wars" Curbs Not Summit Issue, Soviet Aides Hint', *NYT*, December 6 1987, p. A1.

16 Ibid., p. 24.

17 Shipler, David K., 'Strategic Arms Cuts and Afghan Pullout Seen as Offering the Best Prospects', *NYT*, December 7 1987, p. A18.

18 Gordon, '"Star Wars" Curbs Not Summit Issue', *NYT*, p. 24.

19 Brinkley, Joel, 'Gorbachev Begins Summit Trip in US With Plea on Arms', *NYT*, December 8 1987, pp. A1, A14.; 'The Soviet Leader's Remarks on Arrival', *NYT*, December 8 1987, p. A14.

20 For details on the history of Gorbachev's linkage and delinkage of the INF, and SDI and START issues, see Talbott, Strobe, 'The Road to Zero: Behind the Scenes of a Surprising But Potentially Troubling Triumph', *Time*, Vol. 130, No. 24, December 14 1987, pp. 8-15, especially pp. 12-15.; For opposition to the INF Treaty, see Lamar, Jr., Jacob V., Reported by Jay Peterzell/Washington, 'How to Wreck the Treaty: Opponents Will Offer Changes That Seem Reasonable But Are Lethal', *Time*, Vol. 130, No. 25, December 21 1987, p. 14.; For coverage of the Washington summit, see *CQWR*, Vol. 45, No. 50, December 12 1987, pp. 3023-3029, 3062-3070, 3070-3085.; For the text of the INF Treaty and Appendices, see *CQWR*, Vol. 45, No. 50, December 12 1987.; For the 'Text of Treaty on Intermediate Range Missiles', see *CQWR*, Vol. 45, No. 50, December 12 1987, pp. 3070-3076.; For Appendices, see ibid., pp. 3076-3085.; For the text of the INF Treaty as stated in the *New York Times*, see 'The Treaty: Text of the Agreement to Eliminate Some Missiles', *NYT*, December 9 1987, pp. A24-A25.; 'Excerpts From Protocol: How the Missiles Will Be Eliminated', *NYT*, December 9 1987, p. A26.; 'Verifying the Agreement: The Rules Governing Inspections by Both Sides', *NYT*, December 9 1987, p. A26.; For details of the INF Treaty, see 'Highlights of the INF Treaty', *CQWR*, Vol. 45, No. 50, December 12 1987, p. 3024.; Towell, Pat,

'Rules, Timetables: What the Pact Would Do', *CQWR*, Vol. 46, No. 4, January 23 1988, p. 150.; For information on the INF Treaty, see Talbott, Strobe, 'The Road to Zero', *Time*, pp. 8-15.; Shipler, David K., 'A Mood of Warmth: As Summit Talks Begin, the Attention Shifts to Strategic Arms', *NYT*, December 9 1987, pp. A1, A20.; Gordon, Michael R., 'How to Destroy the 2,611 Missiles', *NYT*, December 9 1987, pp. A1, A21.; For Reagan and Gorbachev's comments before the signing of the INF Treaty, see 'Text of Reagan–Gorbachev Comments: Superpowers sign INF Treaty, Join in TV Address to Nations', *CQWR*, Vol. 45, No. 50, December 12 1987, pp. 3068-3069.

21   Shipler, 'A Mood of Warmth: As Summit Talks Begin', *NYT*, p. A20.; 'Highlights of the INF Treaty', *CQWR*, Vol. 45, No. 50, December 12 1987, p. 3024.

22   Towell, 'Rules, Timetables', *CQWR*, p. 150.

23   'Highlights of the INF Treaty', *CQWR*, p. 3024.; Towell, 'Rules, Timetables', *CQWR*, p. 150.

24   Ibid.

25   Ibid.; Shipler, 'A Mood of Warmth', *NYT*, p. A20.; For the INF Treaty, see Shevardnadze, Eduard A., *The Future Belongs to Freedom*, New York, The Free Press, 1991, pp. 91-92.

26   'Senate Now Turns Scrutiny to INF – and Beyond', *CQWR*, Vol. 46, No. 4, January 23 1988, p. 153.; Regarding the issue of verification in US–Soviet relations, according to Eduard Shevardnadze, the Soviet refusal to accept verification and control measures was an effort to 'hide our weaknesses and inadequacies'. Shevardnadze, *The Future Belongs to Freedom*, p. 89.

27   By Trewhitt, Henry with Robert Kaylor, Kenneth T. Walsh, Peter Ross Range and Rene Riley, 'The Big Problems Restarting START', *USNWR*, December 21 1987, p. 28.

28   By Towell, Pat with Mike Mills, 'INF Treaty: Star Vehicle for Political Agendas', *CQWR*, Vol. 46, No. 5, January 30 1988, p. 194.; Eduard Shevardnadze states that 'the Soviet Union destroyed a significantly greater number of missiles than the United States'. Shevardnadze, *The Future Belongs to Freedom*, p. 96.

29   Towell, 'The INF Deal: Apart From the "Hell, No" Votes, Senate Likely to Concur', *CQWR*, Vol. 45, No. 50, December 12 1987, p. 3025.

30   Towell, with Mills, 'INF Treaty: Star Vehicle', *CQWR*, p. 194.

31   All information in paragraph taken from ibid.

32   'Arms Control: is it Good For us?', *USNWR*, December 14, 1987, p. 25.

33   Towell, Pat, 'Treaty–Interpretation Issue Complicating INF Approval', *CQWR*, Vol. 46, No. 14, April 2 1988, p. 868.

34   'Arms Control: Is it Good', *USNWR*, p. 25.

35   Talbott, 'The Road to Zero', *Time*, p. 14.

36   Towell with Mills, 'INF Treaty: Star Vehicle', *CQWR*, p. 192.

37   By Hook, Janet, Macon Moorhouse and Pat Towell, 'Just in Time for Moscow Summit: Senate Votes 93–5 to Approve Ratification of the INF Treaty', *CQWR*, Vol. 46, No. 22, May 28 1988, p. 1435.

38   Towell, 'The INF Deal: Apart from the "Hell, No" Votes', *CQWR*, p. 3025.

39   Garthoff, *Great*, p. 327.; That the INF Treaty represented the complete elimination of an entire class of US and Soviet missiles, see Ekedahl, Carolyn McGiffert and Melvin A. Goodman, *The Wars of Eduard Shevardnadze*, London, Hurst, 1997, p. 116.; The INF Treaty represented less than five per cent of the Soviet and American nuclear arsenals. However, in signing it Moscow accepted 'asymmetric agreement as well as extensive and intrusive verification policies'. Ekedahl and Goodman, *The Wars of Eduard Shevardnadze*, p. 117.

40   Towell, 'Treaty–Interpretation Issue Complicating INF Approval', *CQWR*, p. 868.

41 Towell, Pat, 'Conciliation Colors the Pre-Summit Picture', *CQWR*, Vol. 45, No. 49, December 5 1987, p. 2967.

42 'Reagan Television Address Caps Summit Week', *CQWR*, Vol. 45, No. 50, December 12 1987, p. 3063.

43 Towell with Mills, 'INF Treaty: Star Vehicle', *CQWR*, p. 197.

44 Ibid., p. 193.; Towell, 'Senate Now Turns Scrutiny to INF – and Beyond', *CQWR*, pp. 149, 153.

45 Lamar, Jr., Jacob, V., Reported by Laurence L. Barrett and Alessandra Stanley/Washington, 'An Offer They Can Refuse: Nearly Everyone Likes the Arms Deal But the G.O.P. Conservatives', *Time*, Vol. 130, No. 24, December 14 1987, p. 16; Garthoff, *Great*, p. 325 59n.

46 'Joint Communique Lays Out Talking Points', *CQWR*, Vol. 45, No. 50, December 12 1987, p. 3064.

47 'Remarks by Reagan and Gorbachev at White House Welcome Ceremony', *NYT*, December 9 1987, p. A20.; Transcript, President Reagan, 'The Signing: 'Universal Significance for Mankind'', *NYT*, December 9 1987, p. A21.

48 'Remarks by Reagan and Gorbachev at White House Welcome Ceremony', *NYT*, p. A20.

49 Transcript, Gorbachev, 'After the Signing: "Persevering" and "History"', *NYT*, December 9 1987, p. A22.

50 Barringer, Felicity, 'In Moscow, Heart Felt Joy for Treaty', *NYT*, December 10 1987, p. A20.

51 Tagliabue, John, 'From East Europe, Applause is Heavy', *NYT*, December 10 1987, p. A20.

52 Schmemann, Serge, 'West Germans Greet Arms Treaty With Relief and Anxiety for the Future', *NYT*, December 10 1987, p. A20.

53 Painton, Frederick, Reported by William Rademakers and Christpher Redman/Paris, 'Hope and Fear: The Summit: Sighs of Relief – and Trepidation – Across the Atlantic', *Time*, Vol. 130, No. 25, December 21 1987, pp. 18-19.

54 All information from ibid., p. 19.

55 Gargan, Edward A., 'From Chinese, Tempered Praise', *NYT*, December 10 1987, p. A20.; For the reaction to the INF, see also Sciolino, Elaine, 'NATO Foreign Ministers Praise Treaty and Urge Senate Approval', *NYT*, December 12 1987, p. 10.; Schmenann, Serge, 'Gorbachev Stops in Berlin; Gets a Triumphal Welcome', *NYT*, December 12 1987, p. 10.

56 Shevardnadze, *The Future Belongs to Freedom*, p. 92.

57 Ibid.

58 Shultz, George P., *Turmoil and Triumph: My Years As Secretary Of State*, New York, Charles Scribner's Sons, 1993, p. 1012.; For information on the INF agreement, see Gorbachev, Mikhail, *Memoirs*, London, Bantam Books, 1997, pp. 570-573, 584.; For the Washington summit, December 1987, see Gorbachev, *Memoirs*, pp. 570-575.; For the Washington summit, see Ekedahl and Goodman, *The Wars of Eduard Shevardnadze*, pp. 116-117.

59 Towell, Pat, 'Old Adversaries Turn to Pragmatic Diplomacy', *CQWR*, Vol. 45, No. 50, December 12 1987, p. 3023.

60 Felton, John, 'Afghanistan, Human Rights: Reagan, Gorbachev Agree on Little More Than Good Will', *CQWR*, Vol. 45, No. 50, December 12 1987, p. 3029.; 'Joint Communique Lays Out Talking Points', *CQWR*, Vol. 45, No. 50, December 12 1987, p. 3065.

61   Shipler, David K., 'Protests Today Point to Rights as Summit Issue', *NYT*, December 6 1987, p. A1.

62   'Summit a "Clear Success" Reagan Says ... But Gorbachev Says More Work Ahead', *CQWR*, Vol. 45, No. 50, December 12 1987, p. 3066.

63   Roberts, Steven V., 'Reagan Finds US–Soviet Ties Now Far More Candid', *NYT*, December 11 1987, p. A23.

64   Felton, 'Afghanistan, Human Rights: Reagan, Gorbachev Agree on Little More Than Good Will', *CQWR*, p. 3029; 'Joint Communique Lays Out Talking Points', *CQWR*, p. 3066.

65   'Joint Communique Lays Out Talking Points', *CQWR*, p. 3066.

66   Felton, 'Afghanistan, Human Rights', *CQWR*, p. 3028.

67   Ibid.; see also Shipler, 'Strategic Arms Cuts and Afghan Pullout', *NYT*, p. A18.

68   All information from Felton, 'Afghanistan, Human Rights', *CQWR*, pp. 3028-3029.

69   All information from ibid., p. 3028.

70   'Joint Communique Lays Out Talking Points', *CQWR*, p. 3066.

71   Roberts, 'Reagan Finds US–Soviet Ties', *NYT*, p. A23.

72   'Excerpts from Gorbachev News Conference: 'A New Phase in Relations'', *NYT*, December 11 1987, p. A24.; Taubman, Philip, 'Gorbachev Extols Talks on Leaving: He Calls Meeting a "Major Event in World Politics"', *NYT*, December 11 1987, p. A1.

73   Apple, Jr., R.W., 'Reagan Trip is Due: No New Key Agreement is Reached as Russian Ends His US Visit', *NYT*, December 11 1987, p. A1.; Mikhail Gorbachev felt that 'there is a growing desire in American society for improved Soviet–American relations'. Shultz, *Turmoil*, p. 1014.; To quote George Shultz, the results of the Washington summit 'were a tribute to the persistent effort of Ronald Reagan to stick by his basic objectives, to maintain our strength and the cohesion of our alliances, and to be willing to recognise an opportunity for a good deal and a changed situation when he saw one'. Shultz, *Turmoil*, p. 1015.; For Shultz's account of the Washington summit, see Chapter 46, 'The Long Road to a Washington Summit', Shultz, *Turmoil*, pp. 982-1015.

74   'Exchange of Farewells: "Common Ground" and "Justified Hopes"', *NYT*, December 11 1987, p. A22.

75   Thatcher, Margaret, *The Downing Street Years*, London, Harper Collins, 1993, p. 774.

76   Dowd, Maureen, 'Washington Summit Song is Off Key for Weinberger', *NYT*, December 12 1987, pp. A1, 9.

77   'But Will We Still Love Him Tomorrow?', *USNWR*, Vol. 103, No. 25, December 21 1987, p. 21.

78   Reagan, *An American Life*, p. 701.

79   Jackson, William, D., 'Soviet Reassessment of Ronald Reagan, 1985–1988', *Political Science Quarterly*, Vol. 113, No. 4, Winter 1998–99, p. 639.

80   For the ABM Treaty and the SDI, see the prepared statement of Abraham D. Sofaer, submitted at the October 30 1985 Congressional hearing, 'Prepared Statement of Abraham D. Sofaer, Legal Adviser, US Department of State', in 'Strategic Defense Initiative', *Hearings Before the Subcommittee on Strategic and Theater Nuclear Forces of the Committee of Armed Services, United States Senate*, Ninety-Ninth Congress, First Session, October 30, November 6, 21, December 3, 5 1985, Washington, US Government Printing Office, 1986, pp. 423-425.; For the interpretation of the ABM Treaty, see 'Strategic Defense Initiative', *Hearings Before the Subcommittee on Strategic and Theater Nuclear Forces of the Committee on Armed Services, United States Senate*, Ninety-Ninth Congress, First Session, October 30, November 6, 21, December 3, 5 1985, Washington, US Government Printing Office, 1986, pp. 92, 93, 95.; For the Congressional debate regarding the interpretation of the ABM Treaty, see

'Statement of Hon. Richard N. Perle, Assistant Secretary of Defense (International Security Policy)', in 'Strategic Defense Initiative', *Hearings Before the Subcommittee on Strategic and Theater Nuclear Forces of the Committee on Armed Services, United States Senate*, Ninety-Ninth Congress, First Session, October 30, November 6, 21, December 3, 5 1985, Washington, US Government Printing Office, 1986, pp. 73-74.

81 Gordon, Michael R., 'How the US and Soviet Officials Agreed to Disagree on "Star Wars"', *NYT*, December 12 1987, p. 8.

82 Apple, Jr, R.W., 'Reagan and Gorbachev Report Progress on Long-Range Arms: Mute Quarrel over "Star Wars": Reagan Trip is Due: No New Key Agreement is Reached as Russian Ends His US Visit', *NYT*, December 11 1987, p. A1.

83 Gordon, Michael R., 'Avoiding the Obstacles: US and Soviet Put Aside Thorniest Issues and End Summit Talks on a Positive Note', *NYT*, December 11 1987, p. A1.

84 Taubman, Philip, 'Russian Gains Room to Bargain at Home Through Careful Maneuvers in US', *NYT*, December 12 1987, p. 9.

85 Apple, Jr., 'No New Key Agreement is Reached', *NYT*, p. A22.

86 Roberts, Steven V., 'President Upbeat Over Relationship With Gorbachev', *NYT*, December 12 1987, p. 8.

87 Gordon, Michael R., 'How the US and Soviet Officials Agreed to Disagree on "Star Wars"', *NYT*, December 12 1987, p. A1.

88 Apple, Jr., 'No New Key Agreement is Reached', *NYT*, p. A22.

89 Ibid.

90 'Joint Communique Lays Out Talking Points', *CQWR*, p. 3065.

91 Gordon, 'Avoiding the Obstacles', *NYT*, p. A25.; Towell, Pat, 'On SDI and Cutting Long-Range Missiles … A Combination of Punting and Progress', *CQWR*, Vol. 45, No. 50, December 12 1987, p. 3026.; In his memoirs, Mikhail Gorbachev contended that progress was made during the Washington summit on strategic arms control. However one problem remained: President Reagan's Strategic Defence Initiative. Gorbachev, *Memoirs*, pp. 573-574.; For information on the discussions regarding the limits imposed by the ABM Treaty on SDI testing, see Gorbachev, *Memoirs*, p. 574.

92 Gordon, 'How the US and Soviet Officials Agreed to Disagree', *NYT*, p. 8.

93 Gordon, 'Avoiding the Obstacles', *NYT*, p. A25.

94 'Excerpts From Gorbachev News Conference: "A New Phase in Relations"', *NYT*, p. A24.

95 Gordon, 'Avoiding the Obstacles', *NYT*, p. A25.

96 Ibid.; Gordon, 'How the US and Soviet Officials Agreed to Disagree', *NYT*, p. 8.

97 Towell, 'On SDI and Cutting Long-Range Missiles … A Combination', *CQWR*, p. 3026.; For the role of the SDI at the Washington summit, see Talbott, Strobe, *The Master of the Game: Paul Nitze and the Nuclear Peace*, New York, Vintage Books, 1989, pp. 363-368.

98 All information taken from Gordon, 'How the US and Soviet Officials Agreed to Disagree', *NYT*, p. 8.; Trewhitt, Henry, with Robert Kaylor, Kenneth T. Walsh, Peter Ross Range and Rene Riley, 'The Big Problems Restarting START', *USNWR*, Vol. 103, No. 25, December 21 1987, p. 26.

99 All information taken from Gordon, 'How the US and Soviet Officials Agreed', *NYT*, p. 8.

100 All information From Trewhitt, 'The Big Problems Restarting START', *USNWR*, p. 27.

101 Risse-Kappen, Thomas, 'Did "Peace Through Strength" End the Cold War? Lessons from the INF Treaty', *International Security*, Vol. 16, No. 1, Summer 1991, p. 173.

102 Ibid., p. 173.; For the factors that Mike Bowker highlights as the reasons why Gorbachev made the SDI–INF delink, see Bowker, Mike, *Russian Foreign Policy and the End of the Cold War*, Dartmouth, Aldershot, 1997, pp. 83-84.
103 By Budiansky, Stephen and Henry Trewhitt with Peter Ross Range and Maureen Santini, 'On to the Summit, as Star Wars Waits', *USNWR*, Vol. 103, No. 19, November 9 1987, p. 13.
104 'Start at the Washington Summit', *Survey of Current Affairs*, Vol. 18, No. 3, March 1988, p. 102.; Nitze, Paul H., *From Hiroshima to Glasnost: At the Centre of Decision Making – A Memoir*, London, Weidenfeld and Nicolson, 1986, p. 419.
105 That Gorbachev decided on an asymmetric response is promulgated by Garthoff, *Great*, pp. 764-5.; Yevgeni Velikhov, in O'Neill, Bill, 'Fear and Laughter in the Kremlin', *New Scientist*, 20 March 1993, p. 36.
106 Dunbabin, J.P.D., *The Cold War: The Great Powers and Their Allies*, London, Longman, 1994, p. 185.
107 All information taken from Shipler, 'Strategic Arms Cuts and Afghan Pullout', *NYT*, p. A18.
108 By Church, George J., Reported by David Beckwith/Santa Barbara and James O. Jackson/Moscow, 'The Odd Couple: Will Reagan and Gorbachev Come Up With a Surprise or Two?', *Time*, Vol. 130, No. 23, December 7 1987, p. 17.
109 Gordon, '"Star Wars" Curbs Not Summit Issue', p. A1.
110 Ibid., p. A1.
111 Apple, Jr., 'No New Key Agreement is Reached', *NYT*, p. A22.
112 Gordon, Michael R., 'How to Destroy the 2,611 Missiles: Treaty Details Ways but US Withholds Data on Sites', *NYT*, December 9 1987, p. A21.
113 Trewhitt, 'The Big Problems Restarting START', *USNWR*, p. 27.
114 'But Will We Still Love Him Tomorrow?', *USNWR*, p. 21.
115 Trewhitt, 'Big Problems Restarting START', *USNWR*, p. 27.
116 Ibid.
117 Trewhitt, Henry with Robert Kaylor in Washington, Robin Knight in London and Jeff Trimble in Moscow, 'Arms Control: Is it Good for us?', *USNWR*, December 14 1987, p. 26.
118 'But Will We Still Love Him Tomorrow?', *USNWR*, p. 21.
119 Trewhitt, 'Big Problems Restarting START', *USNWR*, p. 27.
120 Such evaluation was promulgated by Sam Nunn, (the Senate's leading agent on arms control), Chairman of the Armed Services Committee. See 'Conversation with Senator Sam Nunn: Renegotiate the ABM Treaty', in Trewhitt, 'Arms Control: Is It Good for us?', *USNWR*, p. 31.
121 Isaacson, Walter, 'We Meet Again: Why All the World Loves a Summit', *Time*, Vol. 130, No. 24, December 14 1987, p. 7.
122 Roberts, Steven V., 'Hopes Grow for Progress on Long-Range Arms Pact', *NYT*, December 6 1987, p. 24.; By Sancton, Thomas A., Reported by James O. Jackson with Gorbachev, Barrett Seaman and Strobe Talbott/Washington, 'The Spirit of Washington: With Big Smiles and Some Frustrations, Detente Makes a Comeback', *Time*, Vol. 130, No. 25, December 21 1987, pp. 9-10.
123 Roberts, 'Hopes Grow for Progress', *NYT*, p. 24.
124 Raines, Howell, 'In Stopover to See Thatcher, Celebration Rules the Air', *NYT*, December 8 1987, p. A16.
125 Gordon, 'Russian Decision is Aimed at Making Progress on Pact', *NYT*, p. A1.
126 'Excerpts From Gorbachev News Conference: "A New Phase in Relations"', *NYT*, p. A24.

127 Ibid.
128 Taubman, Philip, 'Russian Gains Room to Bargain at Home Through Careful Maneuvers in US', *NYT*, December 12 1987, p. 9.
129 Perle, Richard, 'The Keystone Kops of Arms Control', *USNWR*, June 6 1988, p. 22.; For details on the INF Treaty, including the details yet to be settled, see Towell, Pat, 'Breakthrough Reached on Euromissiles Treaty', *CQWR*, Vol. 45, No. 38, September 19 1987, p. 2233.; For a report on the summit, see Towell, Pat, 'Conciliation Colors the Pre-Summit Picture: But Reagan Sets Tone of Tough Pragmatism', *CQWR*, Vol. 45, No. 49, December 5 1987, pp. 2967, 2970-2971.; For the INF in Congress, see Towell, Pat, 'Before the Ink Is Dry, Key Senate Players ... Are Preparing For Debate on INF Treaty', *CQWR*, Vol. 45, No. 49, December 5 1987, pp. 2968-2969.
130 Bowker, *Russian Foreign Policy and the End of the Cold War*, p. 83.
131 'Reagan Previews US–Soviet Summit', *CQWR*, Vol. 45, No. 50, December 12 1987, p. 3086.
132 Towell, Pat, 'INF Pact to Sweeten Reagan–Gorbachev Summit', *CQWR*, Vol. 45, No. 48, November 28 1987, p. 2927.; That 'The Strategic Defense Initiative was not a 'bargaining chip'', see Reagan, *An American Life*, p. 608. See also p. 666.; That 'The SDI held too much potential for the security of mankind to be traded away at the negotiating table', see Reagan, *An American Life*, p. 608.; That Ronald Reagan would not trade away the SDI, also see ibid., p. 628.; Reagan's diary entry on September 11 1985 (before the Geneva summit, November 19–20 1985), was 'I won't trade our SDI off for some Soviet offer of weapon reductions'. Ibid.; That the SDI is not a bargaining chip, see the following: Berke, Richard L., 'Reagan to Press Senate on Treaty', *NYT*, November 25 1987, p. A13.; Brinkley, Joel, 'Reagan Reaffirms "Star Wars" Stand', *NYT*, November 24 1987, p. A14.; George Shultz, in his memoirs, writes that the SDI 'in fact proved to be the ultimate bargaining chip. And we played it for all it was worth'. Shultz, *Turmoil*, p. 264.
133 'Reagan UN Speech Focuses on World Peace', *CQWR*, Vol. 45, No. 39, September 26 1987, p. 2328.
134 'Reagan Television Address Caps Summit Week', *CQWR*, Vol. 45, No. 50, December 12 1987, p. 3063.
135 All information taken from Brand, David, Reported by Dick Thompson/Los Alamos and Bruce Van Voorst/Washington, '"Star Wars" Hollow Promise: Funding Cuts and Technical Delays Beset SDI', *Time*, December 7 1987, pp. 19-20.; The space-based chemical laser was intended to 'shore up Phase I and overcome possible countermeasures' to it. For more information on the chemical laser – 'Zenith Star', see Tammen, Ronald L., James T. Bruce, and Bruce W. MacDonald, 'Star Wars After Five Years: The Decisive Points', *Arms Control Today*, July/August 1988, p. 5.; However, the 1984 Fletcher study 'recommended against deployment of the chemical laser in the 1998–2000 time period'. Tammen, Bruce, and MacDonald, 'Star Wars After Five Years: The Decisive Points', p. 5.; That the US planned to test Zenith Star, and for information on the Zenith Star test, see Sanger, David E., 'Pentagon Plans First Laser Test in Space in 1990s', *NYT*, November 25 1987, p. A13.
136 All information taken from Brand, David, Reported by Dick Thompson/Los Alamos and Bruce Van Voorst/Washington, '"Star Wars" Hollow Promise: Funding Cuts and Technical Delays Beset SDI', *Time*, p. 20.
137 Towell, Pat, 'No Clear Winners, Losers: Administration, Hill Revisit Debate Over ABM Pact, SDI', *CQWR*, Vol. 45, No. 7, February 14 1987, p. 274.; For information on NSDD-192, 'The Strategic Defense Initiative (SDI) Program and US Interpretation of the Anti-Ballistic Missile (ABM) Treaty', (Classified), October 11 1985, see Simpson,

Christopher, *National Security Directives of The Reagan and Bush Administration's: The Declassified History of US Political and Military Policy 1981–1991*, San Francisco, Westview Press, 1995, pp. 460-462.; For NSDD-261, 'Consultations on Adoption of the 'Broad' Interpretation of the Anti-Ballistic Missile (ABM) Treaty', (Secret), February 18 1987, see Simpson, *National Security Directives of the Reagan and Bush Administration's*, pp. 734-735.; That it was worked out by the Reagan administration that from a legal point of view, the broad interpretation of the ABM Treaty was well justified, but that the SDI would be developed within the traditional narrow interpretation, see Dobrynin, Anatoly, *In Confidence: Moscow's Ambassador to America's Six Cold War Presidents 1962–86*, New York, Random House, 1995, p. 579.

[138] Towell, 'No Clear Winners, Losers: Administration, Hill Revisit Debate Over ABM Pact, SDI', *CQWR*, p. 271.

[139] Ibid., pp. 272-273.

[140] Towell, 'Nunn Blasts Administration on ABM Treaty', *CQWR*, Vol. 45, No. 11, March 14 1987, p. 457.

[141] Ibid.

[142] 'The Legal Issues in the ABM Treaty … Fuel Debate Over the SDI Program', *CQWR*, Vol. 45, No. 7, February 14 1987, p. 272.

[143] Towell, 'Nunn Blasts Administration on ABM Treaty', *CQWR*, p. 457.

[144] 'The Legal Issues in the ABM Treaty', *CQWR*, p. 272.

[145] Towell, 'Nunn Blasts Administration on ABM Treaty', *CQWR*, p. 457.

[146] 'The Legal Issues in the ABM Treaty', *CQWR,* p. 272.; 'Nunn Blasts Administration on ABM Treaty', *CQWR*, p. 457.

[147] Towell, 'Nunn Blasts Administration on ABM Treaty', *CQWR*, p. 457.

[148] Ibid.; 'The Legal Issues in the ABM Treaty', *CQWR*, pp. 272-273.

[149] 'The Legal Issues in the ABM Treaty', *CQWR*, pp. 272-273.

[150] Towell, 'Nunn Blasts Administration on ABM Treaty', *CQWR*, p. 458.

[151] Perle, Richard, 'The Political Trials of SDI', *USNWR*, Vol. 103, No. 11, September 14 1987, p. 45.

[152] Towell, 'Nunn Blasts Administration on ABM Treaty', *CQWR*, p. 458.

[153] Towell, Pat, 'ABM Debate: Aides Defend the Reagan View', *CQWR*, Vol. 45, No. 13, March 28 1987, pp. 558-559.

[154] Ibid., p. 560.

[155] Ibid.

[156] Ibid., p. 560. See also p. 558.

[157] Ibid., pp. 558-559.

[158] Ibid, p. 559.

[159] Perle, 'The Political Trials of SDI', *USNWR*, p. 46.; For Richard Perle's rebuttal of Sam Nunn's arguments, see ibid., pp. 45-46.

[160] Richard Perle argued that it was the Soviets who rejected US calls to ban future space-based ABM weapons. Towell, 'ABM Debate: Aides Defend the Reagan View', *CQWR*, p. 558.

[161] Towell, 'ABM Debate: Aides Defend', *CQWR*, p. 559.

[162] Ibid., p. 558.

[163] Towell, Pat, 'Senate Deals Reagan a Major Defeat on SDI', *CQWR*, Vol. 45, No. 38, September 19 1987, p. 2229.; For Pentagon officials' disclosure on the need for a 'broad' interpretation, see Gordon, Michael R., with John H. Cushmann Jr., 'Pressure Rises for US Flexibility on "Star Wars"', *NYT*, May 25 1988, pp. A1, A4.

[164] Towell, 'ABM Debate: Aides Defend', *CQWR*, p. 559.

[165] Towell, Pat, 'House Panel Deals Setbacks to SDI Program', *CQWR*, Vol. 45, No. 14, April 4 1987, p. 614.

[166] Ibid., pp. 614-615.

[167] Ibid., p. 615.

[168] Towell, 'Senate Deals Reagan a Major Defeat on SDI', *CQWR*, p. 2229.

[169] Towell, 'House Panel Deals Setbacks to SDI Program', *CQWR*, p. 615.

[170] Ibid.

[171] Ibid.

[172] Ibid., p. 614.

[173] Towell, Pat, 'House Deals Reagan Defeat on SDI, MX Missile', *CQWR*, Vol. 46, No. 19, May 7 1988, p. 1207.; For the proposed reductions in SDI, see ibid., p. 1209.

[174] Towell, Pat, 'Senate Panel Lays Groundwork For Showdown on "Star Wars"', *CQWR*, Vol. 45, No. 19, May 9 1987, p. 904.

[175] Towell, Pat, 'House Slashes President's SDI Request … In Move To Slow Push for Deployment', *CQWR*, Vol. 45, No. 20, May 16 1987, p. 974.

[176] All information from ibid.

[177] Ibid., p. 975.; For information on the SDI tests, including the Delta Star test, the BEAR (Beam Experiment Aboard Rocket) Test and the Kinetic Kill Vehicle, see MacDonald, Bruce W., 'Lost in Space: SDI Struggles Through Its Sixth Year', *Arms Control Today*, September 1989, p. 25.

[178] Towell, Pat, 'House Slashes President's SDI Request … In Move To Slow Push for Deployment', *CQWR*, p. 975.; For another reference on the House and the SDI, see Hook, Janet, 'Parliamentary War Erupts Over Defense Bill', *CQWR*, Vol. 45, No. 20, May 16 1987, p. 977.; For information on the Accidental Launch Protection System (ALPS), see MacDonald, Bruce W., 'Lost in Space: SDI Struggles Through Its Sixth Year', pp. 22-23.

[179] Towell, Pat, 'Dispute Over the ABM Treaty Stalls Defense Bill in Senate', *CQWR*, Vol. 45, No. 21, May 23 1987, p. 1064.

[180] Towell, 'Senate Deals Reagan a Major Defeat on SDI', *CQWR*, p. 2228.

[181] Ibid.

[182] Towell, Pat, 'Critical Showdown over SDI Under Way on Capitol Hill', *CQWR*, Vol. 45, No. 20, May 16 1987, p. 978.

[183] 'Weinberger Leaves Reagan Administration After 7 Years', *NYT*, November 18 1987, p. A1.

[184] All information from Halloran, Richard, 'Weinberger Departs to the Cannon's Roar', *NYT*, p. B5.

[185] Ibid.

[186] Ibid.

[187] Rasky, Susan F., 'Shultz Urges Vote on Missile Treaty in Time for Summit', *NYT*, May 24 1988, pp. A1, A13.

[188] For details on the Soviet demonstration (the destruction by the military of a launching vehicle for Soviet SS-20 missiles) staged to show how the Soviet Union plans to comply with the INF Treaty, see Taubman, Philip, 'In the Sparks From a Soviet Torch, a First Whack at Destroying Arms', *NYT*, June 4 1988, pp. A1, 6.

[189] Towell, Pat, 'Putting a Spin on the Treaty: Three Options', *CQWR*, Vol. 46, No. 4, January 23 1988, p. 152.

[190] Towell, 'Senate Now Turns Scrutiny to INF – and Beyond', *CQWR*, p. 149.

[191] Towell, Pat, 'INF Treaty Shows Strength in Senate Mark Up', *CQWR*, Vol. 46, No. 13, March 26 1988, p. 800.; For details, see Towell, Pat, 'Old Battle Complicates Treaty's Hill Journey', *CQWR*, Vol. 46, No. 13, March 26 1988, p. 802.

192 Towell, 'Senate Now Turns Scrutiny to INF – and Beyond', *CQWR*, p. 153.; For another reference for this, see Towell, Pat, 'Treaty Interpretation Issue Complicating INF Approval', *CQWR*, Vol. 46, No. 14, April 2 1988, p. 868.

193 Towell, Pat, 'Senator Nunn Remains Concerned: "Futuristic" Weapons Prove a Sticky INF Issue', *CQWR*, Vol. 46, No. 14, April 2 1988, p. 871.

194 Towell, with Mills, 'INF Treaty: Star Vehicle for Political Agendas', *CQWR*, p. 192.

195 Towell, Pat, 'INF Treaty Shows Strength in Senate Mark Up', *CQWR*, Vol. 46, No. 13, March 26 1988, p. 801.

196 By Hook, Janet, Macon Morehouse and Pat Towell, 'Senate Votes 93–5 to Approve Ratification of the INF Treaty', *CQWR*, Vol. 46, No. 22, May 28 1988, pp. 1431, 1434.

197 Towell, Pat, 'Nunn Suggests Redirecting the SDI Program', *CQWR*, Vol. 46. No. 4, January 23 1988, p. 154.

198 Ibid.

199 Towell, Pat with John Felton, 'Senate Debates Defense Authorization Measure', *CQWR*, Vol. 46, No. 20, May 14 1988, p. 1301.

200 Ibid.

201 Morehouse, Macon, 'House Approves Defense Bill, Arms Provisions', *CQWR*, Vol. 46, No. 20, May 14 1988, p. 1308.

202 Ibid.; For information on the SDI's 'Phase 1' deployment, see Tammen, Bruce, and MacDonald, 'Star Wars After Five Years: The Decisive Points', pp. 3-7.; For information on 'Phase 1', see MacDonald, 'Lost in Space: SDI Struggles Through Its Sixth Year', pp. 21-26.; It was believed that even if a way could be found to 'lift Phase I into space at a reasonable cost' it would be 'obsolete the day it is deployed'. It is stated that the 'likely Soviet use of innovative tactics, offensive proliferation, and other active and passive countermeasures will reduce Phase I effectiveness dramatically'. Tammen, Bruce and MacDonald, 'Star Wars After Five Years: The Decisive Points', p. 4. See also p. 6.; 'One well-known countermeasure is the fast-burn booster ... A second countermeasure facing Phase I is the release of decoys by Soviet offensive missiles in midcourse flight'. Tammen, Bruce and MacDonald, 'Star Wars After Five Years: The Decisive Points', p. 4.

203 Trewhitt, Henry and Peter Ross Range in Moscow, 'A Triumph of Symbols: Process is now the Substance of Superpower Relations', *USNWR*, Vol. 104, No. 23, June 13 1988, pp. 40-41.

204 Gordon, Michael R., and John H. Cushman Jr., 'Pressure Rises for US Flexibility on "Star Wars"', *NYT*, May 25 1988, p. A1.; For the discussions leading to the Moscow summit, and the issues concerned, see Church, George J., Reported by Ken Olsen/Moscow and Bruce Van Voorst/Washington, 'The Road to Moscow', *Time*, Vol. 131, No. 14, April 4 1988, pp. 28-30.

205 Gordon and Cushman Jr., 'Pressure Rises for US Flexibility on "Star Wars"', *NYT*, p. A1.

206 First quote by author, Roberts, Steven V., 'Reagan in Finland to Rest Before Summit', *NYT*, May 26 1988, p. A12.; For Garthoff quote see ibid.

207 Gordon, Michael R., 'Outlook for Summit: Not Much Chance of Breakthrough on Arms Accords', *NYT*, May 26 1988, p. A12.; For the US ideas and US–Soviet disputes regarding the strategic arms accords, see ibid.

208 Apart from the difference with the Soviets, there were differences within the administration itself regarding the issue. Gordon, Michael R., 'US–Soviet Talks Fail to Complete New Arms Accord', *NYT*, May 29 1988, p. 18.

209 Felton, John, 'Moscow Summit: Upbeat Tone, Limited Results', *CQWR*, Vol. 46, No. 23, June 4 1988, p. 1514.; For the outlook for the strategic arms treaty prior to the

summit, see Gordon, Michael R., 'Outlook for Summit: Not Much Chance of Breakthrough on Arms Accords', *NYT*, May 26 1988, p. A12.; For figures of the US and Soviet nuclear arsenals, see Gordon, Michael R., 'US–Soviet Talks Fail to Complete New Arms Accord', *NYT*, May 29 1988, pp. A1, 18.; For the strategic arms discussions, see Gordon, Michael R., 'Talks on Strategic Arms Treaty Move Ahead, But Major Problems Remain', *NYT*, May 30 1988, p. 6.; Gordon, Michael R., 'Signing of Two Modest Arms Accords is Expected', *NYT*, May 31 1988, p. A12.; Gordon, Michael R., 'Hope, But No Promises', *NYT*, June 2 1988, pp. A1, A17.

[210] Gordon, 'US–Soviet Talks Fail to Complete New Arms Accord', *NYT*, p. A18.; Felton, 'Moscow Summit: Upbeat Tone, Limited Results', *CQWR*, p. 1514.

[211] Gordon, 'US–Soviet Talks Fail to Complete New Arms Accord', *NYT*, pp. 1, A18.

[212] Gordon, 'Talks on Strategic Arms Treaty Move Ahead', *NYT*, p. 6. See also Gordon, 'US–Soviet Talks Fail to Complete New Arms Accord', *NYT*, p. A18.; For details of the Soviet proposal, see Gordon, 'Talks on Strategic Arms Treaty Move Ahead, but Major Problems Remain', *NYT*, p. 6.

[213] Gordon, 'Signing of Two Modest Arms Accords is Expected', *NYT*, p. A12.

[214] Gordon, 'Talks on Strategic Arms Treaty Move Ahead, but Major Problems Remain', *NYT*, p. 6.

[215] Felton, 'Moscow Summit: Upbeat Tone, Limited Results', *CQWR*, p. 1514.

[216] Gordon, 'Hope, But No Promises', *NYT*, p. A1.

[217] 'Joint Document Underlines Progress, Good Relations', *CQWR*, June 4 1988, Vol. 46, No. 23, p. 1546.; Felton, 'Moscow Summit: Upbeat Tone', *CQWR*, p. 1514.

[218] Gordon, 'Signing of Two Modest Arms Accords is Expected', *NYT*, p. A12.

[219] Gordon, 'Hope, But No Promises', *NYT*, p. A17.

[220] Felton, 'Moscow Summit: Upbeat Tone', *CQWR*, p. 1514.

[221] Ibid., p. 1514.

[222] Ibid.; Gordon, 'Hope, But No Promises', *NYT*, p. A17.; Gordon, 'Signing of Two Modest Arms Accords is Expected', *NYT*, p. A12.

[223] Felton, 'Moscow Summit: Upbeat Tone', *CQWR*, p. 1514.; Gordon, 'Hope, But No Promises', *NYT*, p. A17.; Gordon, 'Signing of Two Modest Arms Accords is Expected', *NYT*, p. A12.

[224] Felton, 'Moscow Summit: Upbeat Tone', *CQWR*, p. 1514. For details, see both Gordon references above.

[225] Roberts, Steven V., 'Reagan Aides Call Human Rights "Agenda Item No. 1" at the Summit', *NYT*, May 29 1988, p. A1.

[226] Felton, 'Moscow Summit: Upbeat Tone', *CQWR*, p. 1514.

[227] Ibid.; Taubman, Philip, 'Reagan Presses Gorbachev on Church and Civil Rights; "Sermonizing" Annoys Hosts: Criticism is Sharp', *NYT*, May 31 1988, p. A14.

[228] Felton, 'Moscow Summit: Upbeat Tone', *CQWR*, p. 1514.

[229] Roberts, Steven V., 'A Mighty Russian Pulpit for Reagan', *NYT*, May 31 1988, p. A13.

[230] Keller, Bill, 'An Expectant Air Hits Muscovites Who Also Face Struggles at Home', *NYT*, May 29 1988, p. 14.

[231] Rosenbaum, David E., 'Reagan Widely Chided on Soviet Rights Issue', *NYT*, June 3 1988, p. A10.

[232] 'Reagan in New Tack on Rights in Soviet', *NYT*, June 4 1988, p. 6.

[233] Felton, 'Moscow Summit: Upbeat Tone', *CQWR*, p. 1515.; See also Barringer, Felicity, 'Soviet Warns Reagan About Seeing Dissidents', *NYT*, May 27 1988, p. A8.

[234] Felton, 'Moscow Summit: Upbeat Tone', *CQWR*, p. 1515.; 'Joint Document Underlines Progress, Good Relations', *CQWR*, p. 1547.; See also Gordon, Michael R., 'US and Soviet Agree to Widen Student Exchange', *NYT*, June 1 1988, pp. A1, A15.

235 Ibid.
236 'Excerpts From the President's Talk to Artists and Students', *NYT*, June 1 1988, p. A12.
237 Roberts, Steven V., 'President Charms Students, But His Ideas Lack Converts', *NYT*, June 1 1988, p. A13.
238 Roberts, Steven V., 'Summit Wasn't the World Series, US Says, But Was Still a Success', *NYT*, June 3 1988, p. A1.
239 All information from 'Joint Document Underlines Progress, Good Relations', *CQWR*, p. 1547.
240 Gorbachev, *Memoirs*, p. 582.
241 Felton, 'Moscow Summit: Upbeat Tone', *CQWR*, p. 1515.
242 Ibid.
243 Gorbachev, *Memoirs*, p. 591.
244 Felton, 'Moscow Summit: Upbeat Tone', *CQWR*, p. 1515.
245 Roberts, 'Summit Wasn't the World Series', *NYT*, p. A1.
246 'Transcripts of Reagan and Gorbachev Remarks', *NYT*, May 30 1988, p. 6.
247 Roberts, Steven V., 'Reagan Says He Was Moved By Contacts With Russians', *NYT*, June 2 1988, p. A16.; See also 'Reagan Gives Press Conference in Moscow', *CQWR*, Vol. 46, No. 23, June 4 1988, pp. 1542-1545.
248 Mikhail Gorbachev, in his memoirs, stated that the Soviets wanted Ronald Reagan's visit to Moscow 'to become another milestone marking the end of the Cold War, instead of a mere symbolic act of friendship'. Gorbachev, *Memoirs*, p. 581.; For the Moscow summit, see ibid., pp. 584-592.
249 'Gorbachev's Words: "Soviet–US Relations on Healthy Track"', *NYT*, June 2 1988, p. A18.
250 Ibid.
251 'Gorbachev and Reagan Toasts: "Man's Survival" and "Peace and Freedom"', *NYT*, May 31 1988, p. A14.
252 Taubman, Philip, 'Summitry and Beyond: Gorbachev Used Reagan's Visit to Bolster His Position Before Big Party Conference', *NYT*, June 3 1988, p. A11.
253 Ibid.
254 Ibid, p. A1.
255 'Excerpts From President's Address on US–Soviet Relations', *NYT*, June 4 1988, p. 6.
256 Roberts, Steven V., 'US–Soviet Tension is Now Receding, Reagan Declares', *NYT*, June 4 1988, pp. A1, 6.
257 'Reagan's Words: Differences Continue to Recede', *NYT*, June 2 1988, p. A16.
258 Roberts, 'Summit Wasn't the World Series', *NYT*, p. A1.
259 Ibid.
260 Ibid, p. A11.; Felton, 'Moscow Summit: Upbeat Tone', *CQWR*, p. 1513.
261 Felton, 'Moscow Summit: Upbeat Tone', *CQWR*, p. 1513.
262 Ibid.; For the excerpts from the joint US–Soviet statement issued with information on arms control, nuclear and space talks, and nuclear testing, see 'Joint Document: "Realistic Approach" to Reducing Nuclear Risk', *NYT*, June 2 1988, p. A17.
263 Tagliabue, John, 'East Bloc Reacts to Summit: Much Praise, Some Criticism', *NYT*, June 3 1988, p. A10.
264 Ibid.
265 Ibid.
266 Gargan, Edward A., 'China Says Little About the Summit: Only Foreign Minister Offers Any Comment, and He is Not Too Enthusiastic', *NYT*, June 4 1988, p. 6.
267 Felton, 'Moscow Summit: Upbeat Tone', *CQWR*, p. 1513.

268 By Trewhitt, Henry and Peter Ross Range in Moscow, 'A Triumph of Symbols: Process is Now the Substance of Superpower Relations', *USNWR*, June 13 1988, p. 38.; For the New York Times journalist's analysis of the Moscow summit, see Safire, William, 'The Sobersided Summit', *NYT*, May 30 1988, p. 23.; For the Soviet public's perception of President Reagan during the Moscow summit, see Keller, Bill, 'Veil on Personalities is Drawn Back', *NYT*, June 2 1988, pp. A1, A19.; 'The Moscow summit, as anticipated, resulted in little progress and no surprises in arms control. At the same time, the positive interactions between President Reagan and General Secretary Gorbachev reflected a fundamental improvement in US–Soviet relations which should substantially increase the prospects for arms control'. Keeny, Jr., Spurgeon M., 'Moscow Summit: Half Empty or Half Full?', *Arms Control Today*, July/August 1988, p. 2.; 'In the future, we may look back on the Moscow summit as the moment of lost opportunity for a breakthrough in arms control'. Keeny, Jr., 'Moscow Summit: Half Empty or Half Full?', p. 2.

269 Reagan, *An American Life*, p. 705.; For George Shultz's account of the Moscow summit, see Chapter 49, 'The Last of the Superpower Summits: Making the Most of it', in Shultz, *Turmoil*, pp. 1080-1108.

270 For Gorbachev's United Nations speech, December 7 1988, see 'My Watershed: My Speech to the United Nations', in Gorbachev, *Memoirs*, pp. 592-597.; See also Isaacson, Walter, Reported by John Kohan with Gorbachev, B. William Mader/United Nations and Strobe Talbott/Washington, 'The Gorbachev Challenge', *Time*, Vol. 132, No. 25, December 19 1988, pp. 6-11.

271 'Excerpts From Speech to UN on Major Soviet Military Cuts', *NYT*, December 8 1988, p. A16.

272 Ibid.; 'Highlights of Soviet Leader Gorbachev's Plans Proposals', *CQWR*, Vol. 46, No. 50, December 10 1988, p. 3467.

273 Ibid.

274 For the end of the 'Brezhnev Doctrine', see Gorbachev, *Memoirs*, pp. 599-611.

275 'The Soviet willingness to abandon the Brezhnev Doctrine in the late 1980s in favor of the 'Sinatra Doctrine' – under which any East European country could sing, 'I did it my way' suggests a radical transformation in the prevailing Soviet perception of threat from the West'. Deudney, Daniel and G. John Ikenberry, 'Who Won the Cold War?', *Foreign Policy*, No. 87, Summer 1992, p. 132.

276 'Excerpts From Speech to UN on Major Soviet Military Cuts', *NYT*, p. A16.; 'Highlights of Soviet Leader Gorbachev's Plans Proposals', *CQWR*, p. 3467.

277 'Excerpts From Speech to UN on Major Soviet Military Cuts', *NYT*, December 8 1988, p. A16.

278 Gorbachev, Mikhail, *Memoirs*, p. 593.

279 Ibid.

280 Gordon, Michael R., 'Western Officials Term Troop Cuts Significant', *NYT*, December 8 1988, p. A1.

281 Towell, Pat, 'Gorbachev Initiative Challenges Bush, NATO', *CQWR*, Vol. 46, No. 50, December 10 1988, p. 3466.; For the statistics of Current Warsaw Pact Forces, Current NATO forces and Gorbachev's Plan, see 'Gorbachev's UN Surprise: Soviet Arms Cuts', *NYT*, December 8 1988, p. A18.; For statistics of NATO and Warsaw Pact forces, see 'NATO, Warsaw Pact Conventional Force Balance', *CQWR*, Vol. 46, No. 50, December 10 1988, p. 3468.

282 Safire, 'A Virtue of Necessity', *NYT*, p. A35.; That the Eastern Bloc would have more than a 2 to 1 advantage in tanks is also stated in Gordon, Michael R., 'Western Officials Term Troop Cuts Significant', *NYT*, December 8 1988, p. A18.; *Time* magazine, December 19 1988, stated 'Yet Gorbachev's gambit is fraught with potential dangers for

the US. The announced cuts are substantive enough to lure the West toward complacency, yet they are too small to dent significantly the advantages in men, material and geography that the Soviet bloc has over NATO'. Isaacson, Walter, 'The Gorbachev Challenge', *Time*, p. 6.

[283]   Safire, 'A Virtue of Necessity', *NYT*, p. A35.

[284]   Keller, Bill, 'Departure Today: In UN Address, Soviet Chief Vows to Reduce Forces by 500,000', *NYT*, December 8 1988, p. A17.

[285]   Editorial, 'Gambler, Showman, Statesman', *NYT*, December 8 1988, p. A34.

[286]   Earle, II, Ralph and Elliot L. Richardson, 'Building on Gorbachev's Cuts in Europe', *NYT*, December 8 1988, p. A35.

[287]   Gordon, 'Western Officials Term Troop Cuts Significant', *NYT*, p. A1.

[288]   Ibid., p. A18.

[289]   'In UN Address, Soviet Chief Vows to Reduce Forces by 500,000', *NYT*, p. A1.

[290]   See Towell, Pat, 'Gorbachev Initiative Challenges Bush, NATO', *CQWR*, Vol. 46, No. 50, December 10 1988, p. 3466.

[291]   Trainor, Bernard E., 'Exit of Soviet General Tied to Discord on Cuts', *NYT*, December 8 1988, p. A18.

[292]   Towell, 'Gorbachev Initiative Challenges Bush, NATO', *CQWR*, p. 3467.

[293]   Both quotes taken from ibid.

[294]   Felton, John, 'US Rebels Cool to Afghan Plans', *CQWR*, Vol. 46, No. 50, December 10 1988, p. 3469.; See also Lewis, Paul, 'Concessions by Gorbachev Are Seen an Aid to Afghans', *NYT*, December 8 1988, p. A17.

[295]   Towell, 'Gorbachev Initiative Challenges Bush, NATO', *CQWR*, p. 3468.

[296]   Keller, 'In UN Address, Soviet Chief Vows to Reduce Forces by 500,000', *NYT*, p. A17.

[297]   Roberts, Steven V., 'Table for Three, With Talk of Bygones and Best Hopes', *NYT*, December 8 1988, p. A17.; For Reagan's account of the New York summit, see Reagan, *An American Life*, pp. 720-721.; For Gorbachev's account of the Governor's Island meeting, see Gorbachev, *Memoirs*, pp. 597-598.

[298]   Roberts, 'Table for Three, With Talk of Bygones and Best Hopes', *NYT*, p. A17.

[299]   'Excerpts From Shultz's News Conference', *NYT*, December 8 1988, p. A18.

[300]   Keller, 'In UN Address, Soviet Chief Vows to Reduce Forces by 500,000', *NYT*, p. A1.; 'Thousands Feared Dead in Soviet Caucasus Quake', *NYT*, December 8 1988, pp. A1, A18.; For the New York summit, see Isaacson, Walter, 'The Gorbachev Challenge', *Time*, p. 8.

[301]   Gorbachev, *Memoirs*, p. 598.

[302]   Reagan, *An American Life*, p. 720.

[303]   Ibid., pp. 720-721.

Chapter 5

Strategic Defence: The Post-Cold War and Post-September 11 World

The SDI after President Ronald Reagan

The George Bush and Bill Clinton Years

The plan that the SDI would protect only missile silos, not cities, marked the end of Ronald Reagan's original idea of SDI.[1] On October 6 1988, it was announced that the SDI was to be deployed in phases. The first phase which used space-based interceptors ('Smart Rocks') would destroy 30 per cent of Soviet warheads.[2] On November 8 1988, George Bush won the Presidency and vowed to continue the SDI.[3]

 The following year, on April 23 1989, the Pentagon replaced 'Smart Rocks' with 'Brilliant Pebbles'. This used smaller and smarter rockets.[4] In 1990, Congress reduced SDI's budget to $2.89 billion in 1991. This was the programme's first large cutback.[5] A 'Theater Missile Defense' programme was created in October–November 1990.[6] The 'Missile Defense Act' of December 1991 required the Defense Department to pursue the development of theater missile defence systems. The system was to be 'designed to protect the United States against limited ballistic missile threats, including accidental or unauthorized launches or Third World attacks'.[7]

 On January 29 1991, SDI plans were further cut back. The new plan was called 'Global Protection Against Limited Strikes', or 'GPALS'. Under the plan, a few missiles (launched by accident or by terrorists) would be shot down.[8] There were three main components to the new GPALS system: a ground-based 'Theater Missile Defense' (TMD), a ground-based 'National Missile Defense' (NMD) and a (Brilliant Pebble) 'Space-Based Global Defense'.[9] A new space-based sensor called 'Brilliant Eyes' (BE) was now known as the 'Space and Missile Tracking System' (SMTS).[10] The GPALS plan failed due to technical and political reasons. It was considered expensive in the face of a perceived disappearing threat. Although its failure was often attributed to the Clinton administration, it started two years earlier with the declining Congressional support.[11]

 President Bush said, during the Gulf War, that the US Patriot missiles intercepted 41 Iraqi Scud missiles out of 42 attempts. This was 'Proof positive that missile defence works'.[12] Consequently, Congress approved a record SDI budget of $4.15 billion for 1992.[13] On January 1 1992, the Soviet Union dissolved into the Commonwealth of Independent States. A month later, Russian President Boris

Yeltsin proposed a joint US–Russian programme. He stated that 'We are ready jointly to work out and subsequently to create and jointly operate a global system of defence in place of SDI'.[14]

On April 7 1992, the Army admitted that during the Gulf War, the Patriot may have only hit 24 Scuds in 85 attempts. Other government investigators revealed that only one Scud may have been hit.[15] Congress later approved a reduced $3.8 billion budget for SDI in 1993. Up until 1992, the total funding for SDI was $32 billion.[16] Regarding theater missile defences, the strategy was to upgrade defensive capabilities such as the Patriot, and to produce a new generation system with greater range and effectiveness: the 'Theater High Altitude Area Defense' (THAAD).[17]

President Bill Clinton, in 1992, pledged to cut SDI spending but still supported the 'option of deploying a limited ground-based defence' for the US.[18] The election of President Clinton speeded the conversion to the Theater Missile Defense programme.[19] On May 13 1993, Les Aspin, Secretary of Defense, announced that the Strategic Defense Initiative Organization was being redesignated the name 'Ballistic Missile Defense Organization'.[20] It was stressed that the change signalled the end of the SDI era.[21]

Les Aspin noted that the end of the Cold War meant that the US no longer faced the threat of a Soviet attack, which the SDI programme had concentrated on. Instead, the US faced theater ballistic missiles from Third World dictators. Such missiles could pose a threat to the US and its allies.[22] The second priority of the post-Cold War era was developing defences for the American people.[23] At the time it was believed that the break up of the former Soviet Union and Warsaw Pact meant that a return to the SDI ('star wars') system would be unlikely.[24] The BMDO had programmes for Theater Missile Defense (to meet the existing missile threat to deployed US and allied forces), National Missile Defense (against the emergence of long-range ballistic missile threats) and Technological Readiness (advanced ballistic missile defense technologies).[25]

The Bottom-Up Review (BUR) of September 1993 allocated top priority to the theater missile defense (TMD) programme, which was to receive $12 billion over five years.[26] The TMD programme consisted of three projects; a modification of the Navy's Aegis air defense system, improvements to the Army's Patriot missile system, and a new Army missile defence system.[27] This was known as Theater High Altitude Area Defense (THAAD).[28] It was designed to destroy attacking missiles at a greater range than that of the Patriot system. Under the BUR, National Missile Defense was to receive $3 billion.[29] $3 billion was allocated to technology readiness – a programme that was to provide advances to both theater and national defences.[30]

TMD and NMD were intended to defend the US against the proliferation of theater ballistic missiles. In the late 1990s, the Patriot system had become 'integral' to the US theater missile defense (TMD) plan.[31] Iraq's use of the Scud in the Gulf War demonstrated the potential of the theater missile threat as a 'weapon of terror'.[32] The North Korean launch of the Taepo-Dong 1 missile, on August 31 1998, was indicative of the 'rogue nation missile threat' to the US.[33] The end of the Cold War ensured that there was a reduction 'in the likelihood of global conflict'.[34]

However, the emerging threat posed to the US was the proliferation of ballistic missiles 'both in terms of numbers of missiles and in terms of the technical capabilities of those missiles'.[35]

According to Martin Anderson, speaking on September 21 1998, 'In today's paper, *The New York Times*, the US and Japan signed an agreement to build a missile defense system against North Korea'.[36] Speaking in 1998, Martin Anderson stated that 'in recent months there has been a push towards the issue of ballistic missile defence'. He stated that 'The allies, Japan, Israel are very concerned because Iran has missiles. The US and Japan have a missile defense agreement. The US has one with Israel'.[37] Anderson explained that 'The Rumsfeld Commission's conclusion was that it was very likely other nations could in a very short period of time threaten to attack us. This was *before* Iran shot a missile'.[38]

The Rumsfeld Commission was 'The Commission to Assess the Ballistic Missile Threat to the United States'.[39] Established by Congress, the Rumsfeld Commission's July 15 1998 report warned that the US might have 'little or no warning before hostile countries such as North Korea fielded ballistic missiles able to reach U.S. territory with nuclear, chemical or biological warheads'.[40] These hostile countries, termed 'rogue states' had the capability to 'strike the US' with long-range ballistic missiles within a period of approximately five years, without the US knowing (or ten years in the case of Iraq). The 'rogue states' had obtained the technologies from unrestricted export controls among the industrial nations, and from other rogue states.[41]

The 'newer, developing threats' were from 'North Korea, Iran and Iraq'. They were threats 'in addition to those still posed by the existing ballistic missile arsenals of Russia and China'.[42] Russia and China were 'nations with which the United States is not now in conflict but which remain in uncertain transitions'.[43] The anti-missile system being developed in 1999 in the US was not intended to deal with the Russian threat alone, but from the rogue states in general.[44] The two events, in the summer of 1998, which 'fundamentally altered the missile defense debate' (and showed the need for a missile defence system) were the Rumsfeld Commission's conclusions, and the North Korean launch of its Taepo-Dong 1 missile.[45]

The 'Clinton administration's anti-missile defense program' was 'actually several different initiatives designed to meet the variety of threats' that could face the US.[46] Ballistic missile defences fell 'into two main categories: theater and national, designed to intercept short-range and long-range missiles, respectively'.[47] 'National Missile Defense' would counter intercontinental warheads. 'Theater Defenses' – the PAC-3, THAAD and airborne laser – would protect 'US military forces and allied nations from shorter-range missiles. Satellites could detect launches'.[48]

The US deployed a version of theater missile defense (TMD) – the Patriot. However, the US did not operate a more advanced TMD system or a national missile defense (NMD) system.[49] In the Clinton administration, the US had improved the 'Patriot' missile defense system. It was developing the 'Navy Area Defense System', and was 'chipping in' on the 'Medium Extended Air Defense

System' (MEADS). The US was working on the 'Theater High-Altitude Area Defense System' (THAAD), and the 'Navy Theater Wide System' (NTW).[50]

The SDI, or the 'ballistic missile defense' (BMD) system in the year 2000 was known as 'National Missile Defense' (NMD).[51] NMD was dubbed the 'son of star wars'. The 'official Russian position' to the US National Missile Defense (NMD) system, according to Keith Payne writing in 2000, was 'one of implacable opposition to any American NMD and to any modification of existing treaties',[52] namely the 1972 ABM Treaty. On March 15 1999, the US Senate and House passed bills calling for the development of a national anti-missile defence system, much to the delight of the Republicans, who had been pushing for a national anti-missile defence system for years.[53] In fact, President Clinton's support for a national missile defence system was due to the 1995 Republican take over of Congress following the 1994 Congressional elections.[54]

President Clinton signed the National Missile Defense Act of 1999 which committed the US to deploy such a defence (a national missile defence) 'as soon as it is technologically possible'.[55] However, interestingly, the US public had 'shown little or no interest' in the anti-missile defence debate. There was no public pressure on Congress or the Clinton administration to make the decisions.[56] In the year 2000, the White House planned to decide whether to deploy a national anti-missile system with the deployment deadline schedule targeted to be 2005, instead of 2003.[57]

At the Moscow summit, on June 4 2000, US President Bill Clinton and Russian President Vladimir Putin 'clashed' over US plans for a national missile defence system. Both leaders agreed that there was a threat from 'rogue states and the proliferation of ballistic missile technology'. However, they differed on how to 'tackle the dangers'.[58] Vladimir Putin contended that the row over the NMD system was 'one of the most difficult issues to solve. There are a lot of problems there'. He also contended that 'We're against having a cure which is worse than the disease', meaning that the NMD system was worse than the 'disease' it was designed to treat.[59] To proceed with the NMD system, the US had to 'persuade Russia to amend the 1972 anti-ballistic missile treaty ... or ditch it altogether'.[60] However, Vladimir Putin insisted there would be no amendments to this ABM Treaty.[61]

China warned that it would increase 'the size of its nuclear missile force' if the US went through with its 'controversial' NMD system.[62] Chinese 'President Jiang Zemin criticised NMD' in a 'joint statement with Russian president, Vladimir Putin'. The two leaders stated that the US NMD plan 'could trigger a new arms race'.[63] Russia, like China, perceived that the US NMD system was 'designed primarily to fend off its own weapons'. Both countries indicated that they 'may abandon all previously signed disarmament treaties' if the US went ahead with the NMD system.[64]

On July 7–8 2000, the US unsuccessfully tested its NMD technology, in California, USA.[65] China and Russia 'expressed fury at Bill Clinton's decision to test' NMD technology and 'vowed' to 'speed up plans to build their own missile shields'.[66] Commander-in-chief of Russia's defence force, Vladimir Yakovlev, attested that the tests of July 7-8 2000, at Vandenberg Air Force, California, USA, were 'the first step towards global nuclear instability', and were a 'flagrant violation' of the 1972 ABM Treaty.[67]

The US's European allies believed 'that the NMD project would provoke Russia into taking countermeasures', and 'would prompt China into building more long-range missiles which would provoke an arms race in south Asia'.[68] The Europeans welcomed Russian President Vladimir Putin's proposal for a defence system 'to cover the whole of Europe – designed to attack incoming missiles soon after they have been fired'.[69] National Missile Defence became a major issue in the 2000 US Presidential election.

Strategic Defence in the George W. Bush Presidency

Within a few weeks of George W. Bush becoming the new US President, US Secretary of Defense Donald Rumsfeld (on February 3 2001) announced the new administration's plans to build a national missile defence system (NMD) (dubbed 'the Son of Star Wars'). He promised the European allies that they would be involved. The following day, Sergei Ivanov, advisor to President Vladimir Putin, responded that the proposed US defence system would cause an arms race and undermine world stability. As the Soviets had done so with the SDI predecessor, the Soviets offered to hold talks on arms cuts if the US abandoned their NMD plan. Similarly, as the French had previously opposed the SDI, they opposed the NMD in 2001, saying that it was an 'incitement' to nuclear proliferation. Russia proposed an alternative European system to the NMD. Its President stated on March 6 that NMD jeopardized arms control.

On May 1 2001, George W. Bush committed the US to a NMD system. On May 2, China stated that the NMD system would instigate a new arms race.[70] Soviet analyst Andrei Piontkovsky stated, on May 2 2001, that the NMD would not adversely affect Russia's nuclear deterrrent. On May 2, Bush stated that the US must work on the NMD because of the threat from 'irresponsible' countries which had nuclear weapons and from countries which promoted terrorism. What the US called 'rogue states' were now called 'countries of concern'.

Like the previous SDI, in Congress there was opposition to the NMD. Democrat leader Dick Gephardt called the NMS system 'unproven' and 'costly'. According to him, it jeopardized arms control.[71] The EU, China and Russia were all sceptical of Bush's proposal.[72] Like with the previous SDI, Moscow (which could overwhelm the US proposed NMD system) maintained that the adherence to the 1972 ABM Treaty was vital. Moscow wanted to begin talks to ensure 'strategic stability'.[73] Germany, too, believed that the ABM Treaty should be built upon.[74]

The Americans wanted two bases in Britain to be used for their NMD. The bases would be at RAF Fylingdales and RAF Menwith Hill. RAF Fylingdales (near Whitby) would be one of five early warning radar stations (the others are already in operation, looking for missiles which could threaten the US). RAF Menwith Hill (near Harrowgate) would be the 'European ground relay station' for America's 'Space Based Intra-Red System'.[75] The British bases, however, would put the stations 'in the front line' as a 'target for any missile strike'.[76] In 2001, it was stated that America was 'vulnerable to nuclear and chemical–biological blackmail by countries such as Iran and North Korea'.[77]

President George W. Bush's May 1 2001 speech was his strategy for post-Cold War defence policy. In it, he urged the replacement of the 1972 ABM Treaty. This was a Cold War relic as 'mutual assured destruction' (which it codified) was obsolete for the realities of today's post-Cold War world.[78] In President Bush's speech, he stated that the US and Russia should 'develop a new framework for peace ... that moves beyond the adversial legacy of the Cold War'. He believed that a new defence was needed which reflected the post-Cold War realities and suggested that both countries 'contemplate a joint defence'. Bush contended that the threat to peace was 'not from thousands of ballistic missiles'. It was from 'a small number of weapons in the hands of those nations for whom terror and blackmail is a way of life'.[79] Bush asserted that the NMD system was intended for protection against 'rogue' states like North Korea and Iraq, not against Russia.[80] In his speech, Bush urged consultations on the defence with China and Russia. Donald Rumsfeld stated that even a partial NMD would be a deterrent to countries of concern to strike at the US.[81] In February 2001, Donald Rumsfeld called Russia an 'active proliferator' of missiles.[82]

Interestingly, Russia and China claimed that President Bush's NMD plan could hasten the very nuclear proliferation that it was intended to counter. The US NMD system would render Russian and Chinese nuclear missiles ineffective. This could result in corrupt officials selling the missiles to 'rogue nations' and 'international terrorists'.[83] President Bush indicated that he was 'ready to abandon' the 1972 ABM Treaty 'with or without' Russia's approval. He said that he was ready to make unilateral cuts in the US's nuclear forces in order to appease Russia's disapproval over the US's proposed abandonment of the ABM Treaty.[84] NATO officials welcomed Bush's proposal of cutting the US's nuclear missiles.[85]

After its initial 'hostile' reaction to the US NMD, Germany appeared to have 'come round' to the proposal. France feared that it would encourage China to increase its arsenal of long-range missiles.[86] Moscow 'was pleased by the non-confrontational tone' of George W. Bush's speech on missile defence. Russian Foreign Minister Igor Ivanov welcomed Bush's proposal of reducing the number of the US's missiles.[87] Reminiscent of Reagan's earlier statement to Gorbachev, Bush declared that he wanted to 'look' Vladimir Putin 'in the eye' and reassure him that the US NMD system did not threaten Moscow.[88] The Russian missile arsenal, however, was 'much too large to be affected' by the US NMD system.[89]

On July 15 2001, the Pentagon successfully carried out a $100 million missile defence test, boosting the credibility of Bush's NMD system, and demonstrating the success of 'hit-to-kill' technology. A mock Minuteman ICBM warhead (carrying a mock warhead and decoy balloons) was fired from Vandenberg Air Force base in California. It was shot down by an interceptor rocket (kill vehicle) launched form the Kwajalein in the Western Pacific. The kill vehicle successfully distinguished the dummy missile from the decoy balloon, which was designed to test its ability to test a real missile from a fake one.[90]

Russia and China reacted with 'unbridled hostility' to America's successful missile defence test. Both countries issued warnings that the NMD plan would upset disarmament treaties and provoke a new arms race.[91] Russia denounced the US tests as threatening the 1972 ABM Treaty and a threat to nuclear disarmament. Russia stood by its position to strengthen the ABM Treaty. At a summit in Moscow, Vladimir Putin and the Chinese President Jiang Zemin, issued a statement reaffirming their support for the 1972 ABM Treaty which was threatened from the US plans for its NMD system.

Alexander Yakovenko, Russia's Chief Foreign Ministry spokesman, wanted to know why all 'nuclear disarmament and non proliferation agreements' based on the 1972 ABM Treaty should be 'placed under threat'.[92] Russia maintained that the ABM Treaty was responsible for global stability, and was responsible for all arms control accords. Russia warned that if the US continue with its NMD proposal it would consider all US–Soviet arms control pacts void. Vladimir Putin stated that if the US withdrew from the ABM Treaty, Russia would place multiple warheads on its ICBMs.[93] Putin declared that the new weapons could overwhelm the US NMD system. Admittedly, Russia's response to the US missile defence shield would be to launch an arms race.[94]

Experts stated that Russia could upgrade its Topol-M ICBM with multiple warheads. Interestingly, the Topol-M missiles were designed to 'wobble' during re-entry into the atmosphere. This facility would enable them to evade the missile defence shield which Ronald Reagan originally planned.[95] The success of the US test of July 15 2001 was described as hitting a 'bullet with a bullet, and it does work'.[96] This was reminiscent of the rhetoric of the Reagan administration. China responded to the US tests with the declaration that the US missile defence plan was 'opposed by the international community'. China stated that the missile plan would 'not only spark a new arms race ... but stimulate nuclear proliferation'.[97]

In a scene reminiscent of the Reagan–Gorbachev summits, during the talks in Genoa, Italy, George W. Bush and Vladimir Putin agreed to tie the US plans for its NMD system to talks on reducing nuclear weapons (offensive strategic missiles). Interestingly, Bush had advocated linkage between offensive and defensive talks since his campaign speech in May 2000. In the speech he said that it was possible that the US build a missile defence system whilst defusing confrontation with Russia by reducing nuclear weapons to 'the lowest possible number consistent with out national security'. In his speech on May 1 2001, Bush also encouraged 'further cuts in nuclear weapons'.[98]

Following the successful US missile defence test (and 20 years after President Ronald Reagan proposed the SDI), the Pentagon had reverted to Reagan's original SDI proposal for its NMD plans. The successful July 15 2001 test used a ground-launched interceptor. After the tests, the Pentagon wanted space-based defences used in its missile defence plans (in addition to its ground-based system).[99] The Pentagon wanted chemical lasers in space (or the atmosphere), 'thousands of interceptors' in space and 'dozens of sensor-laden satellites' in orbit. The aim was to have a 'layered defense', which would be able to shoot down a missile at various stages of its flight (trajectory) including whilst they were in their boost phase.[100] However, in contrast to Reagan's original proposal, the Bush proposal would omit the 'nuclear powered X-ray lasers and high-energy particle beams'. It was stated that the US 'weaponry in space' would 'force other nations to counter' the NMD with 'anti-satellite weapons of their own, leading to an arms race in space'.[101]

Regarding the US–Soviet decision to link reductions in missiles to the NMD system, and Vladimir Putin's opposition to modification of the ABM Treaty, Russian newspaper *Kommersant* carried the headline 'Russia has capitulated'. It stated that the leaders of America and Russia had 'effectively put an end to the ABM Treaty'.[102] *Vedemosti* declared that after Russia's threat of equipping its 'warheads with extra missiles' the Russian President 'says that this is unlikely to be necessary'.[103] In response to Russian criticism, Vladimir Putin defended his stance as the correct approach to take. As with the previous SDI, critics described the NMD as 'the first step towards the militarisation of space'.[104] On August 23 2001, President Bush declared that the US would unilaterally pull out of the ABM Treaty which he declared hampered US efforts to 'defend America'. In Britain, in September 2001, it was revealed that a House of Commons motion was signed by more than 200 Labour MP's opposing the NMD.[105] In contrast, the Conservative Party welcomed the US missile defence scheme.

On December 13 2001, George W. Bush announced that the US was withdrawing from the 1972 ABM Treaty. He said that the US would phase-out its treaty obligations over a period of six months. Bush called the treaty unfair because it forbade the right to build a national missile system. In response to Bush's announcement Vladimir Putin called the US decision 'a mistake'. On January 25 2002, the US successfully carried out a further national missile defence test. The test was a precedent in using an interceptor that was fired from a ship rather than land. Launched from the warship USS Lake Eerie, the interceptor rocket was launched into space hitting and destroying a dummy missile that had been fired form Hawaii. The US withdrew from the 1972 ABM Treaty in June 2002. Russia and China reacted with criticism.

On December 17 2002 the US announced that it would begin deploying a limited NMD system in 2004. George W. Bush announced that the missile interceptors for the NMD system would be deployed in Alaska and California.[106] On December 17, it emerged that the US had formally asked for RAF Fylingdales in Yorkshire, Britain, to be part of its planned NMD system. The base would provide early warning intelligence for the US Alaska interceptors which Bush had ordered to be deployed. George W. Bush announced that he ordered the installment of ten interceptor missiles to be deployed in Alaska by 2004. A further ten would be deployed in 2005 or 2006.[107]

The ten interceptor missiles at Fort Greely, Alaska, would counter any threats to the US from the Asia–Pacific region (especially North Korea).[108] The second stage of the NMD proposal (for which Bush had ordered ten further rockets) would neutralize missile attacks emanating from the Middle East (from Libya, Iran and Iraq). It is for this eastern 'front' which George W. Bush had requested basing interceptors on British soil.[109] The US's plans to base BMD interceptor rockets in Britain is part of this 'second front' of defence against ballistic missiles launched by the 'states of concern'.[110] The US is also seeking bases for its interceptor missiles in other areas of north-west Europe.[111] George W. Bush ordered sea-based missile systems to be placed 'aboard Aegis destroyers'.

There would also be 'possible airborne laser weapons' and satellites in space.[112] The Pentagon plans to defend the US from the 'axis of evil' with a 'layered defence'. This involves space, air, and sea-based weapons. The Pentagon does not want to use nuclear 'kill vehicles' in its missile defence.[113]

The US deployment decision came despite the December 11 2002 NMD test failure over the Pacific. The interceptor failed to come close to a dummy warhead in what constituted a third test failure in eight tests for the Pentagon.[114] George W. Bush asserted, on December 17 2002, that the goal was to protect US citizens against the 'catastrophic harm that may result from hostile states or terrorist groups armed with weapons of mass destruction and the means to deliver them'.[115] Bush cited the September 11 2001 terrorist attacks on America as evidence that the US faced 'unprecedented threats' from states which are acknowledged to include Iran, Iraq, North Korea and Libya. Bush's NMD deployment decision coincided with fresh tensions with North Korea which Bush had described as being a member of the 'axis of evil'.[116]

The British Government supported George W. Bush's NMD policy. British Defence Secretary Geoff Hoon stated that the US request to use Fylingdales would be considered 'very seriously'. Approval was expected to be granted for the work to be 'carried out at Fylingdales'.[117] Geoff Hoon promised a public and parliamentary debate on the US Fylingdales request, which has 'provoked protests from Labour MPs and disarmament campaigners'.[118]

Donald Rumsfeld acknowledged that the missile defence system would be deployed before it was fully developed. He revealed that he liked the idea of putting 'something in the ground or in the air or in the sea' with the intention of 'getting comfortable with it ... using it and testing it, and learning from that'.[119] According to Rumsfeld, the NMD system would have a 'deterrent effect', as 'The other countries will know what we are capable of'.[120] Like President Ronald Reagan's SDI offer, Donald Rumsfeld offered to share NMD technology with the British. Robert Einhorn, a former Assistant Secretary of State for non-proliferation asserted that the US administration was 'predicting a rather rapid advance' of the 'problem of ballistic missile proliferation'.[121]

In response to the US NMD deployment decision (of December 17 2002), on December 18 2002 Moscow stated that the NMD system would lead to a 'new, senseless arms race' which would destabilize the world. Moscow's Foreign Ministry stated that the NMD system would distract the US from the war on terror and other important 'challenges and threats'.[122] The two-page statement issued by Moscow said that the NMD would weaken strategic stability and result in the spreading of 'weapons of mass destruction'.[123] Moscow stated that it regretted 'the activation of the attempt by the United States to create a so-called "global anti-missile defence"'. The statement continued that 'the realisation of these plans has entered a new destabilising phase'.[124]

Igor Ivanov warned that the US NMD plan 'must not hurt Russia's security interests' or 'prompt a new arms race'.[125] However, the Soviets were examining possible cooperation possibilities on the NMD system which the Americans offered. This was stated by Dmitri Rogozin (Head of the Russian Parliament's International Affairs committee).[126] The *International Herald Tribune* noted that there was 'little reaction' from other countries to the December 17 US announcement that it would deploy the NMD in 2004. The Chinese Foreign Ministry did not respond to it. There was no reaction from Japan. Yasuo Fukuda, Japan's Chief Cabinet Secretary, said that the NMD decision was Washington's.[127]

China fears that a missile defence shield protecting US troops in Japan and South Korea could be extended to cover Taiwan. China threatened to regain Taiwan (which is America's ally) by force if it 'refuses to reunite with the Communist mainland'.[128] However, Moscow's reaction to the US decision to proceed with the NMD system appears to give credence to the argument that an arms race will be averted. The Russian rhetoric – when contrasted against their rhetoric towards the earlier SDI – appears restrained. It reduces the likelihood that an arms race will take place.

On December 19 2002, the editorial of the British newspaper *The Guardian* concluded that the NMD system was not in the British interest for it could not deter 'the principal security threat facing Britain – that posed by terrorists'.[129] The newspaper concluded that if Britain cooperated with the US it would be 'colluding' in 'weapons proliferation' at a time when the British Government was 'committed to achieving the exact opposite'.[130] It was pointed out that the threat against which NMD was supposed to operate against 'may not materialise'. *The Guardian* stated that the 'Billions of dollars' that would be spent on the NMD system was 'a high price to pay for a false sense of security'.[131]

The deployment over the coming decade of the NMD system will cost the US hundreds of billions of dollars. Congress has approved requests of '$7.8 billion in research, development and testing funds' for the system during each of the last two fiscal years.[132] Although *The New York Times* editorial in *The International Herald Tribune* newspaper, on December 19 2002, concluded that a workable NMD system was in the US's national interest, it concluded that 'rushing to construct a system based on the present unreliable technology seems premature'.[133]

On January 15 2003, Geoff Hoon announced that the British Government agreed 'to the US request to use Fylingdales radar station in Yorkshire for its missile defence system'.[134] He stated that this decision would mean that Britain would have 'an invaluable extra insurance' against the threat of ballistic missiles which were 'a still uncertain but potentially catastrophic threat to the citizens of this country'.[135] It was 'made it plain' that the Government's decision was 'the first step towards a deeper British involvement' in missile defence.[136] According to Geoff Hoon, 'batteries of interceptor rockets' would need to be based in Britain to protect against 'incoming missiles fired by "rogue states"'.[137] Hoon contended that 'Britain would have to pay the cost of the interceptors', whilst the 'US would pay to upgrade Fylingdales'.[138] However, the US 'has made it clear' that 'it eventually wants to install a large x-band radar to track missiles as well as simply detect them' at Fylingdales.[139] The British Government claimed that the Fylingdales 'radar base could also be a "key building block" for a future British or European missile defence system'.[140] The British Government had previously stated that Britain's defence companies could benefit from the NMD project.[141]

After Geoff Hoon's speech, 'The Government was hit by a fierce backlash from Labour MPs'.[142] Former Defence Minister Peter Kilfoyle 'accused the

Government of embracing every "crackpot notion" advanced by "ideologues" in Washington'. He stated that the UK's 'slavish devotion to American policy' added 'further to global destabilisation'.[143] Shadow Defence Secretary Bernard Jenkin 'welcomed' Hoon's announcement. Jenkin stated that the Conservative Party had 'consistently' supported 'the case for missile defence'.[144] Geoff Hoon contended that the 'threat from ballistic missiles in the hands of countries such as Iraq and North Korea' should not be underestimated.[145]

Developments Since the End of the Cold War

Relations between the US and Russia

The relationship between the US and the former Soviet Union has been one of cooperation after the end of the Cold War. Although there have been moments of tension between America and Russia, generally US–Russian relations have been positive. Russia has inevitably sided with America over issues of concern. During the wars in the Balkans (during the 1990s) between the Serbs, Croats and Bosnian-Muslims, as the former Yugoslavia disintegrated, Russian–American relations were strained. America advocated a pro-Croat–Bosnian-Muslim stance whilst Russia was a traditional ally of the Serbs. However, Russia perceived its relations with America as more important than defending its Slavic ally – the Serbs – and so caved in to America's anti-Serbian demands. During the Gulf War (1990–1991) Gorbachev had supported the US position after Iraq invaded Kuwait on August 1 1990. Gorbachev abstained from voting at the UN Security Council, which voted to authorize the use of force to expel Iraq from Kuwait. The Soviets perceived their relations with America as more important than defending their ally Iraq. This would not have occurred during the Cold War.

Post-Cold War; Post-September 11 Threats

The years following the end of the Cold War have bought about a plethora of threats/problems that concerned the US, Russia and the rest of the world; political instability and the concern for the political situation in Russia, Nationalism, immigration, refugees, overpopulation, environmental issues, the search for new economic markets to enhance prosperity, human rights, democracy promotion, drugs, poverty, disease (like AIDS), conventional weapons, nuclear proliferation, the threat of weapons of mass destruction (WMD), biological and chemical weapons. Most pertinently, the greatest threat to the US today (after September 11 2001) appears to be terrorism. Terrorism combined with an ideological anti-American fundamentalism resulted in the September 11 2001 attack on the World Trade Center in New York, – killing thousands of civilians – and the Pentagon in Washington D.C. Orchestrated by Osama Bin Laden and the al-Quaida network, September 11 was the greatest tragedy to Americans since the bombing of Pearl Harbour on December 7 1941.

The September 11 2001 attack demonstrated that America was vulnerable to attack on American soil. American interests have been targeted throughout the globe, throughout the decade (including the embassy bombings in Africa). The difference was that the September 11 attack was carried out on the territory of America. It showed that despite America's overwhelming military and technological power, the world's superpower was not invulnerable to an attack. Symbols of its economic and military prosperity were attacked. The September 11 attack also represented a new type of threat to the US: that of suicide bombers. Suicide bombings have been a feature carried out by Palestinians during their conflict with the Israelis during the decade. In 2001, the US had encountered this new type of warfare directed against them for the first time since the Japanese Kamikaze attacks during the Second World War.

The September 11 2001 attacks were followed by the biological–chemical Anthrax attacks on America in October 2001. The bio-terrorist attacks occurred in New York, Florida, and Capitol Hill (The heart of America's democracy). At the time, believed to be the work of al-Quaida or Iraq, reports later surfaced that the Anthrax spores came from within the US. On January 7 2003, residue of the lethal toxin ricin was found in a London flat in England. Arrests were made of a 'potential al-Quaida cell' that was suspected of 'plotting some form of chemical attack on the UK'.[146] Two days earlier, British Foreign Secretary Jack Straw stated that 'the proliferation of nuclear, chemical, and biological weapons presents the greatest threat to our national security, and to the peace of the world'.[147] North Korea, meanwhile, maintained that its weapons work was to maintain its national security.

The Future for NMD?

Today, America stands at a crossroads. America has sought to democratize the world by expanding its ideals of democracy. It has sought to engage countries in a global community to solve problems. On December 26 2002, leading an international community, America began to 'prepare for war in Iraq to prevent it acquring nuclear weapons'.[148] However, on December 26 2002, the same day, it emerged that Pyongyang, North Korea 'may have' an atomic bomb 'in 30 days'.[149] The very nuclear proliferation that America has sought to prevent has now become a reality.

A year ago (previous to these two events), on November 30 2001, it emerged that Osama Bin Laden 'may already have a "dirty" nuclear bomb'.[150] Following the September 11 2001 attacks, fears of a 'dirty' nuclear bomb have become a possibility. (It could be delivered inside a van or a lorry.) Even the International Atomic Energy Authority (IAEA) which was once sceptical about the threat has admitted that it is likely. Nuclear devices in the post-Cold War, post-September 11 world are 'relatively easy to snuggle into a US city, inside a shipping container, by plane, boat or car'.[151] 'Suitcase bombs' containing nuclear devices constitute a dangerous threat and can be easily carried to a target. In 1997, Russian General Alexander Lebed claimed that the Russian Government had lost 134 suitcase bombs. There were reports that the Chechen guerrillas had sold 20 of these to al-Quaida.[152] The post-September 11 2001 threat of a terrorist nuclear weapon remains. Accidental launches of missiles also threaten the US.

Introducing the NMD, which America has committed itself to, is the clearest signal yet that America will defend itself against offensive missile threats in a proactive defensive posture. NMD is a deterrent to potential adversaries. However, the reality is that many threats which the US faces cannot be solved by national missile defence alone. NMD cannot protect the US or its allies against the threat of 'suitcase bombs'. NMD cannot protect against nuclear devices inside planes, boats or cars. NMD cannot protect against the post-September 11 threat of a terrorist nuclear weapon attack which is likely to be delivered by non-ICBM means. NMD, if proven feasible, can only protect against ICBM (intercontinental ballistic missile) launches (and this protection itself is questionable, as tests of the NMD system have suffered failures).

It is argued that the rogue states whose behaviour motivated the US to move towards missile defences do not actually possess nuclear weapons or ICBMs.[153] However, this could only be a matter of time. Consequently, there is a need for NMD. The countries which do possess these nuclear weapons and ICBMs are countries which are allies of the US or which have diplomatic dialogue with the US (Russia, China, India etc.) Ironically, the US's proposed NMD system, it is argued, will alienate these very countries, including Pakistan. It has already caused China and Pakistan to become closer. Both countries are 'bitterly opposed to the NMD'.[154]

Although the SDI during the Reagan administration served as an important instrument to both enduce concessions from the Soviets (and ultimately convince them of the Reagan administration's intention for world peace), that was a time when the world was bipolar. There was only one threat to the US: the Soviet Union. Now, we live in a multipolar world, with many sources of conflict, and the reality is that NMD will only respond to one particular threat: that of a first-strike ICBM launch. NMD must not be viewed as a panacea to all post-September 11 threats to US national security. However, the actions of nations engaging in the proliferation of weapons only serves to push the US in its quest to build a missile defence system.

Although in theory it is correct that the post-Cold War threats of 'missile technology and weapons of mass destruction – do argue strongly for effective missile defence',[155] the reality, in practice, is that the NMD system could be obsolete as soon as it would be deployed. Yet surely such an assertion is hypothetical? It relies on the presupposition of a fact before it has occurred. The reality of the situation, however, is that this possibility has to be considered nevertheless. Notwithstanding, as new technologies advance each day, they create alternative possibilities of warfare. Perhaps the next phase of warfare would be information technology? Similarly, terrorists could find new methods of inflicting WMD on the US. NMD technologies themselves have not been 100 per cent proven. Then again, they would not need to be proven 100 per cent in order to deter the enemy from launching an attack. The enemy (as with the previous SDI) would perceive that the risks to it would outweigh the benefits of launching an attack on the US.

Unquestionably, NMD would serve as a deterrent to potential adversaries. This would be of extraordinary significance. However, adversaries could develop more feasible and cheaper counter-measures against the NMD system. (Decoys could confuse the missile system.) Furthermore, the US would still be vulnerable to an attack of weapons of mass destruction 'that exceeds the quite limited capacity of US defences'.[156] The US would still be vulnerable to a WMD attack by alternative means of delivery. NMD can cause rogue states to deliver WMD by alternative means. It is argued that NMD would actually 'push rogue nations toward such delivery systems'. Also, NMD 'cannot protect against attacks by nonstate terrorists'.[157] NMD cannot protect against chemical and biological attacks.

It is argued that the NMD system would actually encourage the proliferation of nuclear weapons as countries would begin an arms race to perfect their offense. So would begin an arms race in South Asia and other parts of the world. Igor Ivanov had earlier stated that nuclear non-proliferation would be harmed as a result of the NMD. He contended that global and regional instability would also increase as a consequence of it.[158] To Igor Ivanov, the post-Cold War threats could only be solved by 'the concerted efforts of the world community'. To decrease the missile threats, the world community must engage in 'joint efforts to strengthen strategic stability'.[159] Political measures which should 'infuse' the global environment with greater stability included 'arms control agreements, preventive diplomacy … provisions of international law … and lengthening the reaction time of missile systems'. It was suggested that surveillance data should be exchanged.[160] Is this too little, too late now as the North Korea episode escalates?

Regarding NMD, a plausible solution is that the US must develop a response to the missile threat by pre-empting their delivery in the first place. The US must question why these WMD are targeted at them and work out political solutions to pre-empt antagonisms, albeit through the UN or by enhancing counter-terrorist units. Yet the US had done this, and nuclear proliferation continues. America must also recognize that because a country has nuclear weapons, or is developing them, this does not mean that the country intends to attack the US. Capabilities do not equate to intentions. However, there does need to be an arbiter in the world to make sure that there is peace. America as the world's greatest superpower fulfils this role with moral obligation. The rest of the world would do well to remember this.

Countries like India and Pakistan have developed nuclear weapons for their own security against attack from each other, not to strike at the US. In today's multipolar world, countries fear attack from their neighbours as regional rivalries proliferate. The countries search to deter potential adversaries from invading them in order to increase their deterrence. It is part of the post-Cold War global situation. However, the nuclear deterrence/other missiles of these countries could fall into the hands of separatists/fundamentalists with destructive consequences. Consequently, America's concern and prudence is justified.

In theory, what is needed is for the US to constructively engage these countries with nuclear weapons/conventional weapons, and other countries (including 'rogue states') in a diplomatic dialogue to avoid the possibility of an attack on the US, rather than building a fortress around America and its allies in the hope of avoiding a first-strike. The US could encourage political moderation in the policies of government of the 'rogue states'. The US could seek to encourage and integrate countries into a multilateral alliance. Helping to democratize hostile nations would reduce the threat to the US. The key is preventative negotiations. America must put emphasis on engaging the nations which sponsor terrorism in diplomacy to prevent attacks. America should work more closely with Russia, China and the UN to achieve its objectives. In practice, the US has tried all of these options, yet nuclear proliferation continues.

NMD appears to be a solution to the threat of attack. It is a defence, and a deterrent. Countries will continue to modernize their weapons (ballistic and conventional missiles) regardless of whether the US deploys the NMD system, as nuclear proliferation continues in today's post-Cold War, post-September 11 society. (This proliferation will also continue to increase should the US and Russia reduce their nuclear missiles, as George W. Bush has stated that they would do.) Consequently, the question remains why should the US not defend itself against ballistic missiles? In theory, NMD can counter rogue states should they obtain ballistic missiles/fire conventional weapons. Consequently, in theory NMD will discourage proliferation as it will pre-empt the delivery of ICBMs, since the US would be protected against them. In practice, as technology advances each day, given time, research and development, NMD can be made to work.

So far, without the US NMD there has been nuclear proliferation. Perhaps with NMD this proliferation can stop. Regarding the legality of the NMD, it is argued that the NMD system will undermine the 1972 ABM Treaty. However, the nuclear and conventional missile proliferation that is happening has undermined this ABM Treaty anyway. Secondly, the ABM Treaty was amended in 1974 to permit one defensive missile site for the US and Soviet Union. Now that the Soviet Union is legally dead the ABM Treaty should be renegotiated. Countries should globally sign up not to engage in missile proliferation. Only then, could the US abandon its NMD. Whilst this proliferation continues the US can not be criticized and condemned for seeking ways in which to protect itself.

NMD is not the only answer to protect America's national security. It should not exclusively be relied upon. It should be used in conjunction with other elements of defence. Perhaps, instead of working on a space-based defence, alternative means of rendering ballistic missiles impotent could be found, such as launching missiles from submarines which attack incoming nuclear weapons high in space.[161] (The Soviets devote a lot of work to submarine technology.) The US could still have a NMD but a sea-based system opposed to a space-based one. Alternatively, they could have both.

The Pentagon has already acknowledged the importance of a sea-based defence in its NMD plans. The proposed US NMD system, which George W. Bush announced, would have interceptor missiles based at sea and in aircraft.[162] The US 'plans to base' its x-band radars (that detect and track missiles) 'on ships as an interim measure'.[163] The Joint Chiefs of Staff have produced a document 'Joint Vision 2020' which advocated the US to 'operate in all domains – space, sea, land, air, and information'.[164] To quell NMD doubters maybe the US's NMD should be exclusively sea-based? The answer is no, not entirely.

Just because the US does not currently have a space-based defence does not mean that this will not be possible. America's ally Israel tested its new Arrow interceptor missile system on January 5 2003.[165] Soon, other nations could follow. Given time, other nations will follow. Perhaps there is nowhere else for nuclear proliferation to go. Perhaps the future strategic policies of nations will be based on defensive rather than offensive systems. A defensive oriented deterrent. It is a shame that arms control and global disarmament are not the way forward. National missile defences are a product of today's environment, which has forced America to defend itself. In theory, NMD is a good idea. It is a deterrent. In practice, only time, and the reaction of other nations to the US NMD system, will tell. Space-based defences will be a reality in the future.

Notes

1   Charles, Dan, 'Rise and Fall of Star Wars', *New Scientist*, March 20 1993, p. 25.; For the history of the SDI after Ronald Reagan, see Towell, Pat, 'Anti-Missile Evolution', *CQWR*, Vol. 56, No. 40, October 10 1998, p. 2756.

2   Charles, Dan, 'Rise and Fall of Star Wars', *New Scientist*, p. 2756.

3   Ibid.

4   Ibid.

5   Ibid., p. 25.

6   Ballistic Missile Defense Organization, 'Missile Defense Milestones 1944–1997', http://www.acq.osd.mil/bmdo/bmdolink/html/milstone.html

7   Ibid., p. 11.

8   Charles, 'Rise and Fall of Star Wars', *New Scientist*, p. 25.

9   Ballistic Missile Defense Organization, 'Ballistic Missile Defense: A Brief History', http://www.acq.osd.mil/bmdo/bmdolink/html/origins.html ; 'A History of the SDIO and BMDO', http://tsi.simplenet.com/tsihtml/sdio.html

10   'A History of the SDIO and BMDO', http://tsi.simplenet.com/tsihtml/sdio.html

11   Ibid.

12   Charles, 'Rise and Fall of Star Wars', *New Scientist*, p. 25.

13   Ibid.

14   Ibid.

15   Ibid., p. 25.

16   Ibid.

17   Ballistic Missile Defense Organization, 'Missile Defense Milestones 1944–1997', http://www.acq.osd.mil/bmdo/bmdolink/html/milstone.html

18   Charles, Dan, 'Rise and Fall of Star Wars', *New Scientist*, p. 25.

19   'A History of the SDIO and BMDO', http://tsi.simplenet.com/tsihtml/sdio.html

20   Ballistic Missile Defense Organization, 'Missile Defense Milestones 1944–1997', http://www.acq.osd.mil/bmdo/bmdolink/html/milstone.html

21   'A History of the SDIO and BMDO', http://tsi.simplenet.com/tsihtml/sdio.html

22   Ballistic Missile Defense Organization, 'Missile Defense Milestones 1944–1997', http://www.acq.osd.mil/bmdo/bmdolink/html/milstone.html

23   Ibid.

24 'A History of the SDIO and BMDO', http://tsi.simplenet.com/tsihtml/sdio.html

25 Ibid., p. 1.; Ballistic Missile Defense Organization, 'Theater Missile Defense Programs',
    http://www.acq.osd.mil/bmdo/bmdolink/html/tmd.html

26 Ballistic Missile Defense Organization, 'Ballistic Missile Defense: A Brief History',
    http://www.acq.osd.mil/bmdo/bmdolink/html/origins.html ; Ballistic Missile Defense
    Organization, 'Missile Defense Milestones 1944–1997',
    http://www.acq.osd.mil/bmdo/bmdolink/html/milstone.html

27 Ballistic Missile Defense Organization, 'Ballistic Missile Defense: A Brief History',
    http://www.acq.osd.mil/bmdo/bmdolink/html/origins.html

28 Ibid.

29 Ibid.

30 Ballistic Missile Defense Organization, 'Ballistic Missile Defense: A Brief History',
    http://www.acq.osd.mil/bmdo/bmdolink/html/origins.html ; 'A History of the SDIO and
    BMDO', http://tsi.simplenet.com/tsihtml/sdio.html ; BMDO Fact Sheet PO-99-01,
    'Ballistic Missile Defense Fiscal Year 1999 Budget', April 1999, web address unknown.

31 BMDO Fact Sheet AQ-99-04, 'PATRIOT Advanced Capability-3', February 1999, web
    address unknown.

32 'Theater Missile Defense (TMD)', http://www.zeltech.com/TMD.htm

33 This was stated by William S. Cohen on January 20 1999. BMDO Fact Sheet JN-99-05,
    'National Missile Defense Program', March 1999, web address unknown.

34 Ballistic Missile Defense Organization, 'Why Ballistic Missile Defenses? The Threat',
    http://www.acq.osd.mil/bmdo/bmdolink/html/threat.html

35 The Nuclear Roundtable Background Document, 'S.1124 National Defense
    Authorization Act for Fiscal Year 1996, Signed by the President on February 10 1996:
    Title II, Subtitle C, Ballistic Missile Defense Act of 1995', http://www.stimson.org/rd-
    table/bmd96.htm

36 Anderson, *Interview*.

37 Ibid.

38 Ibid.

39 The bipartisan commission was headed by former Secretary of Defense in the Gerald R.
    Ford administration Donald H. Rumsfeld.

40 Pomper, Miles A., and Pat Towell, 'GOP's Agenda Makes Little Headway Despite
    Clinton's Political Woes', *CQWR*, Vol. 56, No. 36, September 12 1998, p. 2414.

41 All information taken from *Report of the Commission to Assess the Ballistic Missile
    Threat to the United States*, Executive Summary, Pursuant to Public Law 201, 104th
    Congress, July 15 1998, pp. 51, 25, 18-19, respectively.

42 Ibid., p. 5.

43 Ibid.; That it is 'China, not Russia', or any 'rogue' state 'whose nuclear weapons policy
    will concern America most', see Roberts, Brad, Robert A. Manning and Ronald N.
    Montaperto, 'China: The Forgotten Nuclear Power', *Foreign Affairs*, Vol. 79, No. 4,
    July/August 2000, pp. 53-63, especially p. 53.

44 Towell, Pat, 'Hurry Up and Wait: Despite Goading by Hill, a Long Process Lies Ahead',
    CQWR, Vol. 57, No. 12, March 20 1999, p. 716.; The term 'rogue states' has recently
    been 'downgraded to 'countries of concern''. For an assessment of the threat from these
    countries, see Norton-Taylor, Richard, and Ewen MacAskill, 'Assessing The Threat',
    The Guardian, July 7 2000, p. 16.

45 Lewis, George, Lisbeth Gronlund and David Wright, 'National Missile Defense: An
    Indefensible System', *Foreign Policy*, No. 117, Winter 1999–2000, pp. 121-122.

46 Towell, Pat, 'Anti-Missile Defense: Supersonic Duel ... With Almost No Room For
    Mistakes', *CQWR*, Vol. 55, No. 20, May 17 1997, p. 1146.

47 O'Hanlon, Michael 'Star Wars Strikes Back', *Foreign Affairs*, Vol. 78, No. 6, November/December 1999, p. 68.; For information on Taiwan's security and Theater Missile Defense, see Christensen, Thomas J., 'Theater Missile Defense and Taiwan's Security', *Orbis: A Journal of World Affairs*, Vol. 44, No. 1, Winter 2000, pp. 79-90.

48 Towell, Pat, 'Anti-Missile Defense: Supersonic Duel', *CQWR*, p. 1147.

49 O'Hanlon, 'Star Wars Strikes Back', p. 68.

50 Ibid., pp. 75-76.

51 Payne, Keith B., 'The Case For National Missile Defense', *Orbis: A Journal of World Affairs*, Vol. 44, No. 2, Spring 2000, p. 187.; Nelson, Lars-Erik, 'Fantasia: A Book Review of FitzGerald, Frances, 'Way Out There in the Blue: Reagan, Star Wars and the End of the Cold War', New York, Simon and Schuster, 2000', *The New York Review of Books*, Vol. XLVII, No. 8, May 11 2000, p. 7.

52 Payne, 'The Case For National Missile Defense', p. 195.; For Moscow's objection to America's National Missile Defense (NMD) system, see ibid., pp. 194-196.

53 Towell, Pat, 'Effort to Build Anti-Missile System Gets a Strong, If Symbolic Lift', *CQWR*, Vol. 57, No. 12, March 20 1999, p. 715.; Pomper, Miles A., and Pat Towell, 'GOP's Agenda Makes Little Headway Despite Clinton's Political Woes', *CQWR*, Vol. 56, No. 36, September 12 1998, p. 2414.

54 For information on the Pentagon's '3 plus 3' plan, whereby a system would be developed in three years and fielded in another three, see Towell, Pat, 'Picking The Best Missile Defense: Cold War Treaty or New Weapons', *CQWR*, Vol. 56, No. 16, April 18 1998, p. 1001.

55 Walt, Stephen M., 'Two Cheers For Clinton's Foreign Policy', *Foreign Affairs*, Vol. 79, No. 2, March/April 2000, p. 73.

56 'Report Buoys Supporters of Anti Missile System', *CQWR*, Vol. 56, No. 29, July 18 1998, p. 1963.

57 Towell, Pat, 'Hurry Up and Wait: Despite Goading by Hill, a Long Process Lies Ahead', *CQWR*, Vol. 57, No. 12, March 20 1999, p. 716.

58 All information taken from Traynor, Ian, 'US and Russia Clash Over Missile Shield', *The Guardian*, June 5 2000, p. 1.

59 Ibid.

60 Ibid.

61 Ibid.

62 By Gittings, John in Beijing, and Amelia Gentleman in Moscow, 'Chinese Threaten Nuclear Arms Race', *The Guardian*, July 8 2000, p. 15.

63 Ibid.

64 Ibid.; That Moscow and Beijing 'fear a successful US anti-missile system could neutralise their own nuclear arsenals', see Barnett, Antony, 'Missed! $100m Foul-up For Star Wars', *The Observer*, July 9 2000, p. 2.

65 For information on the failed NMD test at Vandenberg Air Force Base, July 7–8 2000 (as reported on July 9 2000, in the newspaper *The Observer*), see the following: Barnett, 'Missed! $100m Foul-up For Star Wars', *The Observer*, pp. 1-2.; Vulliamy, 'Star Wars Falls To Earth', *The Observer*, July 9 2000, p. 22.

66 Barnett, 'Missed! $100m Foul-up For Star Wars', *The Observer*, p. 1.

67 Gittings and Gentleman, 'Chinese Threaten Nuclear Arms Race', *The Guardian*, p. 15.

68 Borger, Julian in Washington and Richard Norton-Taylor, 'Hit or Miss Trial for Son of Star Wars', *The Guardian*, July 7 2000, p. 16.

69 Ibid., p. 16.

70 Norton-Taylor, Richard, and Martin Kettle in Washington, 'Russia and Europe Ready to Hear Bush Plan', *The Guardian*, May 3 2001, p. 13.

[71] Ibid.
[72] White, Michael and Patrick Wintour, 'Labour Under Fire Over "Son of Star Wars" Policy', *The Guardian*, May 3 2001, p. 2.
[73] La Guardia, Anton, Diplomatic Editor, and Marcus Warren in Moscow, 'US Shield May Trigger Arms Race, Says China', *The Daily Telegraph*, May 3 2001, p. 8.
[74] Ibid.
[75] Smith, Michael, Defence Correspondent, 'Two Bases in Britain Will Play Key Role', *The Daily Telegraph*, May 3 2001, p. 8.
[76] Jones, George, Political Editor, 'Blairs Aide End Dither on Star Wars: No. 10 Comes off Fence to Back Bush', *The Daily Telegraph*, May 3 2001, p. 1.
[77] Editorial Comment, 'Blair and the Missiles', *The Daily Telegraph*, May 3 2001, p. 29.
[78] Cornwell, Rupert and Mary Dejevsky, 'Bush Launches New Space-Based Arms Juggernaut', *The Independent*, May 2 2001, p. 12.
[79] Macintyre, Ben, in Washington, 'US aims to Have Early Version of Missile Defence System by 2004', *The Times*, May 2 2001, p. 12.
[80] MacAskill, Ewen, in Genoa, 'Bush, Putin Link Shield to Arms Cuts', *The Guardian*, July 23 2001, p. 5.
[81] Macintyre, 'US aims to Have Early Version of Missile Defence System by 2004', *The Times*, p. 12.
[82] Whittell, Giles, in Moscow, 'Russia Says Bush Strategy Could Backfire', *The Times*, May 2 2001, p. 12.
[83] Ibid.
[84] Ibid.
[85] Kettle, Martin, in Washington, Richard Norton-Taylor, Michael White and Ian Traynor in Moscow, 'Bush Starts Selling "Son of Star Wars"', *The Guardian*, May 2 2001, p. 11.
[86] Ibid.
[87] Cockburn, Patrick, in Moscow, and Mart Dejevsky, in Washington, 'Russians Calmed by Promise of "Star Wars" Talks', *The Independent*, May 3 2001, p. 12.
[88] Ibid.
[89] Ibid.
[90] Kettle, Martin, in Washington, and Duncan Campbell, 'A Hit for Son of Star Wars', *The Guardian*, July 16 2001, p. 10.; Kettle, Martin, in Washington, and Richard Norton-Taylor, 'US Relief at Missile Test Success', *The Guardian*, July 16 2001, p. 2.
[91] Gentleman, Amelia, in Moscow, and John Gittings, in Shanghai, 'Russia and China Blast American Success', *The Guardian*, July 16 2001, p. 10.
[92] Ibid.
[93] Ibid.
[94] Whittell, Giles, in Moscow and Ben MacIntyre in Washington, 'Putin Threat to Launch New Arms Race', *The Times*, June 20 2001, p. 1.
[95] Ibid.
[96] Republican leader Trent Lott quoted in Kettle and Norton-Taylor, 'US Relief at Missile Test Success', *The Guardian*, p. 2.
[97] Gentleman and Gittings, 'Russia and China Blast American Success', *The Guardian*, p. 10.
[98] Allen, Mike and Peter Baker, Washington Post Service, 'Bush and Putin Agree to Link Missile Shield With Arms Cutbacks', *International Herald Tribune*, July 23 2001, p. 3.
[99] Glanz, James, 'Reagan's "Star Wars" is Making a Comeback: Pentagon Broadens Plans For Space Defense', *International Herald Tribune*, July 23 2001, p. 3.
[100] Ibid.
[101] Ibid.

[102] Norton Taylor, Richard and Amelia Gentleman in Moscow, 'Bush and Putin Open the Way to New Arms Deal', *The Guardian*, July 24 2001, p. 14.

[103] Ibid.

[104] Ibid. Quote is by the author.

[105] Grice, Andrew, 'Labour Revolt on Missile Defence', *The Independent*, September 11 2001, p. 1.

[106] Broad, William J., of The New York Times, 'US Ignores Early Failures in Missile Tests', *International Herald Tribune*, December 19 2002, p. 5.

[107] Monaghan, Elaine, in Washington, and Michael Evans, Defence Editor, 'US Requests British Base for "Son of Star Wars"', *The Times*, December 18 2002, p. 16.

[108] Tisdall, Simon and Richard Norton-Taylor, 'Star Wars Missiles May Be Based in UK', *The Guardian*, December 19 2002, p. 1.

[109] Editorial, 'Not in Our Interest: Missile Defence is the Wrong Road For Britain', *The Guardian*, December 19 2002, p. 21.

[110] Tisdall and Norton-Taylor, 'Star Wars Missiles May Be Based in UK', *The Guardian*, p. 1.

[111] Ibid.

[112] Ibid.

[113] Rennie, David, 'Bush Puts British Base in the Frontline', *The Daily Telegraph*, December 18 2002, p. 4.

[114] Ibid.

[115] Ibid.

[116] Ibid.

[117] Monaghan and Evans, 'US Requests British Base for "Son of Star Wars"', *The Times*, p. 16.

[118] Tisdall and Norton-Taylor, 'Star Wars Missiles May Be Based in UK', *The Guardian*, p. 1.

[119] Goldenberg, Suzanne, in Washington, and Richard Norton-Taylor, 'America Announces Premature Birth of Son of Star Wars', *The Guardian*, December 18 2002, p. 12.

[120] Ibid.

[121] Ibid.

[122] From News Reports, 'US Defense Shield Plan is Attacked by Russia: It Warns of "New Senseless Arms Race"', *International Herald Tribune*, December 19 2002, p. 5.

[123] Ibid.

[124] Tisdall and Norton-Taylor, 'Star Wars Missiles May Be Based in UK', *The Guardian*, p. 1.

[125] From News Reports, 'US Defense Shield Plan is Attacked by Russia: It Warns of "New Senseless Arms Race"', *International Herald Tribune*, p. 5.

[126] Ibid.

[127] Ibid.

[128] Rennie, David, 'Bush Puts British Base in the Frontline', *The Daily Telegraph*, p. 4.

[129] Editorial, 'Not in Our Interest: Missile Defence is the Wrong Road For Britain', *The Guardian*, p. 21.

[130] Ibid.

[131] Ibid.

[132] Monaghan and Evans, 'US Requests British Base for "Son of Star Wars"', *The Times*, p. 16.

[133] The New York Times Editorial Commentary, 'Unreliable Missile Defense', *International Herald Tribune*, December 19 2002, p. 8.

[134] Norton-Taylor, Richard, 'Star Wars Deal is Just First Step, Admits Hoon', *The Guardian*, January 16 2003, p. 11.

[135] Ibid.

[136] Ibid.

[137] Ibid.

[138] Ibid.

[139] Wintour, Patrick and Richard Norton-Taylor, 'Hoon to Let US Use Base For Son of Star Wars', *The Guardian*, January 15 2003, p. 8.

[140] Ibid.

[141] Ibid.

[142] Helm, Toby, Chief Political Correspondent, 'Labour Anger at Decision to Back "Son of Star Wars"', *The Daily Telegraph*, January 16 2003, p. 10.

[143] Ibid.

[144] Ibid.

[145] Ibid.

[146] Hopkins, Nick and Tania Branigan, 'Poison Find Sparks Terror Alert', *The Guardian*, January 8 2003, p. 1.

[147] La Guarda, Anton, Diplomatic Editor, 'Britain Will Back US Over Axis of Evil, Says Straw', *The Daily Telegraph,* January 6 2003, p. 12.

[148] Rifkind, Malcolm, 'North Korean Crisis is More Menacing Than Baghdad', *The Times*, December 27 2002, p. 22.

[149] Browne, Anthony, 'Pyongyang May Have A-Bomb in 30 Days', *The Times*, December 27 2002, p. 17.

[150] Borger, Julian in Washington and Ewen MacAskill, 'Black Market Means Bin Laden May Already Have a "Dirty" Nuclear Bomb', *The Guardian*, November 7 2001, p. 3.

[151] Ibid.

[152] Ibid.

[153] Miller, Steven E., 'The Flawed Case For Missile Defence', *Survival*, Vol. 43, No. 3, Autum 2001, p. 97.

[154] Harding, Luke, 'India is the New Pakistan', *The Guardian*, May 16 2001, p. 22.

[155] Arnold, Klaus, 'Making Missile Defence Beningn', *Survival*, Vol. 43, No. 3, Autumn 2001, p. 84.

[156] Miller, 'The Flawed Case For Missile Defence', p. 99.

[157] Levine, Robert A., 'Deterrence and the ABM: Retreading the Old Calculus', *World Policy Journal*, Vol. XVIII, No. 3, Fall 2001, p. 30.

[158] Ivanov, Igor, 'The Missile Defense Mistake: Undermining Strategic Stability and the ABM Treaty', *Foreign Affairs*, Vol. 79, No. 5, September/October 2000, p. 18.

[159] Ibid., p. 19.

[160] Newhouse, John, 'The Missile Defense Debate', *Foreign Affairs*, Vol. 80, No. 4, July/August 2001, p. 98.

[161] This is supported by the following works which highlight the importance of launching missiles from submarines: Regarding the importance of submarines: That US submarines had a 'devastating and invulnerable nuclear deterrent' and 'could have destroyed the Soviet Union as a functioning society', see Nelson, Lars-Erik, 'Fantasia: A Book Review of FitzGerald, Frances, 'Way Out There in the Blue: Reagan, Star Wars and the End of the Cold War', New York, Simon and Schuster, 2000', *The New York Review of Books*, p. 6.; Further documenting the importance of submarines is David Greenberg. He states that 'even a working antimissile system would not render nuclear weapons 'obsolete' as Reagan dreamed, since submarines and airplanes could still deliver apocalyptic payloads'. Greenberg, David, 'Review Essay: The Empire Strikes

Out: Why Star Wars Did Not End the Cold War: A Review of FitzGerald, Frances, 'Way Out There in the Blue: Reagan, Star Wars and the End of the Cold War', New York, Simon and Schuster, 2000', *Foreign Affairs*, Vol. 79, No. 2, March/April 2000, p. 139.; The importance of ships was apparent by the *Report of the Commission to Assess the Ballistic Missile Threat to the United States*, also known as the report of the Rumsfeld Commission. It asserted that countries could 'threaten the United States with medium-range missiles launched from ships'. See O'Hanlon, Michael, 'Star Wars Strikes Back', p. 71. See also p. 82.; For the feasibility of cruise missiles launches from 'boats or submarines', see O'Hanlon, Michael, 'Star Wars Strikes Back', p. 74.; For 'new submarines with ballistic missile launching capability', see Roberts, Manning and Montaperto, 'China: The Forgotten Nuclear Power', p. 55.; Regarding the importance of ship launched ballistic missiles: Writing in Winter 1999–2000, George Lewis, Lisbeth Gronlund and David Wright contended that 'The Rumsfeld Commission noted, it would be easier for an emerging missile state to develop shorter-range, ship-launched ballistic missiles than ICBMs'. See Lewis, Gronlund and Wright, 'National Missile Defense: An Indefensible System', p. 124.; See also the Rumsfeld Commission Report – *Report of the Commission to Assess the Ballistic Missile Threat to the United States*, Executive Summary, Pursuant to Public Law 201, 104th Congress, July 15 1998.; Regarding the importance of submarine launched ballistic missiles, George Lewis, Lisbeth Gronlund and David Wright, affirmed that 'Even as the United States builds its missile defense, it will retain large numbers of highly accurate ICBMs and submarine-launched ballistic missiles (SLBMs), which have considerable first-strike capabilities against Russia's nuclear forces'. They also state that 'U.S. nuclear-powered attack submarines continue to operate near Russian ballistic missile submarine bases, posing a direct threat to the few missile submarines Russia is able to maintain at sea at any given time'. Lewis, Gronlund and Wright, 'National Missile Defense: An Indefensible System', p. 131.; Writing in the journal *Foreign Policy*, in Summer 2000, John Deutch, Harold Brown and John P. White highlight the importance of submarine-launched ballistic missiles. They write that the US remained 'vulnerable to a large Russian attack with ICBM and submarine-launched ballistic missile (SLBM) strikes'. They also contended that the US remained 'vulnerable to nuclear, chemical, and biological attacks delivered by various means'. According to them 'Potential attackers' had a variety of options 'cruise missiles, aircraft, short-range ballistic missiles launched from a ship or submarine, or surreptitious transfer by truck or suitcase'. Deutch, John, Harold Brown and John P. White, 'National Missile Defense: Is There Another Way?', *Foreign Policy*, No. 119, Summer 2000, pp. 92-93.

[162] Goldenberg and Norton-Taylor, 'America Announces Premature Birth of Son of Star Wars', *The Guardian*, p. 12.

[163] Norton-Taylor, 'Star Wars Deal is Just First Step, Admits Hoon', *The Guardian*, p. 11.

[164] Newhouse, 'The Missile Defense Debate', p. 105.

[165] McGreal, Chris, 'Israel Tests New Missile System', *The Guardian*, January 6 2003, p. 9.

Conclusion

To answer the question whether the SDI was important in the end of the Cold War, it is necessary to determine whether the SDI was important in US–Soviet relations, and, consequently, whether it affected Mikhail Gorbachev. Then it is important to analyse in what way did it affect Gorbachev's policies which in turn resulted in the end the Cold War; the cessation of hostilities with the West. That is not to say that Mikhail Gorbachev initially came to power with the intention of ending the Cold War. Gorbachev's policies were ones of retrenchment; he sought to modify Soviet policy by updating it to the circumstances that required change. He saw that to survive, the Soviet Union had to reform. Unquestionably, Soviet overstretch caused by its Cold War 'competition' with America had exacerbated the inherent weaknesses of its economy which was a legacy of the Leninist–Stalinist system. American policy exacerbated the Soviet crisis. The crucial question is whether America wanted to bring the Soviet Union to 'collapse' through its SDI?

As attested by Peter Schweizer, looking at the end of the Cold War, the timing of its ending has to be answered. Why did the Cold War end when it did? The flaws in the Soviet system and the productivity of capitalism were always present. That the Cold War ended when it did, therefore, must have been due to either Ronald Reagan or Mikhail Gorbachev. Schweizer contends that Ronald Reagan was the man who ended it.[1] Whilst technically the Cold War ended under George Bush's presidency, the foundations for this end were undoubtedly laid in the Reagan–Gorbachev era.

The Reagan administration policies played an important role in affecting the Soviet Union. Whether it was because of the defence build-up (which too cost the American economy) and caused the Soviets to similarly 'build-up' their weapons procurement, and further 'spend their way to oblivion'. Or whether it was the American simultaneous desire to engage the Soviets in arms control talks, which reinforced in the Soviet minds that the Americans were not the great enemy that they were perceived to have been during the Cold War hostilities. Ronald Reagan believed that a US arms build-up would put a strain on the Soviet economy and eventually force the Soviets to the bargaining table on arms control.[2] Reagan's policy was to 'bargain from strength'. In the end 'Reagan Victory' had achieved its aim.

Was the SDI an instrument of Reagan's 'squeeze strategy' that was designed to overburden the USSR's economy? If it were, why exactly did the Reagan administration negotiate arms reductions with the Soviets during the second term Reagan administration? Would not it have been easier to keep squeezing the Soviet Union until it collapsed?

The most plausible explanation is that SDI was not part of the arms build-up 'squeeze strategy'. That is not to say that the strategy did not exist. (The fact that the SDI was as a surprise to the US foreign policy bureaucracy is evidence that the

SDI was not part of the 'squeeze strategy'.) The Reagan administration wanted to negotiate arms reductions with the Soviets because it wanted to terminate Cold War hostilities through peaceful dialogue. To make sure that peace was achieved with the Soviets through diplomacy, (so that the Soviet Union did not threaten the US again), not forged in a battle which would result in the Soviets being humiliated and later avenging their defeat. Its squeeze strategy was merely a way of ensuring that the Soviets would be present at the talks, and that the Soviet options would be narrowed to them.

The Reagan administration wanted to bring about a reduction of weapons, both conventional and nuclear. Reagan himself was surprised of Soviet fears that the West was to launch a nuclear attack (The NATO Able Archer 83 exercise held on November 11 1983)[3] and was keen to get the Soviet leader in a room and persuade him that the US would never launch a first-strike. It is not an issue here, albeit correct, whether Reagan was more flexible in his first term and stronger in his second.

Evidence points to the contention that Ronald Reagan, even before his election as President was committed to reducing the stockpile of nuclear weapons. In his presidential election debate with President Jimmy Carter, on October 28 1980, Reagan affirmed that the Soviets had 'managed, in spite of all our attempts at arms limitation, to go forward with the biggest military build up in the history of man'.[4] Reagan strongly opposed 'the one-sided SALT II Treaty' (strategic arms limitation treaty) to limit nuclear arms on the ground that it was advantageous to the Soviets. Reagan said that he would negotiate a treaty 'to genuinely limit strategic nuclear weapons'.[5]

In a campaign advertisement, on November 2 1980, Ronald Reagan stated that amongst his foreign policy approach would be 'to work non-stop for the world's greatest course: the cause of *peace*'.[6] In a subsequent interview, President-elect Reagan said of one of his objectives in foreign policy 'I want to make certain that the entire world understands that peace is our first priority'.[7] Ronald Reagan in both his first term and second term administration was conducive to talks with the Soviets.

So if the SDI was not part of the squeeze strategy, then what was it? To President Reagan, the SDI was a means of achieving a peaceful world. It was a way of superceeding nuclear weapons altogether. The President had an inherent hatred and fear of nuclear war, and to him the SDI would be a guarantee that this would never happen. That is why he proposed to share SDI technology with the Soviet Union. That is why, when urged to use the SDI as a bargaining chip, (by many in his administration) in the US–Soviet summits, Reagan refused to do so. On many occasions he reaffirmed that the SDI was not a bargaining chip.

Reagan did not want to make the SDI a condition for talks with the Soviets – unlike Gorbachev – and he certainly did not want to exchange the SDI for a reduction of Soviet offensive missiles – unlike Gorbachev, again. Reagan wanted to guarantee that the world was safe from a nuclear holocaust once he and Gorbachev were no longer leaders, as who knew what 'madman' would come along long after they were both gone. Gorbachev came to recognize that Reagan was genuine in his ideal of peace and so felt confident to make the concessions which he later made, and which he knew that the US would not exploit, which eventually resulted in the 'end of the Cold War'. SDI, therefore, contributed to the Soviet reassessment of foreign, military and strategic policy, which ultimately ended the Cold War through conciliation.

Yet the path to this did not run this smooth. It was a long journey played out over many years and through many summit meetings. The initial perception of the SDI in Soviet minds was one of fear of an American first-strike. It was only when Gorbachev had made his concessions at the US–Soviet summits and the US President refused to abandon his SDI did the Soviet leader become convinced that the President was genuine in his SDI rhetoric. Who else would fail to abandon a yet unready system in exchange for already deployed offensive weapons, if one was not resolutely faithful in ones conviction.

It is argued that the SDI bankrupted the Soviet Union. Critics assert that this cannot be proven, as we do not have access to Soviet defence expenditure and archives. Yet we do not necessarily need to have this to make an assertion regarding the importance of the Soviet response to SDI. This is demonstrated by the public pronouncements that the Soviets gave (in response to the US SDI) as well as the concessions that they proposed during the summit meetings in exchange for it.

The Soviets responded to the SDI by unleashing a campaign against it, whilst simultaneously proposing arms talks with Washington. There was a discrepancy between the Soviet rhetoric towards and actual reaction to the SDI. For a project that the Soviets deemed unfeasible, their response to it was disproportionate to the contention which they espoused. The Soviets were against the proposed US SDI, yet they themselves were working on their own strategic ballistic missile defence (BMD) programme. They also had their own operational Moscow Galosh anti-ballistic missile (ABM) system.[8] If the SDI were unfeasible (as the Soviets claimed) why did they work on strategic defences? Could this not have been a reason for them to discontinue their own BMD programme? If BMD were unfeasible, the Soviet Union could have encouraged the US to overstretch its resources on a wasted project.[9] The contradiction in the Soviet statements (such as that the SDI was 'technologically infeasible' and 'well within the reach of Soviet military scientists'[10]) was reconciled to the fact that the Soviets genuinely feared being overtaken by an American strategic defence system. Evidence corroborates the interpretation that the Soviets wanted to maintain a monopoly in strategic defences and feared the superior technology of their US competitors.

The SDI was perceived to have proposed a competition with the US in the production of modern military systems, in which the US had the comparative advantage in, and the Soviets had relatively fallen behind in. The Soviets feared the comparatively superior US technology. The SDI was an important psychological weapon against the Soviet Union.[11] Was their perception of SDI overexaggerated? Ronald Reagan himself recognized that SDI could not be deployed for another 20 years. He never viewed the shield as impenetrable, but it offered a greater hope of protection than what the US currently relied on; mutual assured destruction. Even though the shield could not be 100 per cent effective, the SDI could still deter the enemy from launching an attack.

Critics of the SDI state that if the SDI were feasible why did the US not object to the Soviets having an ABM system already deployed? This, critics assert, must demonstrate that ballistic missile defences were not feasible, and, that consequently the SDI was not a plausible concept. The answer to this question is tied in to the other claim made by SDI critics, namely 'if the SDI could not be deployed for another 20 years, how did this consequently demonstrate to the Soviets that they were no longer competitive?'.

The answer is a simple one. Even though the Soviets had an ABM defence deployed, whilst the US did not, the US had a strong history of ABM defence (its 'Sentinel' and 'Safeguard' systems). The US was capable of recreating its former technology to create an ABM defence, if it had chosen to do so. However, what the US proposed to do with its SDI proposal was to have a 'full' space-based defence, as opposed to a ground-based system which is what the Soviets had, with their Moscow ABM system. The Soviet ABM system did not concern the Americans, as they did not plan to launch a ballistic missile attack on Moscow. What bothered Moscow was that the Americans planned a space-based anti-ballistic missile system. This involved the technologies which the Soviets had fallen behind in. The SDI, therefore, was a representation of what the Soviets once had expertise in, but now could not do as well. It represented their inability to compete at a time when their resources were strained, through their military excursions in Afghanistan.

SDI critics should turn their attention to the question of if the Americans proposed to share SDI technology with the Soviets, why then were the Soviets concerned with SDI? Does that mean that the Soviets planned to strike at the US? The answer is that the Soviets did not intend to launch a first-strike, just like the Americans did not intend to strike at the Soviet Union. That is why by definition the Cold War was called the Cold War. It was fought by proxy in the 'Third World', for superpower global domination. A first-strike by either nation was out of the question by the very nature of the Cold War logic and nuclear confrontation. True, the nuclear threat remained. It was very real. Yet so did the stability in the global balance of power. There was no turmoil, as had occurred when the Soviet Union ceased to exist, and there was a vacuum at the heart of international politics, when the enemy was 'unknown'. A feeling initially felt when the World Trade Center was attacked in September 2001.

When President Reagan announced the SDI, the rules of the Cold War were perceived, by the Soviets, to have changed. To them, Reagan had changed the status quo. The perception of a 'threat' – in this case the SDI – (although it was actually intended to guard against threats and was not a threat in itself) meant that the Soviets feared a potential first-strike by the Americans. Allegedly proposing a 'competition' in the technological systems which the Soviets had fallen back in could only arouse the suspicions of the Soviets as to SDI's true motivation. The reality was that SDI was just a defence.

The US President recognized that 'defensive systems have limitations and raise certain problems and ambiguities'. Pairing them with offensive systems they could be viewed as 'fostering an aggressive policy'.[12] However, Ronald Reagan maintained that no one wanted that. What he wanted was for nuclear weapons to become redundant. Reagan spoke of his desire for a nuclear-free world in his memoirs *An American Life*. Ronald Reagan's plan was to introduce the SDI, and simultaneously eliminate nuclear weapons. Then both the US and the Soviet Union could deploy the SDI and there would be a non-nuclear utopia.

It was due to the fact that there was the stalemate in US–Soviet relations, in that the Soviets continued their offensive force increases and arms control had broken down, that the SDI was introduced at the time it was, in 1983. The timing is important. Introduced to render ballistic missiles impotent and obsolete if they were fired at the US, it was hoped that the SDI could contribute successfully to arms control, by engaging the Soviets in talks on getting rid of nuclear and conventional weapons. The SDI filled a void in policy. It offered various solutions. As well as enhancing strategic stability and leading away from mutual vulnerability, it was a response to the anti-nuclear and 'nuclear freeze' movement.

Mikhail Gorbachev had threatened to defeat the US SDI with counter-measures. He claimed that the Soviets had developed a response to the SDI. One must pose the question here of why were the Soviets responding to a system which they declared unfeasible? This is tied in to the question of why the Soviets were against the US SDI when they themselves were involved with their own programme, and had their own mini SDI around Moscow. One can only conclude, again, that they were scared of the potential US technology.

This would have socio–political ramifications on the Soviet ability to project world power. The USSR had to be seen, especially in its satellite nations, to be a superpower. A superpower during the Cold War era could not afford to fall behind in the 'arms' or 'space' race. When the Soviets were the first superpower to go into space in 1961, President John F. Kennedy announced that the US would put a man on the moon within ten years. Ronald Reagan's proposal of a space-based defence would incite the Soviets to follow suit. Interestingly, Gorbachev revealed to Reagan, during the 1985 Geneva summit, that the Soviet Union had developed their response to the US SDI. The Soviets attempt at trying to get the Americans to abandon the SDI, even as late as 1987 and 1988 – despite the fact that they had actually developed their response to it as early as 1985 – is evidence that the Soviets feared the SDI.

Mikhail Gorbachev admitted Soviet strategic defence research on November 30 1987. Was Gorbachev's claim a smokescreen for actual Soviet capabilities? Could it have been a ploy to exaggerate their state of technology and capability in order to get the US to overstretch its capability? The answer will appear yes to SDI critics. However, upon analysis of private Gorbachev–Reagan correspondence and the Soviet conditions imposed on the SDI at the Reagan–Gorbachev summits, then the answer is no.

The SDI was a greater threat to the Soviets than what they wanted everyone to believe. Private correspondence from the *Donald T. Regan Papers* (located at the Library of Congress) shows that that SDI was a crucial issue between the two leaders. Gorbachev's December 24 1985 letter to Reagan shows that he was extremely worried about the SDI. Gorbachev devoted four out of five pages of the letter to the issue of defensive systems in space. Reagan wrote three out of five pages on the issue in his February 12 1986 draft reply to Gorbachev's letter. (In his letter Gorbachev wrote that SDI should not go 'beyond the walls of the laboratory'.)[13]

Yet, the Soviets had actually conducted their own anti-missile weapons tests in space which were, in fact, the type of tests which they wanted banned in the 1972 ABM Treaty. At Reykjavik they proposed to ban such anti-missile weapons tests for a ten-year period. This proposal corroborates the interpretation that the Soviets feared the American SDI.[14] In the Soviet minds, it was acceptable for them to conduct anti-missile tests, yet they tried to prevent the US from doing so.

Evidence that the Soviets were concerned about the SDI was most apparent at the US–Soviet summit meetings. The Reykjavik summit (1986) was a success in terms of the improving relations between the superpowers, and heralded a turning point in US–Soviet relations towards a safer world. Further US–Soviet summits built upon the success of the diplomatic relations which Reykjavik consolidated, and Geneva instigated. Mikhail Gorbachev was frightened of the SDI. At the Reykjavik summit, Gorbachev, in what appeared to be a concession, no longer demanded that SDI research be banned. However, he insisted that SDI research be confined to the laboratory, and that all anti-ballistic missile tests in space be banned. This would prohibit the SDI. The most contentious issue at the Reykjavik summit was the ABM Treaty. To Gorbachev, every agreement made, during the summit, was conditional upon SDI abandonment. Gorbachev hoped to achieve such an abandonment by urging a stricter interpretation of the ABM Treaty.

Despite Gorbachev's SDI–INF–START delink (in February 1987) the Soviet leader was still preoccupied with the SDI, as his September 1987 letter to Reagan showed. Previous to the Washington summit (December 7–10 1987) Gorbachev still insisted on concessions on the SDI. The Soviets rejected a START deal unless the US would limit SDI under the terms of the ABM Treaty. Seeking a 50 per cent cut in strategic weapons, Gorbachev tried to incorporate the SDI into the discussions, but left it to one side when the US refused. During the Washington summit, Gorbachev stated that negotiations would proceed on START and the US and Soviet Union would leave the SDI aside. This was Gorbachev's SDI–START delink.

Two days before the summit, the Soviets revealed they would cast aside their differences with the US over the ABM Treaty interpretation. This was because the Soviets recognized that Congress refused to let the US implement a broad interpretation of the treaty, thereby limiting SDI testing. The Soviets agreed to drafting an agreement on strategic arms, which would not prevent SDI testing, because Congress prohibited the Reagan administration from SDI tests except those permitted under the narrow interpretation of the ABM Treaty which Moscow favoured. This was an 'agreement to disagree', which would allow for progress on the START Treaty.[15]

At the Washington summit, the US and the Soviet Union did not try to resolve what SDI testing was allowed under the ABM Treaty. Instead, using intentionally ambiguous instructions they deferred the resolution. Gorbachev had advocated a new approach in stopping the US SDI. Gorbachev's new policy was one of stopping the SDI by trying to strengthen the 1972 ABM Treaty, by pressing for a stricter interpretation of it. He was aided in his hope of SDI abandonment by the fact that Congress had restricted the SDI (by limiting SDI testing). The Soviets rarely mentioned SDI anymore. Rather, they talked about strengthening the ABM Treaty. This, however, was designed to stop SDI.

Gorbachev tried to negotiate arms reductions, whilst trying to agree on a period during which both sides would observe the ABM Treaty. (Gorbachev's signing of the INF Treaty appeared a way of destroying the SDI, as the (medium-range) missiles destroyed in the INF Treaty would not be used in the SDI tests.) Gorbachev wanted to conclude a START agreement separately whilst letting Congress kill SDI for him. The conclusion of the START Treaty would mean the death of the SDI. A START accord and Treaty was not reached or signed, at the Moscow summit. SDI precluded a START agreement. The dispute over how much SDI testing was allowed was the principal obstacle to the START Treaty (as was the issue of sea-launched cruise missiles). On June 1 1988, Gorbachev repeated his opposition to the SDI. He perceived it as an obstacle to START and did not believe it to be a defensive weapon.

The fact that the joint US–Soviet communique, regarding the ABM Treaty and strategic offensive arms, did not clarify what SDI testing was permitted, shows that Gorbachev upheld his conviction of abandoning SDI by forcing a narrow interpretation of the ABM Treaty. This shows that the SDI still troubled the Soviet Union as a START Treaty was not signed. Demonstrating that the SDI troubled the Soviet Union is that the Soviets continued to insist that the SDI be confined to the narrow ABM Treaty interpretation in exchange for strategic offensive arms reductions.

If Gorbachev was so concerned about the SDI, as was demonstrated at the US–Soviet summits, why did he make the concessions that he made? Is this not an inherent paradox? The SDI prevented an agreement at the Washington summit, so, consequently, how can one give the SDI credit for causing the Soviets to seek a more cooperative course in the US–Soviet negotiations?

Although Gorbachev made the concessions that he made, he continued to regard the SDI as a threat to the Soviet Union, which is why he did not sign a START accord. As long as the US hung onto their SDI, Gorbachev failed to sign a START Treaty. This accounts for why when Reagan's successor George Bush was elected President, he no longer clung onto Reagan's SDI plan, and so the START Treaty was signed between Gorbachev and the USA.

As for the significant signing of the INF Treaty between Reagan and Gorbachev, it can be argued that both countries found it conducive to sign this treaty for the weapons that it dealt with (the Pershing II and SS-20s) had outlived their usefulness as both political and strategic weapons. They had become obsolete. The SDI–INF delink that Gorbachev made was more an issue of pragmatism, not a good will gesture. His SDI–INF delinkage policy was, to Gorbachev, like killing two birds with one stone. Simultaneously, he hoped to get rid of his obsolete weapons, and force the US to abandon the SDI. When the US refused to do so, Gorbachev nevertheless signed the INF agreement, with an aim of defeating the SDI by a new method: strengthening the ABM Treaty.

Therefore, it is not a paradox to say that SDI prevented agreements, yet made the Soviets seek a more cooperative course in negotiations. Gorbachev was forced by the realities of his domestic situation (exacerbated by competition with the US during the Second Cold War) to adopt the policies which he did. Gorbachev was concerned about the SDI. Gorbachev did make concessions. His new approach (advocating a strict adherence to the ABM Treaty) was just a different way of trying to defeat the SDI. The INF Treaty, however, was useful to both leaders. It was a symbolic accord. The reality was that the current situation in both countries necessitated it. If two other leaders would have been in power an INF Treaty might have been signed sooner or later.

Stating that, however, is not to deny that without Reagan and Gorbachev's mutual rapport that was emerging at the summits, the subsequent relations that followed the signing of the INF Treaty would not have happened if any other two leaders would have been in power. The Cold War would not have ended the peaceful way it did – without a war – and with the resulting friendly relations between the two nations (with which it ended), that has continued to characterize today's relations between the US and Russia.

The Soviets would not have necessarily made the concessions that they made had any leader other than Ronald Reagan been in power. Albeit for reasons of retrenchment and pragmatism, Gorbachev would not have made the unilateral concessions which he made if he had not been sure that the US side would not exploit the Soviet actions. Gorbachev was sure that Reagan would not exploit the Soviet actions. Similarly, without Gorbachev, if there had been a hard-line Soviet leader in power Reagan's policies would have resulted in a hardening anti-American Soviet policy.

Quite simply, Reagan and Gorbachev got on well and they had a mutual respect for each other. They liked each other and saw that they could do business with each other. Gorbachev admired Reagan as a former Hollywood actor, and Reagan admired Gorbachev as being a new unique leader that was different from all previous Soviet leaders. To Reagan, Gorbachev was one who had not died in office. Reagan did not even want to blame human rights problems on Gorbachev, but on the Soviet 'bureaucracy'.

In March 2000, a letter was released which was written by Mikhail Gorbachev in which he urged Congress to give a US Congressional Gold medal to Ronald Reagan. In the letter, Gorbachev wrote that 'together' he and Reagan had taken the 'first, most important steps to end the Cold War and start real nuclear disarmament'. Gorbachev stated that from their Geneva summit meeting Reagan had engaged Gorbachev in an 'honest and respectful dialogue'. He wrote that their 'human rapport' had continued between them after they had both left their respective governments.[16]

So it was that what started out as an issue of pragmatism, (for both countries) albeit wanting to improve US–Soviet relations, that the INF Treaty was signed. So began a journey that would unravel in the end of the Cold War for two leaders who quite simply were in touch with an emotion that previous US–Soviet leaders were not in touch with. Ronald Reagan and Mikhail Gorbachev, by agreeing to meet with each other and by actually finding themselves agreeing with each other on issues of mutual human benefit, demystified each other as the enemy. They saw that their positions on issues were not so far apart. They were two human beings wanting to improve their country's relations and improve the prospects of peace throughout the world, which had been endangered by the Cold War.

Ronald Reagan and Mikhail Gorbachev were both a new type of leader who recognized the futility in carrying on with the Cold War. Whether it was because they wanted to increase their military spending in order to compel the opposition to surrender (Reagan's 'bargaining from strength' approach), or propose a series of unprecedented unilateral concessions (Gorbachev's policy); both leaders wanted to bring about a reduction of hostility with the other. They wanted to end the futile Cold War that had cost both countries a great deal in terms of money, hatred and mutual suspicion.

It was only after the Reagan–Gorbachev summits that US–Soviet cooperation (that we have in the last decade become accustomed to) was possible. Whether it was relations between US Presidents George Bush, Bill Clinton or George W. Bush and Russian Presidents Boris Yeltsin or Vladimir Putin, the foundations for each leaders relations with his counterpart was shaped by what Reagan and Gorbachev had achieved. This Reagan–Gorbachev cooperation was the foundation for today's relations between the US and Russia. Reagan and Gorbachev shaped modern politics. After Gorbachev's December 7 1988 United Nations speech, the credibility of the UN was enhanced. Global cooperation was required to solve the world's instabilities. Gorbachev's UN speech gave credibility to the UN which it lacked before. To make the speech though, Gorbachev must have changed his perception of the West. For this, Reagan could take credit.

Ronald Reagan's friendship with Mikhail Gorbachev – based on trust – was a major factor in dissipating the mistrust of the Cold War.[17] Gorbachev's later relationship with President George Bush was nowhere near as warm as with Reagan. This relationship was a breakthrough in genuine cooperation and friendly relations between the two countries. This 'humanism' factor was notably highlighted as important at the February 1993 'Retrospective on the End of the Cold War', Princeton University Conference by former Cold War officials.[18]

Notwithstanding, Gorbachev was concerned about the SDI, but he made concessions because he knew that the US would not exploit them. Also they were imperative to the Soviet situation, at the time (the need for retrenchment). Although Gorbachev made concessions, these when examined do not negate the contention that the SDI made Gorbachev concede. SDI by itself was not responsible for the Soviet military withdrawals, or for Gorbachev's call for an increased UN role in the world. However, this did not mean that he was not concerned about the SDI. Gorbachev had a new means of responding to the SDI that did not preclude him from making Soviet concessions.

In the short-term, SDI did cause the Reykjavik summit to fail, and it did prevent an agreement at Washington. In the long-term it caused the Soviets to seek a more cooperative course in negotiations, as they became convinced that Ronald Reagan genuinely wanted to eliminate the threat of ballistic missile attack. Reagan's failure to abandon SDI convinced Gorbachev that the US President was ardent in his desire to achieve a world free of the nuclear threat. Even when Reagan faced the prospect of the elimination of Soviet and American nuclear weapons he did not want to abandon SDI in case other countries could threaten the global community.

This brings one to question why if the SDI reinforced in the Soviets mind Reagan's commitment to a world free of nuclear weapons did the Soviets continue to regard the SDI a threat? The answer is that the perceived threat of SDI changed. The Soviets were concerned about the SDI as late as June 1988. Today, Russia is similarly concerned about the possible National Missile Defense (NMD) deployment, despite its allied status with the USA. Yet, in both cases this was not because they viewed the SDI/NMD as a potential US first-strike weapon. They were/are concerned with the effect that SDI/NMD would have on arms control, as it was/is practiced.

In conclusion, it can be resolutely asserted that the SDI confronted Gorbachev with the option of an ever-increasing arms race or cooperation with the US, which he chose. The technological 'threat' that SDI posed the Soviets ultimately persuaded realists in Moscow that cooperation with the US was preferable to a military–technological competition of unlimited duration.[19] The Soviets consequently embarked on a cooperative course with America, whilst simultaneously trying to persuade the US to abandon the SDI. In this respect, the SDI contributed to the Soviet reassessment of foreign, military and strategic policy.

Soviet defence expenditure on strategic defence once declassified will confirm or deny the veracity of the proposition that the SDI was the straw which broke the back of the Soviet Union, exacerbating Soviet economic difficulties. In the meantime, it is plausible to contend that SDI did cause the Soviets a great deal of concern, and contributed to Gorbachev's reassessment of policy which played a crucial role in the end of the Cold War. If the SDI did not cause the Soviets to reassess their position, it clearly did substantiate the assessment that they were unable to compete with the US. The SDI was a significant factor in US–Soviet relations. John Lewis Gaddis claimed that the timing of the SDI proposal was significant, as it came at a Soviet 'moment of exhaustion'. According to Gaddis, although it was 'never even intended' for this purpose, of all the US 'efforts to promote internal reform in the Soviet Union' the SDI 'may have been the most effective'.[20]

Notes

[1] Schweizer, *Interview*.
[2] Mashek, John W., 'Reagan: What Kind of President', *USNWR*, July 21 1980, p. 17.
[3] Fischer, Beth A., *The Reagan Reversal: Foreign Policy and the End of the Cold War*, Columbia, University of Missouri Press, 1997, pp. 122-131.
[4] 'How Much More Can Moscow Spend on Arms?', *NYT*, November 2 1980, p. E5.
[5] Rosenbaum, David E., 'The Candidates' Stands on the Economy, Defense and Other Issues', *NYT*, November 3 1980, p. D14.; Kneeland, Douglas E, 'A Summary of Reagan's Positions on the Major Issues of This Year's Campaign', *NYT*, July 16 1980, p. A14.; Rosenbaum, David E, 'On the Issues: Ronald Reagan', *NYT*, March 22 1980,

p. 8.; See also Gest, Ted, 'Foreign Policy: The Main Arena', *USNWR*, November 3 1980, p. 62.

6   'Before You Vote' (Ronald Reagan Election Campaign Advertisment), *NYT*, November 2 1980, p. 67.

7   'Post Election Interview with President-Elect Reagan', *USNWR*, November 17 1980, p. 41.

8   Chalfont, Alun, *SDI: The Case for the Defence*, Occasional Paper No. 12, Institute for European Defence and Strategic Studies, London, Alliance Publishers Ltd., 1985, p. 32.

9   Jastrow, Robert, 'The Technical Feasibility of Ballistic Missile Defense', *Journal of International Affairs*, Vol. 39, No. 1, Summer 1985, p. 52.; Brzezinski, Zbigniew, *Game Plan*, New York, Atlantic Monthly Press, 1986, p. 153.; Cannon, Lou, *President Reagan: The Role of a Lifetime*, New York, Simon and Schuster, 1991, p. 331.; Chalfont, *SDI: The Case for the Defence*, p. 31.

10   Chalfont, *SDI: The Case for the Defence*, pp. 31-32.

11   That SDI's role was a 'psychological role', see Patman, Robert G., 'Reagan, Gorbachev and the Emergence of "New Political Thinking"', *Review of International Studies*, Vol. 25, No. 4, October 1999, p. 596.

12   'Address to the Nation on Defense and National Security, March 23 1983', *Public Papers of the Presidents of the United States: Ronald Reagan, 1983, (Book I: January 1 to July 1983)*, Washington, US Government Printing Office, 1984, p. 443.

13   'Letter From Mikhail Gorbachev to Ronald W. Reagan', Moscow, December 24 1985, p, 3, *Regan, Donald T., Papers*, Box 214, Folder 9, 'Soviet Union, Reagan–Gorbachev Correspondence', Library of Congress.

14   For the view that the Soviets conducted tests in space which were the type which they wanted banned in the 1972 ABM Treaty, see Broad, William J., 'Experts Say Soviet Has Conducted Space Tests on Anti Missile Weapons', *NYT*, October 15 1986, p. A14.

15   Apple, Jr., R.W., 'Reagan Trip Is Due: No New Key Agreement is Reached as Russian Ends His US Visit', *NYT*, December 11 1987, p. A22.

16   CNN, 'Gorbachev endorses Congressional Gold Medal for Ronald Reagan', http://www.cnni.co.uk/2001/ALLPOLITICS/stories/03/15/reagan.medal/

17   That 'the personal relationship that Ronald Reagan and Mikhail S. Gorbachev eventually built was critical to the diplomatic understandings they reached', see Lewis, Paul 'Ex-Foes Trade Stories From Cold War Trenches', *NYT*, March 1 1993, p. A7.; That 'the end of the Cold War can be told as a story of the development of trust', see Forsberg, Tuomas, 'Power, Interests and Trust: Explaining Gorbachev's Choices at the End of the Cold War', *Review of International Studies*, Vol. 25, No. 4, October 1999, pp. 603-621, especially p. 603.

18   See Wohlforth, William, C., (ed.), *Witnesses to the End of the Cold War*, Baltimore, The John Hopkins University Press, 1996.

19   McMahon, Robert J., 'Review Essay: Making Sense of American Foreign Policy During the Reagan Years', *Diplomatic History*, Vol. 19, No. 2, Spring 1995, p. 373.

20   Gaddis, John Lewis, *The United States and the End of the Cold War: Implications, Reconsiderations, Provocations*, New York, Oxford University Press, 1992, pp. 43-44.

Selective Bibliography

Interviews with the Author (In Alphabetical Order)

Allen, Richard V., 9/16/1998
Anderson, Martin, 9/21/1998 and 10/23/98
Garthoff, Raymond L., 9/16/1998
Graham, William, 9/19/1998
Lee, William (Bill) T., 11/5/1998
Meese III, Edwin M., 9/24/1998
Payne, Keith B., 9/22/1998
Perle, Richard N., 9/24/1998
Schweizer, Peter, 9/25/1998
Weinberger, Caspar W., 9/15/1998

Newspapers

Pravda (London)
The Daily Telegraph
The Guardian
The Independent
The International Herald Tribune
The Observer
The New York Times (NYT)
The Sunday Times
The Times (London)
The Washington Post
The Washington Times

News Magazines

Newsweek
The Economist
Time
US News and World Report (USNWR)

Congressional Sources

Congressional Quarterly Almanac (CQA)
Congressional Quarterly Weekly Report (CQWR)

Congressional Hearings

'Implications of the President's Strategic Defense Initiative and Antisatellite Weapons Policy', *Hearings Before the Subcommittee on Arms Control, International Security and Science of the Committee on Foreign Affairs, House of Representatives*, Ninety-Ninth Congress, First Session, April 24 and May 1 1985, Washington, US Government Printing Office, 1985.

'Review of Arms Control Implications of the Report of the President's Commission on Strategic Forces', *Hearings Before the Committee on Foreign Affairs, House of Representatives*, Ninety-Eighth Congress, First Session, May 17, 19, and 24, 1983, Washington, US Government Printing Office, 1983.

'SDI Program', *Hearings Before the Defense Policy Panel and Research and Development Subcommittee of the Committee on Armed Services, House of Representatives*, One Hundredth Congress, First Session, March 26, July 8 and September 15 1988, Washington, US Government Printing Office, 1988.

'Strategic Defense and Anti-Satellite Weapons', *Hearing Before the Committee on Foreign Relations, United States Senate*, Ninety-Eighth Congress, Second Session, April 25 1984, Washington, US Government Printing Office, 1984.

'Strategic Defense Initiative', *Hearings Before the Subcommittee on Strategic and Theater Nuclear Forces of the Committee on Armed Services, United States Senate*, Ninety-Ninth Congress, First Session, October 30, November 6, 21, December 3, 5 1985, Washington, US Government Printing Office, 1986.

'Strategic Defense Initiative [SDI] Program', *Hearing Before the Committee on Armed Services, House of Representatives*, Ninety-Ninth Congress, First Session, June 6 1985, Washington, US Government Printing Office, 1985.

Administration/Executive Sources

Department of Defense, *Soviet Military Power 1985*, Washington D.C., US Government Printing Office, 1985.

Department of Defense, Strategic Defense Initiative, *Report to the Congress on the Strategic Defense Initiative*, June 1986.

General Advisory Committee on Arms Control and Disarmament, *A Quarter Century of Soviet Compliance Practices Under Arms Control Commitments: 1958–1983*, Washington D.C., October 1984, pp. 1-15.

Public Papers of the Presidents of the US: Ronald Reagan 1983, Washington, US Government Printing Office, 1984.

Report of the Commission to Assess the Ballistic Missile Threat to the United States, Executive Summary, Pursuant to Public Law 201, 104th Congress, July 15 1998.

Strategic Defense Initiative Organization, *1989 Report to the Congress on the Strategic Defense Initiative*, March 13 1989.

The President's Strategic Defense Initiative, January 1985.

United States Arms Control and Disarmament Agency, *Arms Control and Disarmament Agreements 1982 Edition*, Washington D.C., US Government Printing Office, 1985.

United States General Accounting Office, Report to the Congress, *Strategic Defense Initiative Program: Expert's Views on DoD's Organizational Options and Plans For SDI Technical Support*, November 1986.

US Department of Defense, *Anti-Missile and Anti-Satellite Technologies and Programs: SDI & ASAT*, Office of Technology Assessment, The Heritage Foundation, 1986.

Memoirs

Anderson, Martin, *Revolution: The Reagan Legacy*, Stanford, California, Hoover Institution Press, 1990.

Dobrynin, Anatoly, *In Confidence: Moscow's Ambassador to America's Six Cold War Presidents 1962–86*, New York, Random House, 1995.

Gates, Robert M., *From the Shadows: The Ultimate Insider's Story of Five Presidents and How They Won the Cold War*, New York, Simon and Schuster, 1996.

Gorbachev, Mikhail, *Memoirs*, London, Bantam Books, 1997.

Meese III, Edwin M., *With Reagan: The Inside Story*, Washington D.C., Regnery Gateway, 1992.

Nitze, Paul H. with Ann M. Smith and Steven L. Rearden, *From Hiroshima to Glasnost: At the Centre of Decision Making – A Memoir*, London, Weidenfeld and Nicolson, 1986.

Reagan, Ronald, *An American Life*, London, Hutchinson, 1990.

Regan, Donald T., *For The Record: From Wall Street to Washington*, London, Hutchinson, 1988.

Shevardnadze, Eduard A., *The Future Belongs to Freedom*, New York, The Free Press, 1991.

Shultz, George P., *Turmoil and Triumph: My Years as Secretary of State*, New York, Charles Scribner's Sons, 1993.

Thatcher, Margaret, *The Downing Street Years*, London, Harper Collins, 1993.

Weinberger, Caspar W., *Fighting For Peace: Seven Critical Years in the Pentagon*, New York, Warner Books, 1990.

Private Papers

'Letter From Mikhail Gorbachev to Ronald W. Reagan', Moscow, December 24 1985, pp. 1-5, *Regan, Donald T., Papers*, Box 214, Folder 9, 'Soviet Union, Reagan–Gorbachev Correspondence', Library of Congress.

Reagan, Ronald, 'Draft Reply to Handwritten Letter From Gorbachev', February 12 1986, pp. 1-5, *Regan, Donald T., Papers*, Box 214, Folder 9, 'Soviet Union, Reagan–Gorbachev Correspondence', Library of Congress.

Conference Proceedings

Greenstein, Fred I., and William C. Wohlforth, (eds), 'Retrospective on the End of the Cold War', *Report of a Conference Sponsored by the John Foster Dulles Program for the Study of Leadership in International Affairs*, Center of International Studies, Monograph Series No. 6, Princeton University, 1994, pp. 1-51.

Audio Visuals

'Cold War: Star Wars 1981–1988', *Television Programme*, BBC2, Sunday April 25 1999, 8pm-8.50 pm.

Books

Baucom, Donald R., *The Origins of SDI, 1944–1983*, Kansas, University Press of Kansas, 1992.

Beschloss, Michael R. and Strobe Talbott, *At the Highest Levels: The Inside Story of the End of the Cold War*, London, Warner Books, 1994.

Bowker, Mike, *Russian Foreign Policy and the End of the Cold War*, Dartmouth, Aldershot, 1997.

Broad, William J., *Teller's War: The Top Secret Story Behind the Star Wars Deception*, New York, Simon and Shuster, 1992.

Cannon, Lou, *President Reagan: The Role of a Lifetime*, New York, Simon and Schuster, 1991.

Cimbala, Stephen J, *US Military Strategy and the Cold War Endgame*, London, Frank Cass and Co. Ltd., 1995.

Dumbrell, John, *American Foreign Policy: Carter to Clinton*, London, Macmillan Press Ltd., 1997.

Ekedahl, Carolyn McGiffert and Melvin A. Goodman, *The Wars of Eduard Shevardnadze*, London, Hurst, 1997.

Fischer, Beth A., *The Reagan Reversal: Foreign Policy and the End of the Cold War*, Columbia, University of Missouri Press, 1997.

FitzGerald, Frances, *Way Out There in the Blue: Reagan, Star Wars and the End of the Cold War*, New York, Simon and Schuster, 2000.

Gaddis, John Lewis, *The United States and the End of the Cold War: Implications, Reconsiderations, Provocations*, New York, Oxford University Press, 1992.

Garthoff, Raymond L., *The Great Transition: American–Soviet Relations and the End of the Cold War*, Washington D.C., The Brookings Institution, 1994.

Goldman, Marshall, I., *What Went Wrong With Perestroika*, 2nd ed., London, W.W., Norton and Company, 1992.

Gorbachev, Mikhail, *Perestroika: New Thinking For Our Country and the World*, New York, Harper and Row, 1987.

Kaufmann, William W., *Glasnost, Perestroika, and US Defense Spending*, Washington, D.C., The Brookings Institution, 1990.

Lee, William T., and Richard F. Staar, *Soviet Military Policy Since World War II*, Stanford, California, Hoover Institution Press, 1986.

MccGwire, Michael, *Perestroika and Soviet National Security*, Washington, The Brookings Institution, 1991.

Mikheyev, Dmitry, *The Soviet Perspective on the Strategic Defense Initiative*, Washington, Pergamon-Brassey's, 1987.

Oberdorfer, Don, *The Turn: How the Cold War Came to an End, The United States and the Soviet Union, 1983–1990*, London, Jonathan Cape, 1991.

Payne, Keith B., *Strategic Defense: 'Star Wars' in Perspective*, London, Hamilton Press, 1986.

Pressler, Larry, *Star Wars: The Strategic Defense Initiative Debates in Congress*, New York, Praeger, 1986.

Sakwa, Richard, *Gorbachev and His Reforms 1985–1990*, New York, Prentice Hall, 1991.

Sakwa, Richard, *Russian, Politics and Society*, London, Routledge, 1993.

Schweizer, Peter, *Victory: The Reagan Administration's Secret Strategy That Hastened the Collapse of the Soviet Union*, New York, Atlantic Monthly Press, 1994.

Simpson, Christopher, *National Security Directives of The Reagan and Bush Administrations: The Declassified History of US Political and Military Policy 1981–1991*, San Francisco, Westview Press, 1995.

Talbott, Strobe, *The Master of the Game: Paul Nitze and the Nuclear Peace*, New York, Vintage Books, 1989.

Wohlforth, William, C., (ed.), *Witnesses to the End of the Cold War*, Baltimore, The John Hopkins University Press, 1996.

Journals

'A Consensus on Missile Defence', *Survival: The IISS Quarterly*, Vol. 43, No. 3, Autumn 2001, pp. 61-128.

Allen, Richard V., 'The Man Who Changed the Game Plan', *The National Interest*, Vol. 44, Summer 1996, pp. 60-65.

Baker, David, 'The Making of Star Wars', *New Scientist*, July 9 1987, pp. 36-40.

Barnes, Fred, 'Brilliant Pebble', *The New Republic*, April 1 1991, pp. 10-11.

Baucom, Donald R., 'Hail to the Chiefs: The Untold History of Reagan's SDI Decision', *Policy Review*, No. 53, Summer 1990, pp. 66-73.

Berkowitz, Bruce D., 'Who Won The Cold War and Why It Matters', *Orbis: A Journal of World Affairs*, Vol. 40, No. 1, Winter 1996, pp. 164-171.

Brooks, David, 'Reagan was a Reaganite: A Book Review of 'Reagan, in His Own Hand. The Writings of Ronald Reagan That Reveal His Revolutionary Vision for America', Edited by Kiron K. Skinner, Annelise Anderson and Martin Anderson, Foreword by George P. Shultz, New York, The Free Press', *The New York Times Book Review*, Vol. CVI, No. 4, January 28 2001, p. 5.

Brown, Neville, 'A Soviet SDI?', *The World Today*, Vol. 43, December 1987, pp. 212-215.

Brown, Neville, 'SDI Revisited', *The World Today*, Vol. 43, April 1987, pp. 57-58.

Brzezinski, Zbigniew, Robert Jastrow, and Max Kampelman, 'Defense in Space is Not Star Wars', *The New York Times Magazine*, January 27 1985, pp. 28, 29, 46, 48, 51.

Chait, Jonathan, 'Still His Party: Why the GOP Can't Get Over Reagan', *The New Republic: A Journal of Politics and the Arts*, Vol. 223, No. 6, August 7 2000, pp. 26-29.

Charles, Dan, 'The Man who Promised the Earth', *New Scientist*, March 20 1993, pp. 26-28.

Charles, Dan, 'The Rise and Fall of Star Wars: Chronology', *New Scientist*, March 20 1993, pp. 24-25.

Christensen, Thomas J., 'Theater Missile Defense and Taiwan's Security', *Orbis: A Journal of World Affairs*, Vol. 44, No. 1, Winter 2000, pp. 79-90.

Cirincione, Joseph, 'Why the Right Lost the Missile Defense Debate', *Foreign Policy*, No. 106, Spring 1997, pp. 39-55.

Coyle, Philip E., and John B. Rhinelander, 'National Missile Defense and the ABM Treaty: No Need to Wreck the Accord', *World Policy Journal*, Vol. XVIII, No. 3, Fall 2001, pp. 15-22.

Deutch, John, Harold Brown and John P. White, 'National Missile Defense: is There Another Way?', *Foreign Policy*, No. 119, Summer 2000, pp. 91-100.

Forsberg, Tuomas, 'Power, Interests and Trust: Explaining Gorbachev's Choices at the End of the Cold War', *Review of International Studies*, Vol. 25, No. 4, October 1999, pp. 603-621.

Garwin, Richard L., 'Star Wars: Shield or Threat?', *Journal of International Affairs*, Vol. 39, No. 1, Summer 1985, pp. 31-44.

Gizewski, Peter, 'The International Politics of Missile Defence', *International Journal*, Vol. LVI, No. 3, Summer 2001, pp. 527-532.

Glazer, Nathan, 'How Important was Reagan?', *The National Interest*, No. 28, Summer 1992, pp. 102-108.

Greenberg, David, 'Review Essay: The Empire Strikes Out: Why Star Wars Did Not End the Cold War: A Review of FitzGerald, Frances, 'Way Out There in the Blue: Reagan, Star Wars and the End of the Cold War', New York, Simon and Schuster, 2000', *Foreign Affairs*, Vol. 79, No. 2, March/April 2000, pp. 136-142.

Haass, Richard N., 'The Squandered Presidency: Demanding More From the Commander-in-Chief', *Foreign Affairs*, Vol. 79, No. 3, May/June 2000, pp. 136-140.

Hamm, Manfred R., and W. Bruce Weinrod, 'The Transatlantic Politics of Strategic Defense', *Orbis: A Journal of World Affairs*, Vol. 29, No. 4, Winter 1986, pp. 709-734.

Hecht, Jeff, 'Blinded by the Light', *New Scientist*, March 20 1993, pp. 29-31.

Herken, Gregg, 'The Earthly Origins of Star Wars', *Bulletin of The Atomic Scientists*, 43, October 1987, pp. 20-28.

Hoff, Joan, 'How The United States Sold its Soul to Win the Cold War (And Now Cannot Develop a Coherent Post-Cold War Foreign Policy)', *International Journal*, Vol. LVI, No. 3, Summer 2001, pp. 373-392.

Ivanov, Igor, 'The Missile Defense Mistake: Undermining Strategic Stability and the ABM Treaty', *Foreign Affairs*, Vol. 79, No. 5, September/October 2000, pp. 15-20.

Jackson, William D., 'Soviet Reassessment of Ronald Reagan, 1985–1988', *Political Science Quarterly*, Vol. 113, No. 4, Winter 1998–99, pp. 617-644.

Jastrow, Robert, 'The Technical Feasibility of Ballistic Missile Defense', *Journal of International Affairs*, Vol. 39, No. 1, Summer 1985, pp. 45-55.

Kanter, Arnold, 'Thinking About the Strategic Defence Initiative: An Alliance Perspective', *International Affairs*, Vol. 61, No. 3, Summer 1985, pp. 449-464.

Kaplan, Lawrence F., 'Why The Best Offense is a Good Missile Defense: Offensive Line', *The New Republic: A Journal of Politics and the Arts*, Vol. 224, No. 11, March 12 2001, pp. 22-25.

Lee, William T., 'US–USSR Strategic Arms Control Agreements: Expectations and Reality', *Comparative Strategy*, Vol. 12, No. 4, October/December 1993, pp. 415-436.

Levine, Robert A., 'Deterrence and the ABM: Retreading the Old Calculus', *World Policy Journal*, Vol. XVIII, No. 3, Fall 2001, pp. 23-31.

Lewis, George, Lisbeth Gronlund and David Wright, 'National Missile Defense: An Indefensible System', *Foreign Policy*, No. 117, Winter 1999–2000, pp. 120-131, 134-137.

Lewis, George N., Theodore A. Postol and John Pike, 'Why National Missile Defense Won't Work', *Scientific American*, Vol. 281, No. 2, August 1999, pp. 22-27.

MacDonald, Bruce W., 'Falling Star: SDI's Troubled Seventh Year', *Arms Control Today*, September 1990, pp. 7-11.

MacDonald, Bruce W., 'Lost in Space: SDI Struggles Through its Sixth Year', *Arms Control Today*, September 1989, pp. 21-26.

Menshikov, S., 'What is Behind the "Star Wars" Debate', *International Affairs*, Moscow, No. 6, June 1985, pp. 67-77.

Meyerson, Adam, 'The Ash Heap of History: Why Communism Failed', *Policy Review*, No. 58, Fall 1991, pp. 4-5.

Nelson, Lars-Erik, 'Fantasia: A Book Review of FitzGerald, Frances, 'Way Out There in the Blue: Reagan, Star Wars and the End of the Cold War', New York, Simon and Schuster, 2000', *The New York Review of Books*, Vol. XLVII, No. 8, May 11 2000, pp. 4-7.

Newhouse, John, 'The Missile Defense Debate', *Foreign Affairs*, Vol. 80, No. 4, July/August 2001, pp. 97-109.

O'Hanlon, Michael, 'Star Wars Strikes Back', *Foreign Affairs*, Vol. 78, No. 6, November/December 1999, pp. 68-82.

O'Neill, Bill, 'Fear and Laughter in the Kremlin', *New Scientist*, March 20 1993, pp. 34-37.

Ovinnikov, R., '"Star Wars" Programme – A New Phase in Washington's Militaristic Policy', *International Affairs*, Moscow, No. 8, August 1985, pp. 13-22.

Patman, Robert G., 'Reagan, Gorbachev and the Emergence of "New Political Thinking"', *Review of International Studies*, Vol. 25, No. 4, October 1999, pp. 577-601.

Payne, Keith B., 'Post-Cold War Deterrence and Missile Defense', *Orbis: A Journal of World Affairs*, Vol. 39, No. 2, Spring 1995, pp. 201-223.

Payne, Keith B., 'The Case For National Missile Defense', *Orbis: A Journal of World Affairs*, Vol. 44, No. 2, Spring 2000, pp. 187-196.

Perle, Richard N., 'The Strategic Defense Initiative: Addressing Some Misconceptions', *Journal of International Affairs*, Vol. 39, No. 1, Summer 1985, pp. 23-29.

Pick, Otto, 'How Serious is Gorbachev About Arms Control?', *The World Today*, Vol. 43, April 1987, pp. 66-69.

Postol, Theodore, 'Hitting Them Where it Works', *Foreign Policy*, No. 117, Winter 1999–2000, pp. 132-133.

Puschel, Karen, 'Can Moscow Live With SDI?', *Survival*, Vol. XXXI, No. 1, January/February 1989, pp. 34-51.

Rearden, Steven L., 'Feature Review: The Cold War: How the Winner Won', *Diplomatic History*, Vol. 25, No. 4, Fall 2001, pp. 707-712.

Risse-Kappen, Thomas, 'Did "Peace Through Strength" End the Cold War? Lessons From the INF Treaty', *International Security*, Vol. 16, No. 1, Summer 1991, pp. 162-188.

Rivkin, Jr., David B., 'SDI: Strategic Reality or Never–Never Land?', *Strategic Review*, Vol. XV, No. 3, Summer 1987, pp. 43-54.

Roberts, Brad, Robert A. Manning and Ronald N. Montaperto, 'China: The Forgotten Nuclear Power', *Foreign Affairs*, Vol. 79, No. 4, July/August 2000, pp. 53-63.

Schell, Jonathan, 'The Folly of Arms Control', *Foreign Affairs*, Vol. 79, No. 5, September/October 2000, p. 22-46.

Schlesinger, James, 'Reykjavik and Revelations: A Turn of the Tide?', *Foreign Affairs*, 65, pp. 426-446.

Schlesinger, James R., 'Rhetoric and Realities in the Star Wars Debate', *International Security*, Vol. 10, No. 1, Summer 1985, pp. 3-12.

Schweizer, Peter, 'Winning the Cold War: Who Broke the Evil Empire?', *National Review*, May 30 1994, pp. 46-49.

Sicherman, Harvey, 'Review Essay: The Rest of Reagan. Review of Morris, Edmund, 'Dutch: A Memoir of Ronald Reagan', New York, Random House, 1999', *Orbis: A Journal of World Affairs*, Vol. 44, No. 3, Summer 2000, pp. 477-499.

Slater, Jerome & David Goldfischer, 'Can SDI Provide a Defense?', *Political Science Quarterly*, Vol. 101, No. 5, 1986, pp. 839-856.

'Start at The Washington Summit', *Survey of Current Affairs*, Vol. 18, No. 3, March 1988, p. 102.

Stevens, Sayre, 'The Soviet Factor in SDI', *Orbis: A Journal of World Affairs*, Vol. 29, No. 4, Winter 1986, pp. 689-700.

Szabo, Michael, 'GPALS: The Bid to Save Star Wars', *New Scientist*, March 20 1993, pp. 32-33.

Tammen, Ronald L., James T. Bruce, and Bruce W. MacDonald, 'Star Wars After Five Years: The Decisive Points', *Arms Control Today*, July/August 1988, pp. 3-7.

Walt, Stephen M., 'Two Cheers For Clinton's Foreign Policy', *Foreign Affairs*, Vol. 79, No. 2, March/April 2000, pp. 63-79.

Yost, David S., 'European Anxieties About Ballistic Missile Defence', *Washington Quarterly*, Fall 1984, pp. 112-29.
Yost, David S., 'Soviet Ballistic Missile Defence and NATO', *Orbis: A Journal of World Affairs*, Vol. 29, No. 2, Summer 1985, pp. 281-292.

Published Works

Chalfont, Alun, *SDI: The Case for the Defence*, Occasional Paper No. 12, Institute for European Defence and Strategic Studies, London, Alliance Publishers Ltd., 1985.
Jones, R. V. Prof, *New Light on Star Wars: A Contribution to the SDI Debate*, Policy Study No. 71, Centre for Policy Studies, London, Donald and Co. Ltd., 1985.
Wilkening, Dean A., 'Ballistic-Missile Defence and Strategic Stability', *Adelphi Paper*, No. 334, May 2000, pp. 1-97.

Internet

'A History of the SDIO and BMDO', http://tsi.simplenet.com/tsihtml/sdio.html

Ballistic Missile Defense Organization, 'Ballistic Missile Defense: A Brief History', http://www.acq.osd.mil/bmdo/bmdolink/html/origins.html

Ballistic Missile Defense Organization, 'Missile Defense Milestones 1944–1997', http://www.acq.osd.mil/bmdo/bmdolink/html/milstone.html

Ballistic Missile Defense Organization, 'Theater Missile Defense Programs', http://www.acq.osd.mil/bmdo/bmdolink/html/tmd.html

Index